EXCHANGE RATE REGIMES IN THE TWENTIETH CENTURY

T0315122

For Alison, wife and friend

Exchange Rate Regimes in the Twentieth Century

Derek H. Aldcroft

Research Professor in Economic History, Manchester Metropolitan University, UK

Michael J. Oliver

Lecturer in Economic History, University of Leeds, UK

Edward Elgar
Cheltenham, UK • Northampton, MA, USA

Published by
Edward Elgar Publishing Limited
8 Lansdown Place
Cheltenham
Glos GL5O 2HU
UK

Edward Elgar Publishing, Inc.
6 Market Street
Northampton
Massachusetts O1060
USA

A catalogue record for this book
is available from the British Library

Library of Congress Cataloguing in Publication Data

Aldcroft, Derek Howard.
    Exchange rate regimes in the twentieth century/ Derek H. Aldcroft, Michael J. Oliver.
    Includes bibliographical references and index.
    1. Foreign exchange rates — History. 2. International finance — History. I. Oliver, Michael J. II. Title.
    HG3815.A45 1998
    332.4'56'09—dc21

98–21063
CIP

ISBN 1 85898 320 7 (cased)

Printed and bound in Great Britain by Bookcraft (Bath) Limited.

Contents

Figures

Tables

Preface

Exchange rate regimes have always fascinated economists and economic historians and have led to an enormous generation of literature through the years. However, for undergraduates in particular, some of the more recent literature has become increasingly technical in nature and a historical in content. This book was conceived to rectify both shortcomings and to provide an accessible account of the different exchange rate regimes of the twentieth century.

DEREK H. ALDCROFT
MICHAEL J. OLIVER

Introduction

Since the golden age of the long nineteenth century, the international monetary mechanism has experienced many changes in exchange rate regimes, alternating between fixed and floating rate systems interspersed with or alongside variants thereof, for example, managed or dirty floats.

In fact the twentieth century has seen virtually every conceivable type of exchange rate regime. Before the First World War most of the major countries were on a pure gold standard with exchange rates fixed within narrow points. The war eventually led to a breakup of this system and what emerged was a short period of floating rates with very little intervention by the monetary authorities. The subsequent slow pace of stabilisation during the 1920s produced a modified form of the gold standard (the gold exchange standard) which lasted until the early 1930s. The collapse of the gold standard under the impact of depression was then followed by a short period of volatility in exchange rates before managed currency systems became the order of the day, grouped around several distinct currency blocs.

After the Second World War, a new system of fixed exchange rates emerged following the negotiations held at Bretton Woods in 1944. This system, under the aegis of the International Monetary Fund (IMF), appeared to work reasonably well until the late 1960s, before disintegrating a few years later. For several years after 1973 world monetary relations bore some resemblance to those of the 1930s; they were conducted:

> in the context of a heterogeneous system characterised by a broad spectrum of exchange rate practices, ranging from independent floating with relatively little intervention to the maintenance of a fixed exchange rate in terms of a single currency. . . . While the greater majority of the IMF members have pegged exchange rates, most of the major countries, which control 80 per cent of the IMF members' trade, are floating independently or are floating jointly or crawl. (Poniachek 1979, 185)

At the end of the decade several European countries devised a more formal fixed rate system within the European Monetary System (EMS), which became the forerunner of the move towards a more permanent monetary integration within Europe. However, in spite of one or two regional currency groupings, the current international monetary arrangements have been described as a 'non-system' (Kenen et al. 1994, 1).

International monetary history raises many interesting issues, many of which have been the subject of vigorous debate in recent years. Why, for example, do monetary regimes change and how do they evolve over time? Are fixed exchange rate systems prone to decay because of inflexibility and disharmony among the members? Why do some regimes appear more successful than others? Casual observation would suggest that fixed exchange rate systems have worked better than others. Most commentators would probably agree that the prewar gold standard and the Bretton Woods system after the Second World War were superior to the systems which followed in the early 1920s, the 1930s and again in the 1970s, when exchange rates were often very unstable. Growth was faster (at least under Bretton Woods), there was a fair degree of price stability and a state of general equilibrium seemed to prevail. Why was this so? Was it the presence of hegemonic leadership, that is Britain before 1914 and the United States after 1945, that was responsible, or was it the political stability and cooperation among the members countries that ensured success? Can economic order reign under pluralistic or disintegrating political systems? Or if no hegemony exists can the same results be achieved by cooperation and coordination of policies of a group of dominant countries in contrast to the lack of it for much of the interwar period? There are, of course, other relevant factors to consider: for example, the absence of major shocks, political stability and the flexibility of factor markets. As Triffin and others have pointed out, it was not fixed exchange rate regimes that were the source of stability (Triffin 1968, 14). Rather, it was the harmony in the real development process and the convergence in price and factor markets which made it possible to generate successful fixed exchange rate systems, as happened before 1914, again after the Second World War, and perhaps more modestly in the 1980s. How far are fixed exchange rate regimes dependent on the contingent policy behaviour of the participating countries?

Of the fixed regimes, the one that stands out, of course, is the prewar gold standard. Throughout the twentieth century the classical gold standard cast a long shadow over the international monetary system. If modern Western philosophy can be seen as a series of footnotes to Plato, so likewise might modern monetary systems be ghosted by the gold standard, which for many was seen as the archetype of a successful monetary system (Cleveland 1976, 5). Nostalgia for the gold standard has been very evident during periods of monetary disorder – witness, for example, the reluctance to abandon the notion of getting back to a gold-based system in the 1930s – not simply because of its gold content *per se*, though for the French this was always the *sine qua non* of monetary probity – but more because it appeared to embody the quintessence of monetary order which no other system has managed to do either before or since to the same degree (ibid, 26–7). On the other hand, there are those who would argue that the shadow of the past has exercised a baleful influence on the search for a satisfactory system of international monetary relations (Eastman 1955, 403).

The phases in between have not always been unmitigated disasters. The exchange disorders following the First World War were probably inevitable given the distortion of cost and price relationships among countries caused by the period of hostilities, but some countries, it has been argued, did benefit from depreciating exchange rates. The exchange rate experience of the 1930s was by no means as chaotic as contemporaries would have us believe, and the general abandonment of gold did help to promote economic recovery from the great depression. Similarly, one could argue that adjustment to the economic disturbances of the 1970s would have been impossible under the straitjacket of the Bretton Woods system.

One disturbing feature of international monetary relations which has prevailed from the days of the classical gold standard through to the present, is that the systems in operation were designed by and for the rich nations of the West. There is no brooking the fact that the Eurocentric or Western approach to international monetary matters leaves much to be desired, at least as far as Third World countries are concerned. Both today and in the past the less-developed countries have borne some of the burden of adjustment of the rich man's monetary club. This was certainly the case under the classical gold standard, and, for much of the present century, Third World countries have had little influence in the design of new monetary systems. Consequently, their interests and needs have been neglected and they have been forced to adapt their currency regimes to those of the metropolitan core countries.

Several of these issues will be taken up in subsequent chapters. The main objectives of the present study are as follows: to trace the evolution of exchange rate regimes since the First World War and to discuss the forces which have brought about change; to determine how different regimes affected the economic environment; to consider the merits or otherwise of the respective regimes; and to assess the evidence and arguments for and against fixed and floating exchange rate systems.

1 The restoration of monetary stability in the 1920s

The background to international monetary reconstruction

Few countries emerged from the war with their monetary and currency systems unscathed. It is true that many countries maintained the legal fiction of the gold standard during the period of hostilities by artificially pegging their exchange rates to those of 1914, which meant that by the end of the war most of the Allied and neutral countries had a pattern of exchange rates not very dissimilar from that of prewar. However, once the formal tie with gold was formally broken and pegging operations ceased, most currencies lost their stability and depreciated against the dollar which was by then the world's strongest currency. Thus by early 1920 (February) sterling had dropped to 35 per cent below its former par value (Yeager 1976, 319). Ex-enemy countries fared rather worse. The German, Austrian and Hungarian exchanges continued to sink during the war and by the end of 1918 they had depreciated by 50 per cent or more. Several other countries, including Belgium, Finland and Portugal, also experienced a substantial deterioration in their exchanges (League of Nations 1920). In the years ahead, many countries were to suffer much greater depreciation of their currencies (see Table 1.1).

The loss in exchange values was scarcely surprising given the fact that the war had seriously weakened the productive mechanisms of many economies; it had given rise to serious balance of payments problems, especially with the dollar area; while inflationary methods of financing leading to large budgetary deficits had been widely practised. Thus before currency stability could be regained it would be necessary, as Moggridge (1989, 258) notes, to clear away much of the financial debris of war, and in many cases that of reconstruction.

The restoration of currency stability was recognised as a matter of some urgency after the war, although initially the turbulent postwar conditions made it difficult to make any progress towards this goal. The return to the prewar liberal economic order – embracing freedom from controls, free trade in commodities and factors of production, and above all, fixed exchange rates under a gold-standard system – was regarded almost universally as a basic priority of policy (Arndt 1944, 223). The virtues of the

Table 1.1   Exchange values of European currencies, selected years (December averages, par value = 100)

	1918	1920	1923
Austria	31.3	3.2	0.01
Belgium	71.2	49.8	23.8
Bulgaria	–	13.7	4.2
Czechoslovakia	–	10.0	14.4
Denmark	101.0	70.1	66.4
Finland	62.6	15.9	12.9
France	95.2	47.9	27.2
Germany	50.8	8.8	(1)
Greece	100.0	84.9	9.8
Hungary	40.7	15.5	0.03
Italy	81.5	39.6	22.5
Netherlands	106.2	94.2	94.5
Norway	103.7	76.9	55.6
Poland	–	6.3	(2)
Portugal	61.5	30.9	3.3
Romania	–	18.2	2.7
Spain	106.8	101.1	67.4
Sweden	108.6	80.6	98.1
Switzerland	106.9	95.5	90.7
United Kingdom	97.8	78.3	89.6
Yugoslavia	–	25.7	5.9

Notes:
(1) 0.000,000,000,084.
(2) 0.000,034.

Source: League of Nations (1943a, 42)

gold standard were never questioned, and its restoration was seen as the key to the return of world prosperity and stability. Both the Brussels and Genoa International Conferences of 1920 and 1922 stressed the urgency of returning to fixed gold parities (Orde 1990, 299; Fink 1984, 235; Kemmerer 1944, 109–10). The same message had already been transmitted loud and clear to the world by the Cunliffe Report of 1918, such that the return to gold 'devint une affaire de prestige, un point de dogme, presque une question de religion' (van der Wee and Tavernier 1975, 79–80).

   Whether the stabilising properties of the gold standard were as significant as most contemporaries imagined is a debatable issue (Yeager 1976;

Triffin 1968) but, notwithstanding any reservations on this score, there was good reason why statesmen should have been anxious to restore the prewar international monetary system. Apart from questions of prestige and national honour, especially relevant to countries such as France and Italy, the fact was that European currencies and international finance generally were in a chaotic state for several years after 1918. The floating exchange rate system which emerged after the war gave rise to large and erratic swings in currency valuations, and these tended to exacerbate inflation. Admittedly many of the more violent movements in the exchanges were no doubt a product of the lax monetary and fiscal conditions in the constrained conditions of the period, but that did not alter the fact that they were seen as a major impediment to European reconstruction and recovery. Pigou, in his memorandum to the Brussels Conference of 1920, had warned that wide fluctuations in exchange rates were a great hindrance to trade and credit transactions (Pigou 1920, 12). A similar view was expressed somewhat later by the Head of the League of Nations' Intelligence Service when he argued that trade could scarcely flourish when

> European exchanges for seven years danced and jumped with spasmodic and tireless energy. ... That instability has not only rendered the transaction of business from day to day extraordinarily difficult and risky, but has for some years excluded the possibility of laying down any elaborate economic programme for the future. (Loveday 1931, 31)

Whether speculative activity on the exchanges exacerbated fluctuations in exchange rates, as many contemporary commentators believed (see League of Nations 1944), is an issue which has given rise to lively debate in recent years, and one to which we shall return below. For the moment, one might recall that more recent experience with the vagaries of floating exchange rates now affords somewhat greater sympathy with the motives of statesmen in the 1920s who were keen to restore an orderly pattern of exchange rates.

Two main themes dominated the process of international monetary reconstruction. It was considered highly desirable that each nation should return as quickly as possible to a fixed gold parity. This belief resulted in a country-by-country approach to stabilisation with little regard to the crucial issue of the viability of the exchange rate selected. Establishing the gold value of the currency was regarded as an act of national sovereignty and the chief concerns of central bankers and governments was whether stabilisation could be maintained at the chosen rate. Second, it was never for a moment questioned that the monetary system should be based on gold. That many nations eventually adopted a variant of the prewar system, the gold exchange standard, was neither here nor there, since most countries regarded it as a first step or half-way house to a return to a gold specie standard, or at least a gold bullion standard (Meyer 1970, 6–7).

Faith in the power of the gold standard was unquestioned. It was seen as the hallmark of a return to 'normalcy'; international imbalances would be readily corrected by the system's 'automatic' adjustment processes, although it was recognised that there might be temporary strains for the domestic economy in the transitional period. Furthermore, adherence to a fixed exchange rate regime would behove countries to put their domestic fiscal and monetary affairs in order.

The process of stabilisation

In contrast to the negotiated settlement on exchange rates following the second world war, the process of currency stabilisation in the 1920s was a long-drawn-out and piecemeal affair. Despite the resolutions of the Brussels and Genoa conferences calling for a degree of coordination, at least among central banks, there was no systematic plan to stabilise currencies, or groups of currencies, simultaneously, and as a consequence insufficient attention was paid to the vast changes which had taken place in world finance and the world economy through the period 1914–20 (Fink 1984, 235; League of Nations 1946, 91). In practice, currency stabilisation was a protracted process, with most countries acting independently of one another by stabilising their exchange rates at different times throughout the decade, as and when it best suited their needs, which usually meant when they had managed to regain control of their domestic financial systems. Delays were encountered due to friction over which groups in society should bear the costs of stabilising. This often involved a war of attrition between different socio-economic groups until the more conservative elements gained the upperhand and imposed the costs on the weaker members of the community, France being the classic case (Alesina and Drazen 1991, 1173–4). In the convoluted process of securing political consolidation, little room was left for rational consideration being given to the relative shifts in costs and prices which had taken place since 1914 when choosing new exchange rates. The chief objective was to choose a rate that was thought to be defensible, although even this was disregarded when prestige or questions of honour were at stake, or when it was felt that a competitive edge could be secured by undervaluation. However, as de Cecco (1995, 122–4) has shown, the timing of formal stabilisation was also influenced by the machinations of Montagu Norman and Benjamin Strong who were keen to ensure that European countries did not select exchange rates that were too competitive. Britain also was anxious to maintain her former role as the leading financial centre, which was one reason why Norman sought to persuade countries to adopt the gold exchange standard.

Table 1.2 provides summary details of some of the main stabilisations effected during the 1920s. One of the first to achieve success was Latvia which, without financial aid, brought a halt to inflation in the summer of

Table 1.2 Dates and levels at which currencies stabilised in the 1920s

Country	Stabilisation date[1]	% of prewar value
Austria	1922	new currency
Belgium	1926	14.3
Bulgaria	1924 (1928)	3.7
Czechoslovakia	1923	14.3
Denmark	1926	prewar parity
Estonia	1924 (1927)	1.1
France	1926 (1928)	20.0
Finland	1926	12.5
Germany	1923 (1924)	new currency
Greece	1928	6.7
Hungary	1924	new currency
Italy	1927	25.0
Japan	1930	prewar parity
Latvia	1921	0.8
Netherlands	1924	prewar parity
Norway	1928	prewar parity
Poland	1926 (1927)[2]	new currency
Portugal	1929 (1931)	4.6
Romania	1927 (1929)	3.0
Sweden	1922	prewar parity
Switzerland	1924	prewar parity
United Kingdom	1925	prewar parity
Yugoslavia	1925 (1931)	9.1

Notes:
1. Dates of *de jure* stabilisation where different from those of *de facto* stabilisation are shown in brackets.
2. Poland initially stabilised the gold value of its currency in 1924 but was forced to abandon it the following year.

Source: League of Nations (1946, 92–3).

1921. Albania and Lithuania followed soon after by introducing new national currencies to replace foreign ones, while Austria was the first of the hyperinflationary countries to bring in a new monetary unit. During the next two years several other countries returned to their prewar parities including Switzerland, Sweden and the Netherlands. By contrast, both Germany and Hungary had to introduce new currency units following the collapse of their currencies through hyperinflation. Britain's return to the gold standard in April 1925 provided the cue for the British

Dominions and several other countries to stabilise their exchanges. By early 1926, exchange stability had been achieved in 39 countries, 17 of which were in Europe, two in North America, 12 in Central and South America, two each in Africa and Asia and four in Oceania.

In the latter half of the decade the process was more or less completed. Several countries such as France, Poland, Estonia and Bulgaria moved from *de facto* stabilisation to a *de jure* basis, while a number of others, including Italy, Norway, Greece, Brazil, Argentina, Ecuador, Paraguay and Peru stabilised their exchanges. By then, most of the countries of the world had returned to gold and the number of gold-standard countries was greater than ever before (Kemmerer 1944, 110–11). Only one or two countries, notably Japan, Portugal, Romania and Yugoslavia, had still to finalise their stabilisations, while Spain and Turkey continued to allow their currencies to fluctuate, with the result that they depreciated significantly during the 1920s (Brown 1940 I, 395–402; League of Nations 1937a, 30; Keyder 1981, 69, 84–5). China, Persia and Abyssinia were the main silver standard bearers. Spain is an interesting case which is worth further study since despite a fluctuating exchange rate the country enjoyed remarkable price stability and avoided a deflationary stabilisation policy – the exception to the rule that paper currencies are more unstable than metallic ones (Hawtrey 1939, 245).

External financial aid played a rather variable role in assisting the process of stabilisation, and only in a few cases was it of crucial importance. Only in the case of Austria, Belgium, Hungary, Poland and Danzig was *de facto* stabilisation effected with the help of specific loans, credits or reconstruction schemes. The majority of countries managed to stabilise without drawing on external aid, although many did in fact arrange temporary forms of credit in case of emergency. The role of the League of Nations in financial reconstruction and currency reform was somewhat limited and haphazard. Only when economies were on the point of disintegration and the damage had been done did the League step in with a reconstruction scheme, and even then its assistance was not always of crucial importance. This was true of Austria (1922), Hungary (1924), Germany (1924), Poland (1927) and Estonia (1927), all of which were helped by the League (League of Nations 1946, 95–7). The League's efforts usually involved some measure of control over the financial affairs of the countries in question, which they were often unwilling to accept until things became really desperate (League of Nations 1930c, 1945). For this reason countries were reluctant to turn to the League for assistance and so most of the credits and loans arranged in connection with stabilisation were provided by the major central banks.

Although lines of credit or loans arranged ostensibly for stabilisation purposes through the banks were fairly common, it is doubtful whether external aid in general was of crucial significance in ensuring the technical success of currency reform. It is true that they could act as an important confidence booster when confidence in the currency was being eroded by capital flight. On the other hand, much of the aid was too small or too late to serve a really useful purpose, or alternatively many of the credits were never utilised. Moreover, none of the specific stabilisation loans were raised for that purpose alone and hence it is difficult to determine what proportion of funds was used for the express purpose of currency reform. In some of the more extreme inflationary situations it is also doubtful whether external aid would have been much use, however large the amount. The German experience provides a good case in point. Stability of the exchanges ultimately depended upon domestic monetary reform, and as long as inflation was allowed to continue no amount of foreign aid would have saved the mark from headlong depreciation. But once inflation had been brought under control and preliminary stabilisation effected, then it was possible for a foreign loan to consolidate the final reform. Even when the basic conditions for exchange stability had been met, external assistance was rarely indispensable, although in the case of Austria and Hungary it may have had a favourable psychological impact (League of Nations 1926a, 1926b). The fact is that many countries never really required foreign assistance and the fact that they had recourse to credits or loans in one form or another was largely because 'they had become almost a fashion in the 'twenties' (League of Nations 1946, 131). A fashion which had unfortunate consequences since, according to Meyer (1970, 3), credit and loan negotiations among central banks gave rise to friction and divisions of opinion which served to destroy international monetary and financial cooperation.

The format of the restored gold standard differed considerably from that of prewar. The consequences of the changes for the operation of the new standard are explored more fully in Chapter 2 and here we simply note some of the salient features. In few countries was the prewar monetary organisation fully restored in its original form. The full gold standard or specie standard, in which gold coins circulate internally and fiat money is readily convertible into gold, was abandoned almost everywhere with the odd exceptions of the United States, Sweden, the Netherlands and a few Latin American countries. Most countries adopted a watered-down version of the full standard with restrictions on the convertibility of non-commodity money into gold and on the export of gold. In the few countries which adopted the gold bullion standard (for example Britain, Denmark and Norway) notes could not be readily converted into gold on demand except for export and then only at a fixed price and in large minimum amounts. Many countries in fact adopted the gold exchange standard whereby a country's monetary authority tied its currency to gold indirectly by dealing on the foreign exchange market to maintain a fixed exchange rate with a foreign currency which was on either a gold coin or gold bullion standard. By the end of the 1920s, 30 or more countries had adopted the gold exchange standard in one form or another and in each case there was legal provision for the central bank to hold foreign exchange reserves against notes and deposits. Only a small number of countries (including the US, the UK, Canada, Australia, New Zealand, South Africa, the Netherlands, Sweden, Norway and Switzerland) were without legal provisions permitting the inclusion of anything but gold in the reserves of their central banks, although in practice most of them were substantial holders of foreign exchange (Brown 1940 **II**, 732; Jack 1927, 43–4; Palyi 1972, 116–17).

Although many countries originally harboured dreams of returning to the full gold standard at prewar parities, in practice the majority could never aspire to this ideal. The wide variation in domestic cost and price changes since 1914 relative to those of the United States, whose currency served as benchmark for the realignment of most other currencies, meant that the crucial question was when they could stabilise, and the rate at which they did was of secondary importance. Thus for most countries the best they could achieve was a gold exchange standard at a depreciated rate, and even this proved a struggle to achieve and maintain in many cases. Much depended on how willing and how quickly countries could get their domestic financial affairs under control and eradicate the inflationary pressures which were such a common feature of the early postwar years.

The manner in which stabilisation was carried out and the consequences of currency reform varied from country to country and it would be impractical to analyse each case. Dornbusch (1992, 418) identifies three indispensable steps which featured in most stabilisations: fixing the exchange rate, balancing the budget and securing the independence of the central bank, although not necessarily either simultaneously or in any specific order. It is possible to classify countries into three broad categories. The first of these comprised a select band of countries which managed to re-establish their prewar parities: the UK and the Dominions, Denmark, Sweden and Norway, Switzerland, the Netherlands and Japan. At the other extreme were five countries – Austria, Hungary, Germany, Poland and Russia – which were forced to bring in new monetary units after hyperinflation had destroyed the value of their original currencies. The third group of countries, and by far the largest, included all the countries which retained their old monetary units but were forced to stabilise at a devalued rate. Stabilisation levels varied widely, as can be seen from Table 1.2, with the largest divergencies from parity occurring in East and South-eastern Europe.

Return to prewar parity

While none of the currencies in this group could look the dollar squarely in the face in the early postwar years, neither did any of them suffer depreciation of continental dimensions. Average depreciation through 1914–20 was about 10–20 per cent, although Denmark fell to 70 per cent of its prewar parity. During the free floating period of the early 1920s, only the Swedish and Swiss currencies showed relative strength against the dollar (League of Nations 1943a, 42). Nevertheless, the question as to whether the parity rates should be changed was rarely entertained, let alone seriously discussed (Moggridge 1969, 1972; Stolper 1948). The prewar monetary system was seen as the ideal goal; the former parity rates were sacrosanct and immutable and should be restored at all possible speed irrespective of the cost. For Britain, which had formed the lynch-pin of the prewar international monetary system, the restoration of the gold standard at the original parity was regarded as crucial, not merely to demonstrate to the world the soundness of Britain's financial and monetary system, but also to ensure that she maintained control over the world's monetary system in the face of the American challenge (Costigliola 1977, 1984; Hogan 1977, 72). In any case, the Dominions were anxious for Britain to lead the way, and had even threatened to take an independent line if action was delayed. It was important for Britain's prestige, therefore, that she took the initiative and ensured uniform action throughout the Empire (Pressnell 1978, 77–9; Tsokhas 1994; Hawke 1971). As Blainey (1958, 313) observed: 'The exchange rate was a sacred cow, to be worshipped in the market place and not to be milked. It was a symbol of Australia's sacrosanct commercial bond with Britain'. Moreover, restoring gold to its former glory symbolised the return to 'normalcy' after which, it was believed, everything would once again be in equilibrium.

The effort required to effect a return to parity was in fact considerable since prices and costs had risen faster in these countries than in America. Severe compression of the domestic economy was necessary to bring about adjustment. Thus in Sweden there was violent deflation between 1920 and 1922 in preparation for the return, intermittent deflation in the UK prior to 1925 and a sharp squeeze in Norway and Denmark between 1925 and 1928. Norway was probably more severely affected than in the depression of 1929–32 (Heckscher 1930, 246–9). Moreover, once the decision to return to parity was made known, speculators moved in and drove the currencies close to their prewar levels, which virtually forced governments to honour their commitments (Aliber 1962, 241). The appreciation of the Norwegian and Danish currencies, for example, from about 50–60 per cent of par to 95–100 per cent between 1924 and 1926 was largely due to an influx of speculative funds in anticipation of the return to parity (League of Nations 1944, 121). Likewise, the British pound was helped back to parity by the speculators, while sharp fluctuations in the yen from 1925 onwards was primarily due to speculators backing Japan's return (Sayers 1976a, 139; Yamamura 1972, 190).

Despite the severe deflationary policies, most of these countries could not fully adjust their cost and price structures and so they ended up with overvalued currencies (Redmond 1984). Deflation coupled with subsequent overvaluation meant that their economies did not achieve their full growth potential in the 1920s, although the impact varied. Norway and, to a lesser extent, Denmark, were badly hit in contrast to the rapid progress of Finland which devalued significantly (Lester 1937, 1939, 222; Broadberry 1984; Haavisto and Jonung 1995, 262, 264). After initial difficulties Sweden made better progress thanks largely to her highly adaptable and structurally progressive economy (Jack 1927, 69; Thomas 1936, 158–61; Dahmén 1970). The UK recorded a rather patchy performance but structural problems were more important than overvaluation, the extent of which has been challenged since Keynes gave his 10 per cent verdict (Redmond 1984, 529–31; Sayers 1960, 320–22; Dimsdale 1981, 328; Matthews 1986a, 582–6; 1986b, 199–201; Walter 1951, 14–16). Japan's economy did not achieve its full growth potential in the 1920s, partly because of spasmodic deflation, an overvalued exchange rate and the uncertainty caused by the instability of the yen (Patrick 1971, 260; Yamamura 1972, 190–95). On the other hand, in the case of the Netherlands the return to gold went fairly smoothly and the economy boomed after 1923, partly because the price structure relative to 1914 was more favourable than that of many other countries. This demonstrates, therefore, that returning to par was not a disaster as long as the economy was competitive and structurally sound (van Zanden 1997, 124–51; van Zanden and Griffiths 1989, 115–16).

Whether the struggle to regain and retain the prewar parity was worthwhile is debatable. The British case is perhaps an exception if one believes in the role of a hegemonic leader demonstrating confidence to the world, although by this time Britain's ability to play the role of a hegemon was waning anyway. But then prestige and rivalry were more important determinants of policy. Conversely, although the adoption of lower exchange rates may not have led to general recovery, each country would have benefited from choosing a lower exchange rate, and there is no reason to believe that had modest adjustments to exchange values been made, this would have sparked off competitive devaluations elsewhere.

Hyperinflation countries

At the other extreme to the Anglo-Saxon parity group were the five countries which experienced the traumas of hyperinflation. The pattern of events was broadly similar even if the details differed in various respects. And the end product was certainly the same, namely that currencies became worthless and had to be replaced by new units of account. At the end of the day prices rose 14,000 times in Austria, 23,000 times in Hungary, 2.5 million in Poland, 4000 million in Russia and one million million in Germany against the prewar base (Aldcroft 1977, 138).

The origins of the extreme inflationary pressures have been much debated and most textbook treatments of inflation usually identify three or four principal causes. First, there is demand–pull inflation where excess demand for goods pushes up prices. To this the monetarists have added a variant. They argue that the inflationary or goods gap is primarily a function of excessive money creation by the authorities, the corollary being that to achieve price stability the money supply growth in the long term should be related to the potential growth in real GNP. Third, there is cost–push inflation where pressure arises from input prices, for example, wages and material inputs. The final possibility is one where inflation arises from the supply side due to an autonomous decline in output as a result of some serious disturbance such as war or revolution. Such occasions are relatively rare but Russia probably falls into this category when, in the 'nightmare conditions' following the revolution of 1917, industrial output collapsed to little more than one-tenth of the prewar level (Nove 1969, 55–63).

In most hyperinflations of any significance all four elements can be discerned in varying degrees, although the most favoured explanation is the demand–pull one. That is, an increase in aggregate demand exceeds the supply capacity of the economy because it is fed by a continuous expansion of the money supply. This was certainly the case in all hyperinflationary episodes, where inflation was preceded or accompanied by monetary expansion, budgetary deficits, trade imbalances and depreciating exchange rates, although not invariably at the same time.

Generalised demand explanations of inflation leave several issues unresolved. The dichotomy between monetarist and Keynesian versions is one of the most important. Hard-line monetarists would argue that inflation is basically a product of autonomous money creation by irresponsible authorities and that little else matters. Thus Cagan (1956) in his study of major twentieth-century inflations argues that changes in the supply of money were critical to the extreme price movements and that the rise in wages and depreciation of exchange rates were merely the effects rather than the causes of inflation. It is true that severe inflations cannot technically occur without monetary expansion, but to deny some independent role to other factors may be straining the evidence. Balance of payments theories of inflation, for example, stress the key role of external deficits in depressing exchange rates and raising import and domestic costs which in turn lead to budget deficits and a rise in the note issue (Laursen and Pedersen 1964, 36–41; Graham 1930, 76; Bresciani-Turroni 1937). There is certainly evidence that exchange rates in several European countries over-tracked at times the internal value of the currency to which the monetary authorities reacted passively. Ranki's study (1983a) of East European infla-tions in the 1920s demonstrates the crucial role of foreign influences. In the early stages of inflation, foreigners bought large amounts of depreciated money in the expectation of making a gain when currencies were stabilised, hopefully at prewar parities (League of Nations 1946, 47). Once it became clear that this was not likely to happen the balances were promptly repatri-ated, which accelerated the decline in currency values. Ranki maintains that in the runaway stages of inflation the fall in the value of currencies caused by capital flight became a crucial factor in inflation, with fiscal deficits losing some of their significance. Austria is often seen as a good example of the exchange influence on the inflationary process (Brown 1988, 122; van Walré de Bordes 1924, 197; Layton and Rist 1925).

The second point to bear in mind is that changes in the money supply and inflation were not always unambiguously related. Prices rose sharply in France between 1920 and 1924 even though the money supply remained fairly stable and budget deficits were declining. By contrast, in post-stabilisation Austria and Hungary the money supply expanded rapidly for a time with relatively little effect on the price level. In Germany the exchange rate, weakened in turn by trade deficits, capital flight and reparations, was at times a potent source of inflation to which monetary growth accommodated.

Third, the relationship between economic variables can only provide a proximate explanation of the mechanics of inflation. It tells us little about the conditions under which inflation thrives. Much recent work on inflation has focused attention on the socio-political factors behind infla-tion. The main premise of the argument rests on the existence of unfulfilled expectations. Because the state cannot meet the aspirations of the population it resorts to inflationary policies to preserve social har-mony. In brief, the state delivers the amount of inflation demanded by the populace. As Maier (1987, 223–4) points out, just as growth became a surrogate for redistribution post-1945, so inflation can be seen as a surro-gate for growth under conditions of instability.

In other words, faced with insurmountable economic and social prob-lems, social strife and inter-group conflict over income shares, weak governments find a temporary solution in inflation financing. In the difficult circumstances of the postwar period, when many governments were struggling to survive amid the welter of reconstruction problems, printing money became a convenient and all too easy way of providing governments with real resources at a time when they lacked the will or strength to impose adequate taxation to provide for their revenue needs. The issue of money was a relatively painless way out of the impasse since it provided revenue by a special kind of tax on real money balances. The potential tax base was equivalent to the volume of real cash balances in the hands of the public, while the tax rate was determined by the rate of depreciation of the value of money which in turn was synonymous with the rate at which prices rose. In other words, the revenue collected in real terms was the product of the rate of increase in prices (the tax rate) and the real cash balances (the tax base).

While politically more acceptable than taxation and easier to administer, the effectiveness of this method of financing tended to diminish over time and hence ever larger doses of money growth and inflation were required to keep the process going. Eventually there comes a point when inflation ceases to act as a social lubricant. When tax rates explode (that is, prices) and confidence in the currency is undermined, the tax-gathering process breaks down. The state's ability to generate real revenue dwindles rapidly as the costs of collection rise and the value of money becomes worthless (Cagan 1956, 77–90; Horsman 1988, 234; Jacobs 1977, 294–8; Brown 1988, 122). In the last throes of hyperinflation in Germany the transaction costs of day-to-day operations became prohibitive and some 'two thousand printing presses turned out bank notes day and night and the economy drowned in a flood of paper money' (Knauerhase 1972, 26). By this stage, the benefits of inflation had long since passed; there were few supporters left and its continuation did more to antagonise intergroup conflict than to promote social harmony (Feldman 1993, 838).

A similar scenario could be written for all the hyperinflationary countries of the 1920s. Although the original inflationary impulses had first originated in wartime, it was the severe conditions arising in the aftermath, including the presence or threat of civil strife, which provided a fertile germination ground for much higher rates of inflation. Conditions in these countries were so deplorable in the immediate postwar years that draconian measures to check inflation with the attendant results in terms of unemployment, income loss and so on, could easily have caused a collapse of the whole social fabric. The German situation provides a classic case of social control. Defeated in battle, burdened with reparations and the war guilt clause, and on the verge of social revolution, the weak Weimar governments lacked an adequate tax base to finance economic and social reconstruction. Inflation, therefore, appeared to be a tempting way of maintaining a degree of social harmony at a time of great inter-group conflict and instability. As Holtfrerich (1986, 153) writes: 'threatened by Allied sanctions on the one hand and the disintegration of the Reich on the other, no German government could have complied with Reparations demands in any way other than resort to the printing of money'. On the other hand, Feldman (1975, 358) sees the inflation tax largely as the outcome of the class struggle. Resort to the printing press was a form of taxation imposed by the powerful industrial classes who were the main beneficiaries, upon the weaker elements in society and sold to them on the basis that the Allies were to blame. Certainly by the time inflation was in full swing Weimar governments found great difficulty in securing the agreement of the business classes to halt inflation, since stabilisation meant deflation and lower profits. The political future of the regime was so precarious that, until the final monetary collapse in the autumn of 1923, governments had not the support to take decisive steps to bring an end to inflation.

Conditions of extreme instability and social disturbance were present in all hyperinflationary countries and provided a fertile breeding ground for inflationary developments. Whether governments fostered inflation deliberately as a conscious economic policy is still a matter of debate, but the evidence does suggest that once it was well under way they were by no means averse to exploiting its benefits as an instrument of recovery and a source of government revenue (Ranki 1983a, 479; Boross 1994, 132). In some countries there were additional strong motives for letting it continue unchecked. In the USSR it was seen as a means of destroying capitalism, while in Germany as a way of demonstrating that the country could not meet the exacting reparations imposed by the Allies (Holtfrerich 1986, 149–53).

At what point inflation becomes a cause for concern and prompts governments to take action to bring it under control is a matter of some debate among economists. There are those who question whether the real costs of control can be justified and hence they seek to minimise the adverse effects of inflation. Monetarists, by and large, would argue that inflation causes so many distortions that there is no justification for delaying counter-inflationary policies.

The cost considerations of stabilisation were certainly uppermost in the minds of statesmen in the early 1920s, a fact borne out by their reluctance to contemplate positive stabilisation measures. It was widely recognised at the time that it was virtually impossible to check inflation, whatever types of policies were employed, without generating adverse effects on the real economy. Empirical research since then strongly supports this view since there have been few, if any, instances (the USSR may be the rare exception due to the fact that output and employment had sunk to such low levels in 1920) of substantial inflations having been laid to rest without causing recession and unemployment (Gordon 1982, 11–12).

This consideration was especially relevant in the hyperinflationary countries since inflation was eventually seen as a way of pushing forward reconstruction and alleviating social disorder. And so long as the majority of the people could be fooled into believing they were gainers, then the process could be continued. Once, however, the majority failed to benefit, or at least could not clearly perceive whether they were gainers or losers, then it was difficult to justify further inaction. In any case, by this time the benefits to governments via the inflation tax had all but disappeared, while the high rates of inflation that had to be imposed to generate more revenue than under constant rates 'very soon reach such tremendous heights that the monetary system verges on chaos, and a return to orthodox methods becomes an economic and political necessity. (Ranki 1983b, 583: see also Cagan 1956, 77–90).

The manner in which these countries eventually stabilised their currencies provides interesting contrasts in methodology. Resolutions of the Brussels Conference in September 1920 had suggested that the way to currency stabilisation was through budgetary equilibrium, but at the time of their deliberations things were much less chaotic than they later became. Once hyperinflation had taken a firm hold no such order of events was possible, since it was difficult to balance fiscal accounts when currencies were rapidly losing value and becoming increasingly unserviceable for assessing and collecting taxes. In reality, two possible options remained open: either the currency could be stabilised by means other than fiscal policy so as to achieve a monetary unit as the basis of an effective fiscal policy; or, following the Latvian model, the national currency could be abandoned for fiscal accounting purposes and taxes collected in terms of gold or some foreign currency.

The first of these approaches was adopted by Austria and Hungary, both of which secured the assistance and supervision of the League of Nations. Although attempts were made to increase taxes, there was no systematic effort to adjust them to the depreciation of the currency through tax valorisation schemes. In both cases the reforms comprised three main elements: the balancing of budgets, the reorganisation of the central banking system and the flotation of foreign loans. However, stabilisation of the currency preceded budgetary equilibrium and in effect it was a prerequisite of fiscal reform. As the League of Nations (1946, 23) noted: 'Stabilisation of the currency, while simultaneous with a plan for budget reform, preceded its accomplishment'. The initial stabilisation of the respective currencies was achieved by a return of confidence as a result of the League of Nations' reconstruction schemes. The League arranged international loans for Austria in 1922 and Hungary in 1924 and the League's staff undertook to supervise their finances until the end of June

1926 (League of Nations 1926a, 1926b). The mere prospect of a loan, even though not issued until 1923, was sufficient to calm the Austrian exchanges in late August 1922 and by the following month prices had peaked. By the end of the year the crown had appreciated by some 16 per cent (Dornbusch and Fischer 1986, 14). Once confidence in the currency had been restored, fiscal policy rapidly became effective and budgetary improvement ran ahead of schedule thanks to a rapid rise in real tax yields as a result of price stability. The Austrian stabilisation was completed in 1925 when a new unit of currency, the schilling, was introduced.

The Hungarian experience was similar, although technically the prospects were better, since following the Red Terror and Romanian invasion Hungary emerged with a strong right-wing government (Dornbusch 1992, 410). However, the Hungarian regime was somewhat more conscious of the deflationary implications of a counter-inflationary policy and according to Dornbusch (ibid., 413) it was not until the big explosion of 1923 that the political conditions were ripe for reform. Much of the credit for the success of monetary stabilisation is attributable to the return of confidence as a result of the government's firm resolve to bring inflation under control, together with the intervention of the League whose reconstruction scheme for Hungary also included the raising of an international loan. The inflationary spiral was halted in mid-1924 and the exchange rate of the crown was stabilised by linking it to the pound sterling. Monetary reform was completed in the following year when a new unit of currency, the pengö, was introduced. Once the currency was secure, fiscal equilibrium was restored in a short space of time with only one-quarter of the international loan being required for this purpose (Horsman 1988, 61–2; Yeager 1981, 52–5; Berend and Ranki 1974a, 99–110; League of Nations 1926b, 37–9).

The Polish and German stabilisations offer a contrast in at least two respects: first, they were more complicated and second, fiscal reform tended to precede currency stabilisation. Of the two, Poland's was by far the more protracted. Up to 1921, little effort had been made to tackle inflation since the executive machinery was far too weak to impose effective fiscal control or for that matter to devise an efficient system of tax collection. In any case it was not until 1920 that Poland had a unified currency, the Polish mark, which replaced the previous four currencies circulating in the foreign monetary zones. Both economically and politically the new republic remained fragmented for several years; there were many competing power factions so that administrations were short-lived and often powerless, while the country was engaged in border hostilities with several nations in the postwar period (Zweig 1944, 35; Heilperin 1931).

Several abortive attempts were in fact made to halt inflation and stabilise by fiscal reform since the large increase in budget deficits between 1919 and 1922 was seen as the major factor in Poland's inflation (Landau 1983, 511). The first two of these occurred between 1921 and 1923 but both failed after temporary success, largely because the fiscal effort was relaxed too soon (Jack 1927, 181–4). A further attempt was made in 1924, by which time Poland was in the throes of hyperinflation. Following the recommendations of Hilton Young's report on Polish financial conditions (1924), stringent fiscal measures were introduced which included valorisation of taxes on a gold basis. For a time these measures were sufficient to check the hyperinflation and stabilise the exchange value of the new currency, the zloty, which replaced the Polish mark. Again success was short-lived; a new depreciation of the currency began at the end of July 1925 and this rekindled fears of hyperinflation, although in actual fact the new inflationary burst proved moderate by past standards. As before, the fiscal stance was relaxed too soon, giving rise to renewed monetary growth, since the parliamentary regime was too weak to maintain the drastic fiscal measures which proper financial reform required (Zweig 1944, 40–46). Other factors also contributed to the renewed weakness of the currency, including a deterioration in the trade balance, a tariff war with Germany, and the virtual absence of any aid from abroad with which to bolster confidence (League of Nations 1946, 24–7; Smith 1936, 148–57; Mlynarski 1926, 27; Bandera 1964, 24–5). Following a further bout of inflation and exchange depreciation, albeit moderate by past standards, a final attempt was made in 1926–27. This time success was assured by the fact that a strong government under General Józef Piłsudski, who assumed control of Poland in May 1926 by military coup, introduced a harsh package of fiscal and monetary reforms designed to call a halt once and for all to the financial disorders of Poland. These measures soon restored confidence in the currency and the new exchange rate was finally legalised in the autumn of the following year with the help of a foreign stabilisation loan (Yeager 1981, 53–4; Horsman 1988, 101–3; League of Nations 1946, 27).

The German inflation, currency collapse and subsequent stabilisation of the currency have been recorded in detail many times and only the salient features need be recalled here. The origin of inflation, as with most other countries, was the wartime method of financing when the government relied heavily on short-term borrowing and currency issue to meet its expenditure (Jacobs 1977, 295). Budgetary conditions deteriorated sharply after the war due to, among other things, the rising cost of debt service, reparations demands, the burden of reconstruction spending coupled with the erosion of the tax yield through inflation. By 1920–21 the budget deficit was 65 per cent of total expenditure. The budgetary position worsened further in subsequent years, not least because of declining revenue yields and the vast expenditure incurred in mounting the passive resistance to the French invasion of the Ruhr. At the peak of inflation, almost all government expenditure was being financed by currency issue and taxes accounted for a mere 1.3 per cent of state spending (ibid.). As Dornbusch and Fischer (1986, 7) observe:

> The German inflation shows the clear pattern of massive deficits continuing for several years, leading to increasing inflation, increasing velocity and falling real tax revenue until some event leads to exchange rate collapse and hence a completely uncontrolled inflation. In Germany the critical event was the French occupation of the Ruhr in January 1923 and the resulting demands made upon the budget.

However, prior to this event the government of the day had made only half-hearted attempts to check inflation and bring the country's finances into order. The main reason for this failure was that the new and inexperienced socialist government fought a losing battle to establish its authority against strong opposition from conservative and business classes. Both Feldman (1975, 1993) and Holtfrerich (1986) have also drawn attention to the international constraints on government action as well as the domestic one of social disorder. Ultimately, however, it was the ability of the business interests, who were the main beneficiaries of inflation, to thwart the state's attempt to pass tax reforms, which proved the chief stumbling block. Ironically, the head of the government which carried out the inflationary financing of the Ruhr industrialists was a man of big business.

Two important measures preceded the stabilisation of the mark in November 1923. First, the passive resistance expenditure in the Ruhr was terminated in September 1923 and taxes were assessed in terms of gold and collected in national currency at the rate of the day. Almost simultaneously with these preparations for restoring budgetary equilibrium, it was announced that a new currency, the *Rentenmark*, would be introduced to replace the now worthless currency in existence. The new mark, valued at one million million old marks, was brought in on 15 November and five days later the exchange rate was fixed. The currency was backed by the security of an internal loan on the basis of real assets (land and buildings); the issue was to be strictly limited to 2400 million marks; and, to prevent the monetisation of public deficits, the Reichsbank was no longer to discount government bills (Dornbusch 1987, 348). Once again, much depended upon the confidence factor. Once there appeared a reasonable prospect that the Rentenmark would retain its value, the public's demand for cash recovered quickly. But there were some anxious moments: the new currency had limited gold backing and for many months its existence remained precarious. Had the government not set about completing its fiscal reforms immediately following the stabilisation it is doubtful if the new currency would have survived for long. Moreover, it was not until 1924, when Germany secured an international loan (the Dawes loan), that the currency was converted to a more solid gold base and renamed the Reichsmark. Angell (1929, 26) suggests that without this Germany might well have suffered another bout of inflation.

Although the German stabilisation proved successful, the episode left lasting and bitter memories, probably more so than in any other country facing a similar experience. The currency was eventually fixed at an undervalued rate, interest rates remained high and savings were adversely affected by the recollection of inflation. But perhaps the most poignant aspect was the failure of the government to come up with an equitable scheme of asset revaluation to compensate the losers. This more than anything else helped to bring about the disintegration of the Weimar Republic (Hughes 1988; Ferguson 1995).

Intermediate stabilisations

Although the majority of countries at least avoided the ignominy of complete currency collapse, their inflations were sufficiently severe to preclude the possibility of returning to prewar parity. However, few countries found currency stabilisation an easy task, and in some cases several attempts had to be made before success was achieved.

The earliest and most exemplary stabilisations were those of Latvia and Czechoslovakia, both of which managed to take firm action to stem inflation at an early stage. Latvia, without a currency of her own and faced with a relatively large reconstruction task, put a stop to inflation in the summer of 1921 and became one of the first countries to stabilise. Even more impressive was the fact that Latvia was able to stabilise without external assistance. From the inception of the new republic a rigorous fiscal policy was enforced and this checked the incipient hyperinflation of the early months of 1921. In May of the same year, legal provision was made for the collection of all taxes in terms of a new unit of currency, the lat, equivalent to one gold franc. This was in fact the first case of 'tax valorisation' in the history of postwar inflation. By July 1921, state recourse to the printing press for budgetary purposes ceased. In the latter half of the year prices stabilised and the exchange rate appreciated, and from early 1922 the dollar rate remained comparatively stable (League of Nations 1946, 121–3).

The Czech experience was not dissimilar in that the policy approach was equally rigorous, although one should bear in mind that the Czech economy was in a much stronger position than those of other Central and East European countries, having inherited a large part of the former

Austro-Hungarian Empire's industrial base. Czechoslovakia was the only successor state to avoid the ravages of a long and severe inflation. Much of the credit for the success is usually attributed to Alois Rasin, the country's first minister of finance, who was a strong advocate of financial prudence. He was determined to provide the new republic with a sound monetary and financial system. His plan involved three major steps. In the first place monetary reform was enacted early in 1919 when a new unit of currency, the Czech crown, replaced the old currency notes of the former empire which were still circulating in Czech territory. Second, Rasin reduced the amount of currency in circulation by 20 per cent and set a ceiling on the note issue to prevent excess creation of money. Third, fiscal reform was undertaken promptly so that state finances were put on a secure basis and the budget balanced in 1920–21. This involved the imposition of new and higher taxes, especially on the increased value of property, which provided support for the monetary reform (Gruber 1924, 200; Pryor 1973, 194–5; Wiskemann 1938, 141–3; Rasin 1923; Seton-Watson 1928, 61–3). The instant success of the Latvian policy was not repeated, however. Prices continued to rise through 1921 and the new currency fluctuated quite sharply in the first few years. On fundamental grounds there was no valid basis for weakness in the currency. The reason seems to have been that initially the crown tended to track the movements of the German mark, in the mistaken belief that it was yet another suspect currency. Once this illusion was dispelled the Czech crown appreciated, partly in response to a flight out of the mark, but also because deflationary policy in 1922 finally brought an end to the rise in prices. The new level of the crown was then maintained, and in 1923 stabilisation was finally completed (Gruber 1924, 183–9; Berend and Ranki 1974b, 181–2; Teichova 1983, 561). Dornbusch (1992, 403) reckons that the hard money strategy led to massive overvaluation of the currency in 1922–23, causing a strong rise in unemployment.

The French stabilisation was a much more complex affair. Although comparatively modest by hyperinflationary standards – retail prices rose less than threefold between the Armistice and the peak of 1926 – inflationary pressures were persistent, and at one stage hyperinflation appeared a distinct possibility. For much of the 1920s the struggle to save the franc occupied the attention of the authorities since, apart from a short deflationary period between 1921 and 1922, it was continually under pressure until stabilised in 1926.

The French depreciation cannot be attributed to any one particular cause. During the war and immediately thereafter the unsatisfactory state of public finances led to a highly inflationary situation, since the government was forced to borrow heavily from the banks and public and this in turn was accompanied by a large increase in paper currency. France's method of war finance has been described as a 'model of ineptitude' (Kemp 1971, 88; Jèze 1921), although it was by no means unique in this respect. After the war, public spending continued at a high level, since the government paid out liberal compensation to war victims and contributed generously to reconstruction in the belief that most of the cost would be defrayed by German reparations. In the event, reparations covered only just over one-third of the costs of reconstruction and the rest had to be financed mainly by large-scale borrowing, amounting to 159 billion francs between 1919 and 1926, which resulted in a doubling of the internal debt (Ogburn and Jaffé 1929, 60, 66; Dulles 1929, 10).

However, despite the huge public outlays on reconstruction the budgetary situation was not a major problem. For most of the period the budget deficit was declining and, excluding interest payments, by 1924 it was already in surplus (Prati 1991, 214; compare Sargent 1984). Nor was excessive monetary growth a crucial factor since, apart from the period 1925–26, the note issue was virtually static (Horsman 1988, 77).

The almost continuous depreciation of the franc was primarily occasioned by persistent capital flight abroad as currency operators lost confidence in the currency. One cause for concern was the structure of the public debt and its financing. Much of the increase consisted of short-term bonds held by the public and the banks, and as the financial demands of business increased from 1923 onwards the government found it increasingly difficult to renew the debt as it matured. The position was complicated by the maturing of a large slice of long-term debt in 1925 and the fear that the leftist coalition governments in power from May 1924 to July 1926 would impose a capital levy to deal with the problem. Consequently, bondholders refused to roll over the debt and the government was forced to resort to monetary financing through the banking system which put pressure on prices and the exchanges (Rogers 1929, 350; Peel 1925; Miller 1930; Prati 1991, 214, 237).

An additional factor which did little to inspire confidence was the political instability in France. Indeed, it has been noted that 'the only periods when the franc was stable were those of the parliamentary recesses' (Patat and Lutfalla 1990, 30). Beth Williams (1994, 168) has stressed the lack of credibility in French finances as a result of political instability, distrust of left-wing coalition governments and the corrupt machinations of the central bank in its attempts to conceal the monetary accommodation of the state's debts. The almost continuous rise in the floating debt from the end of the war when coupled with political instability served as a potent force in undermining financial confidence resulting in currency crises and panic capital flight. Ministries came and went in quick succession – a total of 11 between March 1924 and July 1926 – and in the ten months before Raymond Poincaré came to power no less than eight finance ministers ('the waltz of the portfolios') had tried but failed to deal with the nation's financial and currency problems. Resolution on these matters was made the more difficult by the serious division of opinion as to the measures which should be taken and the rate at which currency stabilisation should be effected (Kemp 1971, 83–4; Schmitz 1930; Williams 1994). The situation was also complicated by the fact that many in France continued to believe that she would eventually return to gold at the prewar parity. The current difficulties were considered to be only temporary and it was genuinely believed that the automatic functioning of the monetary laws would ensure the re-emergence of the franc germinal as had happened in 1848 and 1870 when the gold standard had to be abandoned temporarily (Wolfe 1951, 207–8).

Speculative pressures may also have played a part. Kindleberger (1984, 360) reckons the history of the franc reveals the presence of destabilising speculation, a view highlighted in 1944 by Ragnar Nurkse (League of Nations 1944). As confidence in the country's financial situation waned, investors and speculators moved against the franc and drove it down well below the cost-competitiveness of French goods. This in turn added to the inflationary pressures through higher import costs and the need to generate an export surplus to finance the short-term capital outflow (Aliber 1962, 242–3). According to Dulles (1929, 45–6), by 1925–26 concern about the value of the franc had spread far outside the range of the professional speculators such that 'The cost of the dollar was the subject of conversation in every corner café and one could hardly make a purchase without some discussion of the exchange rate'. Whether the destabilising properties of speculation were as important as many contemporaries believed has been questioned by more recent researchers (Eichengreen 1982; see also below). Be that as it may, it was not until pressure on the franc reached panic proportions, when it sank to two cents in July 1926, that action was finally taken to remedy the situation.

Fortunately, the accession to power of a strong right-wing government under Poincaré in July 1926 was sufficient to allay fears that the franc would be allowed to go the same way as the German mark. A series of rigorous financial measures, including changes in taxation, reductions in public spending and the funding of a large part of the floating debt at an attractive rate of interest were announced (Sauvy 1963, 392). The last item was crucial since it indicated that the authorities no longer intended to monetise the public debt which had been seen as the main factor behind inflation (Prati 1991, 225–8, 237). At the same time, bondholders' reluctance to roll over debt was assuaged by the removal of the threat of a capital levy and a lightening of the taxation burden on capitalists. In August, the Bank of France was able to announce a fixed buying rate for the pound sterling. The package of measures soon re-established confidence and refugee capital returned to France. By the end of the year *de facto* stabilisation of the franc was announced and in June 1928 France completed her currency reform with a return to the gold standard at the then prevailing exchange rate, that is, equivalent to 20 per cent of the prewar value. This rate undervalued the franc, although whether by deliberate intent or not seems still the matter for debate, and so for a time gave a fillip to exports (Sicsic 1992, 88–9; Cohen 1977, 88; Mouré 1996).

The Belgian franc traced a similar course to the French currency in the postwar years, partly because it was closely linked with the latter in the minds of speculators who expected it to exchange on a one-for-one basis with the French franc (van der Wee and Tavernier 1975, 72). Accordingly, despite any success on the domestic front, it was difficult for the Belgian authorities to pursue an independent stabilisation policy (Aliber 1962, 242). That notwithstanding, Belgium's own financial problems made stabilisation difficult. The government had undertaken to finance the whole cost of postwar reconstruction in the same mistaken belief that the Germans would foot the bill. This and other postwar expenditures led to a big increase in public debt and large budgetary deficits, averaging one-third of government spending in the period 1919–26 and more than 12 per cent of GNP at the peak in 1925 (Cassiers 1995, 225). When reparations failed to live up to expectations and the Germans defaulted on their obligations, the debt and budgetary situation became a cause of great concern both at home and abroad. This was soon transmitted to the exchanges as dealers sought to protect themselves, while investors showed an increasing unwillingness to take up long-term government debt. This inevitably forced the government into a policy of monetising the debt by short-term financing and, as in the case of France, the rise in the floating debt exacerbated inflation and spurred on the depreciation of the currency.

The government made an unsuccessful attempt to stabilise the franc between October 1925 and March 1926. Failure to improve the fiscal position, and especially to deal with the large floating debt, was at the root of the problem. The National Bank, on behalf of the Treasury, began to buy up franc notes in exchange for foreign currencies (mainly dollars), but the notes were simply put back into circulation by the Treasury in meeting redemptions on maturing obligations. Consequently there was no reduction in the total note issue. Doubts about the size of the public debt and the near record budget deficit in 1925 led to fears that there would be further recourse to the printing press, with the result that the Treasury had difficulty in renewing maturing obligations (Shepherd

1936, 30–31, 46, 233–5). Then, in the spring of 1926, attempts to secure an international loan to stabilise the franc at 107 to the pound failed. This proved to be the last straw. Panic swept through the exchange markets and the franc plunged to 230 to the pound, a far greater fall than warranted by fundamental factors alone. A coalition government under Emile Franqui was hastily formed with full powers to deal with the crisis (Pringle 1928, 140–41; Baudhuin 1946, 152–72). Drastic monetary and fiscal measures were introduced, on the basis of which an international loan of $135 million was raised in October 1926. Within two years, the mammoth fiscal deficit had been converted to a surplus, a more dramatic turnaround than in the case of France (Cassiers 1995, 225). These radical measures proved sufficient to hold the situation and the franc was then stabilised at one-seventh of its prewar level.

The similarities between Belgium and France are quite close. In both cases public confidence was sensitive to large floating debts which gave expectations of inflationary government policies. Control of the money supply was made difficult by the structure of the public debt. The inability of weak governments to get to grips with the nations' financial problems led to further loss of confidence and probably accounts for the fact that the respective currencies were driven down below their true equilibrium rates which resulted in stabilisation at undervalued levels (Schmid 1974, 377–8). The success of stabilisation was very much dependent on the policy pronouncements, subsequently backed by action, of strong governments.

The Italian case provides something of a contrast because the budgetary problem was scarcely an issue after the advent of the Fascist regime in 1922. Drastic economy measures were taken to counter the inflationary polices of the immediate postwar years when the lira had plummeted on the exchanges (Forsyth 1993, 230–31). Consequently the deficit of the early 1920s was rapidly reduced and by 1924 the budget was more or less in balance, although there was still a high volume of short-term debt outstanding (Welk 1938, 159–62; McGuire 1927, 97). However, although the fall in the lira was halted, an active stabilisation policy had to await settlement of the debt owed to the Allies. Agreements were reached in late 1925 and early 1926 with both the United States and Britain, but by this time the currency was showing renewed signs of weakness due to rapid credit expansion between 1922 and 1926 designed to hasten industrial development. At this point political factors entered the scene. Mussolini was determined to consolidate his power and enhance the prestige of his regime and one way of doing this was to pledge firm support for the currency irrespective of the economic consequences. In a speech to the nation in August 1926 he promised to 'defend the lira to the last breath, to the last drop of blood' (Cohen 1972, 647–9;

Sarti 1970, 642–54). To further his aim he pushed through drastic deflationary measures and thereby ended up overvaluing the lira. The rate was
fixed at 19 lira to the dollar in December 1927 (25 per cent of the prewar
value) as against 25–26 to the dollar which had prevailed over the previous two years. This has been described as the most spectacular and
deliberate overvaluation of the time in an effort to make the lira a stable
and prestigious currency (Sarti 1970, 97). It had unfortunate consequences for the domestic economy, and industry had to be compensated
in other directions. Mussolini had, of course, greater political latitude to
enforce severe compression policies than his counterparts in the prewar
parity countries (Cohen 1972, 651–2; Zamagni 1993, 251–2).

The restoration of fixed exchange rate regimes was of no less importance to many countries outside Europe, although the war had left a legacy
of problems, not least the collapse of staple exports. Latin America, for
example, had fared well during the war when demand for primary commodities had been strong and currencies had often strengthened against
sterling. Once the postwar boom broke in 1920–21, many countries were
left prostrate, the victims of inflation and depreciating exchanges.

The task of currency stabilisation was also complicated by other factors,
including political instability, heavy dependence on the export of one or two
staple crops, and the lack of adequate monetary institutions, most notably
central banks. The creation of central banks, together with a general
strengthening of financial institutions, therefore became the instrument by
which exchange stability was eventually carried out. During the 1920s,
Dr E.W. Kemmerer, a Princeton University don, headed several missions to
Latin American countries and played a similar role to that of Montagu
Norman, Governor of the Bank of England, in Europe and the
Commonwealth. He was instrumental in setting up central banks in several
of the republics including Peru (1922), Colombia (1923), Uruguay (1924),
Chile and Guatemala (1925), Ecuador (1927) and Bolivia (1929). These new
banks were to function within the framework of the gold exchange standard; they had a monopoly of note issue; and they could undertake open
market operations, act as lenders of last resort and determine discount
rates. By these measures it was hoped to regulate the governments' discretionary note-issuing powers, check the monetisation of budgetary deficits
and encourage governments to use sounder methods of public finance.

In the event the experiment, as with Montagu Norman's experience in
Eastern Europe, was not an unqualified success. The rigidities of the gold
standard rates circumscribed the activities of the central banks. They lacked
the means of using interest rates to attract foreign funds and in practice
their role was confined largely to limiting the note issue. The mechanism of
external adjustment proved difficult in economies specialising in the export

of staple products, especially when prices fell sharply as they did in 1929. Under the preconceived rules of the game the banks were faced with a choice of enforcing sharp compression on the domestic economy or abandoning the gold standard (Joslin 1963, 229–31; Furtado 1970, 68–72).

The costs and benefits of floating rates

The stabilisation of currencies following the breakdown of the prewar gold standard was a complex and protracted affair which took the best part of a decade. There was little coordinated action among nations and hence it was a matter of luck whether the correct exchange rates were achieved. The new gold standard had a short life and within a few years it had all but disintegrated. Its operation and demise are the subject of the next chapter, but first we turn to some of the outstanding issues relating to the period of free floating.

For the first few years after the war, that is until currency stabilisation became fairly general, currencies were for the most part allowed to float freely with only very limited intervention on the part of monetary authorities. In fact this period is perhaps the best example of clean floating in the whole of the twentieth century. As already indicated, contemporaries were by no means enamoured with floating exchanges, perhaps scarcely surprising given the very large swings in exchange rates that took place in some countries. Fluctuating rates, it was argued, caused uncertainty and instability and for that reason they could not be good for recovery or sound economic development. The second main contention was that floating exchanges encouraged destabilising speculation which led to overtracking, that is, a departure of exchange rates from their true equilibrium levels based on fundamentals or purchasing power parity calculations. This in turn caused stabilisation to be carried out at inappropriate levels.

Assessing the impact of different exchange rate regimes is not a straightforward matter. For one thing the periods of the alternative regimes are very short, that is, fairly general floating through to 1923–24 and then fixed rates under a resurrected gold standard into the early 1930s. The two regimes also overlap considerably because of the lack of synchronised stabilisation. Second, the early 1920s are somewhat artificial anyway because of the strong scope for recovery from the very low levels of output and trade obtaining in the immediate postwar years and the distortions caused by widespread and severe inflation.

As far as trade is concerned, there may be some substance in the assertion that unstable exchanges hampered the recovery in international intercourse. World trade, and especially European trade, lagged behind production in the first half of the decade so that trade–income ratios declined compared with prewar levels. Subsequently through to 1929, trade expanded more rapidly than output, although it is doubtful whether trade–income ratios were restored to their former values (Loveday 1931, 70; Woytinsky and Woytinsky 1955, 39–42; Svennilson 1954, 292; Maddison 1962, 186–7). Sir Henry Strakosch (1937) noted that Europe's foreign trade expanded rapidly after 1923 when currency fluctuations subsided markedly. A weighted index based on the average monthly percentage variations in the dollar value of European currencies fell from 13.2 per cent in 1922 and 10.3 per cent in 1923 to 2.6 per cent in 1924 and only 1.4 per cent in 1925. But it should also be noted that there was a very strong gain in trade volume between 1921 and 1922 when currency instability was near its peak. There were, of course, exceptional factors in this case, notably the sharp rebound in the trade of the Anglo-Saxon countries following the postwar slump in these countries and also the trade gains arising from currency depreciation in the high-inflation countries. On balance however, the evidence would seem to favour the view that stable exchange rates were more propitious for sound trade growth.

With regard to postwar reconstruction and recovery in general, the evidence suggests that inflation and associated currency depreciation were of some benefit, at least initially. They provided a temporary boost to activity, trade and employment which meant that inflationary countries did not experience the sharp contraction in activity that occurred in the Anglo-Saxon countries between 1920 and 1921, largely as a result of the severe fiscal and monetary measures imposed to check inflation. The stimulus was most evident in industry, which benefited from the boost to exports through currency depreciation and the fall in real interest rates as nominal values lagged inflation. Where real wages were depressed and capital gained at the expense of labour, as in the case of Germany and many East European countries, this provided an artificial stimulus to investment and output. Furthermore, the decline in the value of money encouraged a flight into fixed assets including capital equipment and buildings (Aldcroft and Morewood 1995, 32–3; Eichengreen 1986a).

However, it is not always easy to distinguish the influence of inflation and currency depreciation from other factors. The example of Greece is a good case in point. Until the mid-1920s, Greece suffered severe inflation and currency depreciation due to lax fiscal and monetary policies (caused by war and political instability) under a floating exchange regime. Industrial output surged ahead at the rate of 7.2 per cent a year between 1921 and 1927. While inflation and currency depreciation no doubt imparted a short-term stimulus to industry, one should also note that manufacturers benefited from heavy tariff protection and a sharp fall in real wages after 1921 due to the depressing effect of a large increase in the country's population as a result of the influx of refugees, many of whom were urban workers, following the defeat by Turkey in Asia Minor. It is also notable that the industrial expansion tailed off somewhat when the authorities moved to stabilise the currency in 1927–28 (Lazaretou 1996, 649–50, 664).

While most countries experiencing inflation, whether moderate or hyperinflationary, appear to have gained a stimulus to activity, it is questionable whether there were many lasting benefits. After all, when stabilisation finally occurred, most of the temporary gains were eliminated as output and employment fell sharply, as is usually the case (Gordon 1982). The post-stabilisation setback was especially severe in the hyperinflationary countries where unemployment rose sharply (Wicker 1986). The inflation boom also gave rise to serious resource misallocation and the artificial creation of assets and enterprises as savings were invested in things which would retain real value. Many of the inflation-inspired creations collapsed like a pack of cards once the artificial conditions ceased to exist, leading to a trail of abandoned assets (Kavka 1960, 115). The most famous of these was the collapse of the Stinnes combine in Germany. Others had to be propped up by state protection (Einzig 1935, 77). Feldman (1993, 843) sounds an appropriately cautious note on the longer-term balance sheet for industry:

> The condition of German industry certainly would have been worse without the inflationary reconstruction, but it would be a mistake to overestimate the depth of that reconstruction and an even greater mistake to think that its longer-term consequences were as positive as they could have been or should have been.

Inflation also had an adverse impact on income distribution and savings. The distribution of income and wealth became more uneven since it was businesspeople, landowners, debtors and speculators who tended to gain, largely at the expense of the rest of society. Wages and salaries generally lagged behind prices so that in many cases real incomes were well below those of prewar. Savings were for the most part wiped out unless invested in fixed assets.

Longer term, the episode had serious consequences. The spectre of inflation and currency depreciation haunted many European countries for a generation or more and as such it conditioned reactions to the slump of 1929–32. Fears of rekindling inflation served as an obstacle to the adoption of expansionary policies (Laursen and Pedersen 1964, 11). Einzig (1935, 77) reckoned that economic nationalism was to a large extent the outgrowth of the postwar currency chaos. Certainly in the case of Germany one can trace the roots of the disintegration of the Weimar Republic to the financial events of this period, even perhaps the seeds of the second world war (Feldman 1993, 837; Hughes 1988).

Were fluctuating exchange rates destabilising? Most contemporaries were convinced that floating rates were bad for trade and the economy because they gave rise to destabilising speculation and hence led to over-tracking in exchange rates. In fact, from a reading of the contemporary press it would be easy to gain the impression that all short-term movements in exchange rates had a speculative flavour (Thomas 1972, 147). International exchange rates, it was believed, were often determined by abnormal and frequently speculative short-term capital movements which caused actual rates to deviate from notional equilibrium rates as determined by economic fundamentals or purchasing power parity calculations (Harris 1931, 277–90). As a result, some countries eventually emerged with overvalued currencies, others with undervalued ones. This view soon became part of the conventional wisdom, invested with no lesser authority than the League of Nations in their report on *International Currency Experience*, which was drafted largely by Ragnar Nurkse and published in 1944 (see also Polak 1943). The report referred to a number of cases, for example Czechoslovakia, Denmark, Norway and Italy, where speculation on stabilisation prospects had led to currency overvaluation, but their classic example was reserved for the speculation which led to the undervaluation of the French franc (League of Nations 1944, 32, 117–21, 138–9).

The presence of destabilising speculation in the 1920s was confirmed in some later studies. Aliber (1962) found that in Britain, Belgium, France, Switzerland and the Netherlands, speculative transactions caused actual rates to deviate significantly from equilibrium rates which, he believed, compromised the greater degree of freedom for domestic policy under flexible rates (compare Kindleberger 1984, 360). Similarly, Krugman (1978, 407), found, on the basis of tests on the mark–dollar, sterling–dollar and franc–dollar rates in the first half of the 1920s, that deviations of the rates from their respective purchasing power parity levels were both large and fairly persistent, especially in countries with unstable monetary policies. Foreign speculators operated strongly on the Spanish peseta in the later 1920s as hopes of stabilisation at the prewar gold parity waxed and waned (Harrison 1985, 67–8). On the other hand, there has been a challenge to the conventional wisdom by several writers who have sought to show that there was little in the way of destabilising speculation in this period (Thomas 1973a, 1973b; Tsiang 1959–60; Hodgson 1972; Frenkel 1977, 1978, 1980; Clements and Frenkel 1980). Thomas (1972) found some confirmation for the traditional notion that speculation destabilised the French franc, but warned that the same was not necessarily true for other currencies. Eichengreen (1982) even concluded that speculation reduced the volatility of the franc–pound rate. Sicsic (1992, 88–9) reckons that the jury is still out on this matter, although he suggests that there may be some appeal in the destabilising argument for the large depreciation of the French currency in the first half of 1926.

The traditional argument against floating rates derives largely from the experience of the early 1920s when rates were very unstable and moved erratically and were therefore deemed to be harmful to macroeconomic stability. However, it would be wrong to assume from that episode that free floating is always pernicious, or that it automatically leads to the cumulative overtracking of exchange rates through self-aggravating capital movements, since as Tsiang (1959–60, 245, 273) has pointed out, the underlying instability in the exchanges in this period can be traced to a supply of money and credit which was extremely elastic with respect to interest rates. This would seem to square with Dornbusch's (1983, 4) view that flexible rates perform poorly in conditions of significant monetary and fiscal disturbance (compare Krugman 1978, 407), and that they require as much managing as fixed rate regimes. If that is the case, it follows therefore that the abrogation of sound financial policies will most likely produce chaos in free floating markets (Thomas 1973b, 149).

Whatever the truth of the matter, the fact remains that a solution to the stabilisation problem of the 1920s was conditioned by the market forces of the period rather than regulated or guided by coordinated agreement. How far currencies diverged from their true equilibrium levels due to speculative pressures is still a matter for debate, but that does not alter the fact that many currencies were stabilised at inappropriate levels and this became a source of strain for the restored gold standard. The League of Nations (1944, 117), with the benefit of hindsight, believed that the haphazard and uncoordinated approach to stabilisation sowed the seeds of the subsequent disintegration of the restored gold standard: 'It was partly because of the lack of proper coordination during the stabilisation period of the 'twenties that the system broke down in the 'thirties'. How far the defects of the stabilisation exercise were responsible for the collapse of the new standard in the early 1930s remains to be seen.

2 The new gold standard and its disintegration

For much of the 1920s the dominating factor in economic policy was the currency question: first, the effort of stabilising exchange rates and returning to gold, and then the struggle to maintain the new standard. For rich and poor countries alike the monetary ideal generally took precedence over all other matters of economic policy. At the time its restoration was widely acclaimed, especially by banking and monetary experts, as the panacea for international stability and recovery (Sayers 1976a, 111). O.M.W. Sprague, financial adviser to the US government and for several years also to the Bank of England, had this to say in 1930:

> The gold standard has emerged triumphantly from the welter of disorganised currencies of the World War period and gold has now become more universally than ever before the foundation of the structure of credit throughout the world. This return to the haven of familiar monetary practice is significant of the widespread conviction that the gold standard is an essential factor in the maintenance of a reasonable measure of international stability, for which there is no promising or practical substitute. (League of Nations 1930b, 53)

Even later writers conceded that its resurrection had some merit, even though they were conscious of its shortcomings (Sayers 1960, 324; Kunz 1987, 189–90; Hardach 1995, 187).

The short-term costs entailed in its restoration were considered worthwhile since much was expected from it. Referring to Britain's return to gold, Cassel (1936, 40) believed that the moderate deflation required was a price well worth paying since 'the relatively small sacrifices involved in that step were much more than counterbalanced by the restoration of international confidence and by the stimulus given to international trade through the replacement of the pound sterling in its old position as the principal currency of the world's trade'. Most countries faithfully believed that its restoration would solve the economic problems left outstanding from the war. As Brown (1940 **II**, 801) succinctly put it:

> Before 1925 concentration upon the goal of a return to normal and upon the achievement of stable exchange rates, and after 1925 the splendours of a stable exchange standard blinded the eyes of bankers and of the world in general.

The illusion that the economic maladjustments would be corrected by automatic forces was dominant in the world's financial thinking.

Such cherished illusions were soon to be shattered. The new gold standard was a fragile and short-lived affair. Well over 50 nations were on some form of gold standard (the majority on the gold exchange standard) for an average duration of some six and a half years, with the most effective concentration in the period 1927–31 (Palyi 1972, 116–17; Eichengreen 1984, 64). Far from correcting the underlying maladjustments, the revised gold standard itself was subject to serious strains from the start and within a few years it had disintegrated. Like a damp squib rekindled, it sputtered for a while and then fizzled out. One of the most intriguing and complex problems is to explain why it did not live up to expectations. How was it that a system which apparently served so well before 1914 seemingly failed to function 'properly' after the war? An answer to this question should help to explain why the system collapsed in the early 1930s. However, the underlying weaknesses of the restored standard are not the only possible reasons for its collapse, since the short-term factors associated with depression and financial crisis need to be taken into account. A second point of equal importance is how the gold standard affected the business recession that set in at the end of the 1920s. Recent research has tended to attribute greater causal connection between the gold standard and depression, stressing the role it played in both propagating and aggravating the downturn. In fact not only could it be said to have intensified the deflationary pressures already present, but it also constrained domestic policy action in promoting recovery (Eichengreen 1992b). Writing on the French stabilisation and return to gold for example, Mouré (1996, 150) claims that 'Rather than marking the end of an era of currency instability, it opened a new phase of international disharmony and deflation leading to the breakdown of the gold standard.'

Few subjects have attracted so much attention as the gold standard. Contemporaries wrote profusely on various aspects, although much of the writing was of a mediocre quality and it often tended to portray a stereotyped ideal which had never really existed in practice. In more recent years, interest in the topic has been rekindled and there has been a spate of new work. This has done much to correct or modify some of the more popular notions of the time regarding the operation of the system both before and after the first world war, although several aspects still require clarification. It has also given rise to considerable debate and controversy on some aspects, which has in some respects made the subject even more complex.

That the restored gold standard disintegrated in the early 1930s after such a short time in operation might be seen as a priori proof that it was inherently defective compared with its classical predecessor. This would suggest that its characteristics and *modus operandi* were essentially different from those before 1914 and that these were sufficient to bring about its collapse irrespective of the impact of short-term disturbances. A second possibility is that it did not differ that radically from the classical standard, taking into account that the version painted by contemporaries was not totally accurate, and that longer-term structural and real factors were responsible for its demise. That is, in particular, relative price and structural distortions coupled with shocks to the system forced countries to abandon the standard when its retention became intolerable. A third scenario would be that there was nothing basically wrong with the new gold and that it was undermined by depression and financial crisis which eventually force countries to abandon their golden ideal. In this version, the reasons for the departure of the UK and the US, especially the former, are crucial since they dragged so many other countries with them.

The prewar gold standard, as recent research has emphasised, may not have worked in the idealised way that many contemporaries assumed, but even allowing for this fact there seems little doubt that the postwar standard was a somewhat different beast from its classical counterpart. The differences can best be illustrated by examining a series of key issues which have featured prominently in the literature:

- the use of gold and the role of reserve currencies;
- disequilibrium in exchange rate setting;
- the rules of the game;
- gold stocks and gold supply;
- commitment to the standard;
- management of the gold standard and international cooperation; and
- convergence and harmony in policy and development.

Gold and reserve currencies

The most visible sign of difference between the prewar and postwar gold standards was the decline in the use of commodity money. The postwar gold standard was not a full gold standard since gold coins disappeared from circulation almost everywhere, except in the United States and one or two other countries. However, it is easy to exaggerate the significance of this change. Even in the heyday of the gold standard before 1914, gold was by no means the chief unit of exchange or account. It is true that gold coin and bullion circulated freely both within and across national boundaries and that paper instruments of exchange were readily convertible into metallic money. Indeed, the essence of the gold standard was that the authorities maintained ready convertibility between gold and their national monetary units at fixed rates of exchange and that the movement of gold across national frontiers was free from hindrance. But the use of commodity money (gold and silver) rapidly diminished in importance as a unit of account in the later nineteenth century, to be replaced by a vast expansion of more convenient credit money (paper money and bank deposits). During the first half of the nineteenth century, credit money had constituted little more than one-third of the total money supply of the major countries, while silver at its peak accounted for about one-half. Thereafter gold began to replace silver as many countries moved on to a monometallic standard, but even its importance dwindled rapidly in relation to the total money supply. Thus between 1850 and the early 1870s two-thirds or more of the total monetary expansion in the major developing nations was provided by credit money, and no less than 95 per cent in the years up to 1914. By the latter date, paper and bank money had completely dwarfed metallic circulations, with gold (10 per cent) and silver (5 per cent) making up the difference (Triffin 1968, 20, 26). Such dramatic changes were, of course, essential for servicing the needs of an expanding international economy which could scarcely have taken place under the rigid and cumbersome metallic systems of the past. On the other hand, they do put a rather different complexion on the very nature of the gold standard itself. Not only was it less rigid and less automatic than many earlier writers claimed, but the very name itself was something of an anachronism. As Triffin (ibid., 21) remarked: 'the nineteenth century could be far more accurately described as the century of an emerging and growing credit-money standard, and of the euthanasia of gold and silver moneys, rather than as the century of the gold standard'.

Thus while the prewar gold standard may have been one in which there was a universal right to convert non-commodity money into gold should one so wish, for all practical purposes gold had ceased to play an important part in everyday transactions. Postwar, the right to convert was withdrawn for most citizens since the minimum amounts specified (gold ingots) were beyond the means of most people. But the postwar standard could not be regarded as a pure bullion standard, either, since only in a few countries were currencies directly convertible into gold bullion. As noted in Chapter 1, many countries, through lack of gold reserves and other factors, were forced to adopt a gold exchange standard under which they held their legally required reserves wholly or partly in the foreign exchange of a key currency (sterling and dollars) that was convertible. Again, this practice was not unknown before 1914 when several countries operated a gold exchange standard, while most of the major countries held some reserves in the form of foreign exchange (Lindert 1969). During the 1920s, it was widely adopted throughout Europe and by many countries overseas. The practice had been recommended by the Financial Committee of the Genoa Conference of 1922, with Montagu Norman one of its most ardent advocates, as a way of economising on gold which was deemed to be in short supply (Eichengreen 1989, 263). The effect of the switch was to increase considerably the foreign exchange component of central bank reserves: in 1927, foreign exchange accounted for 42 per cent of the total reserves (gold and foreign exchange) of 24 European central banks, as against 27 per cent in 1924 and only 12 per cent in 1913 (League of Nations 1944, 29, 35).

The widespread adoption of the gold exchange standard, accompanied by the withdrawal of gold coins from circulation, may have eased the pressure on gold supplies, but in itself it was a source of weakness rather than one of strength, since it only transferred the problem by one remove, that is, from gold to key currencies.

One of the main problems with a multipolar reserve system was that it led to a 'pyramiding' of claims on gold centres, so that a crisis in one country might affect a whole series of currencies with serious consequences for the reserve centres (Bernanke and James 1991, 247–8; League of Nations 1944, 29, 35). Gold exchange standard countries built up their exchange reserve holdings through short-term claims on key currencies, notably sterling and the dollar. The accommodation of large holdings of foreign claims put a severe strain on the central money markets because these funds proved highly volatile and could pass from one centre to another, depending on relative interest rates and changes in confidence. The existence of more than one international financial centre of importance (London, New York and later Paris) provided ample opportunity for fund switching, whereas before the war sterling's strength and unchallenged supremacy, together with closer correspondence in interest rate movements among the major countries, gave less incentive for this to take place. Moreover, under the more unstable postwar conditions there was a much greater danger that foreign exchange holdings would be converted into gold. Nor was such conversion solely contingent on a crisis of confidence. Many countries regarded the gold exchange standard as a sort of half-way house on the way to the resumption of a full gold standard, and for this reason they were anxious to build up their gold stocks. France, especially, was very reluctant to sacrifice her national honour by remaining on an exchange standard. Thus following the *de facto* stabilisation of the franc in 1926, the Bank of France acquired the largest stock of foreign exchange (mainly sterling and dollars) in the world. This policy was partly designed initially to prevent the undue appreciation of the French currency, but there was a consistent threat, which in the later 1920s became a reality, that these holdings would be converted into gold to realise French ambitions (Royal Institute of International Affairs 1935, 152–4). The Germans followed a similar policy. Soon after the stabilisation of the mark, the Reichsbank changed its foreign exchange reserves into gold. Official gold holdings more than tripled between 1924 and 1928, by which time foreign exchange accounted for a mere 8 per cent of the total reserves as against 59 per cent in 1924 (Néré 1968, 53–6; Balderston 1995, 181).

Thus the exchange standard, far from taking the pressure off London and restoring its pre-eminence as Norman envisaged, actually intensified the strain on the key reserve centres (compare Cain and Hopkins 1993, 63–4). This meant that they had to hold larger gold stocks than were required for normal balance transactions to protect them in the event of a sudden conversion of foreign claims. The United States, with its large gold stocks and relatively small liabilities, was fairly safe. London, however, was a different matter. Had sterling been as strong as before the war and with no obvious competitors, there would have been little difficulty, in normal times at least, in operating with a slender gold reserve. But sterling was continually under strain in the later 1920s and the burden of reserve currency status increased the pressure. The inherent weakness of sterling and the growing loss of confidence in it as a reserve currency, together with the scramble for gold in the later 1920s, were already beginning to undermine the system well before the crisis of 1931. The wholesale liquidation of foreign balances in that year merely served to complete the process, whence the pressure was then diverted to the dollar (see below).

Disequilibrium in exchange rate setting

Undoubtedly a major source of weakness of the postwar standard arose out of the stabilisation process itself. As noted in the previous chapter, stabilisation was a piecemeal and uncoordinated process extending over several years, carried out unilaterally by each country as and when it thought fit. Insufficient attention was paid to the shifts in relative costs and prices since 1914, and the somewhat haphazard choice of exchange rates, influenced in some cases by short-term capital movements and questions of prestige, meant that many countries ended up with the wrong parities. Indeed, given that so many currencies emerged from the stabilisation exercise out of kilter, it would probably be difficult to find any that were truly in equilibrium (Yeager 1976, 330). Most of the countries which restored their prewar parities – the UK, Switzerland, the Netherlands and the Scandinavian countries – had overvalued currencies, and the same was true of the Italian lira. By contrast, the German, French and Belgium currencies were significantly undervalued. The dollar too, which was used as a yardstick for stabilisation purposes, was probably undervalued in terms of several currencies (Glynn and Lougheed 1973, 694).

Thus unlike the prewar gold standard, when rates of exchange were for the most part in equilibrium, the postwar standard started out from a point of serious disequilibrium. Moreover, once the pattern was set there was very little chance of subsequent adjustment. Countries regarded their new parities as sacrosanct, in much the same way as those under the prewar system had been, so that they were reluctant to adjust them even when they were seen to be incorrect. In any case, countries with undervalued currencies were scarcely likely to be keen to sacrifice the resultant benefits, while those countries with overvalued rates, mainly the prewar parity group, were faced with a more difficult problem. Apart from the fact that to devalue soon after stabilisation would have entailed a serious loss of prestige, there was a more practical issue, namely that a devaluation of a major currency such as sterling, even had it ever been contemplated, was effectively a non-starter since it would have undermined the whole process of stabilisation and thrown the question back into the melting pot.

For the latter countries therefore, the only alternative was to adjust their domestic economies to accord with the new exchange rates, which in the short term at least meant depressing cost and price levels. Contemporaries thought it could be done with a little help from the Americans in raising their prices and that the sacrifice would be worthwhile in the end. Unfortunately it did not quite work out as planned. Moggridge (1989, 278-9) reckons that progress in removing the initial disparities in cost and price structures was limited prior to the collapse of the whole structure. One or two countries managed the task fairly well, although inevitably at the expense of wages and employment. Sweden, for example, acted early with a very sharp deflation in 1920-22 that almost did the trick, while the Dutch economy does not seem to have been deterred by going back to parity. Italy, too, made a brave attempt to adjust for overvaluation in a favourable political climate. But for other countries the task was well-nigh impossible. In particular, the key currency country, Britain, could not deflate to the necessary extent. This may have been partly due to the fact that prices and wages were less flexible in a downward direction than they had been before the war (Gayer 1934, 135). Too much should not be made of this point, however, since both had taken a severe battering in the postwar slump and there was probably little scope for further compression. In any case, if the British economy remained a high-cost one because of structural and technical deficiencies, then no amount of real wage compression would have made it competitive. A further consideration at the time was that the authorities were increasingly reluctant to press deflation too hard, given the high level of unemployment and the dangers of industrial strife. Thus domestic and external objectives came into conflict in a way they had never previously done, and in an effort to attain a compromise neither goal was achieved (Feavearyear 1963, 361). Sterling therefore remained weak, and Britain's resources were not fully employed.

Thus the pattern of exchange rates as it merged under the restored standard was far from an optimal one, from the point of view of either output and employment growth or balance of payments equilibrium (Scammell 1987, 34). Any system of fixed exchange rates depends for its success on convergence in national policies, as Schwartz (1984, 18) has noted, so that when these rates start out from a position of disequilibrium it follows that the need for convergence policies is all the more pressing. The choice of wrong parity rates tended to magnify balance of payments problems and so the system was called upon to make adjustments on a scale far greater than previously and for which it was never designed, and at a time when, for various reasons, the adjustment mechanism operated less smoothly than previously (Redmond 1992, 358–9). Few countries were prepared to sacrifice completely the stability of their domestic economies for the sake of external equilibrium. Those with overvalued exchange rates were reluctant or unable to make full adjustment to their domestic economies, while surplus countries were unwilling to meet the former half-way. The question is, then, how far was adjustment stymied by countries flouting the rules of the game, as conceptualised from the prewar gold standard.

Rules of the game

What were known as the rules of the game did not constitute a formal code of conduct written in tablets of stone; rather they were 'a set of crude signals and signposts' by which central banks were guided in formulating policy (League of Nations 1944, 67; McKinnon 1993, 3). The rules included maintaining convertibility at a fixed mint parity; absence of restrictions on the import and export of gold; gold backing for the currency; inter-bank cooperation in liquidity crises; and the contingent rule that in the event of convertibility being suspended, it would be restored at the original mint parity as soon as possible (McKinnon 1993, 4). For practical purposes the chief operating maxim was that central banks should reinforce rather than counteract or sterilise the effects of reserve flows (gold and foreign exchange) on their money supplies, by which process the adjustment in payments imbalances would be speeded up through changes in prices and incomes in both gold-receiving and gold-losing countries.

How far interwar experience departed from what was regarded as best practice and hence helped to undermine the system is a tricky question. It is true that sterilisation appears to have been quite common during the interwar period. Nurkse (League of Nations 1944, 68–9) found that only for about one-third of the time were central banks abiding by the rules. However, there is no marked trend in the degree of sterilisation over time, so that flouting the rules does not have any specially significant weight in 1930–31. Second, rule breaking seems to have been almost as frequent before 1914 if we are to believe the results of recent research (Bloomfield 1959; Dutton 1984; Giovannini 1986; Jonung 1984; Dick et al. 1996), although Eichengreen (1990b, 93–4) reckons that it was probably of less significance than in the postwar years. In any case, before 1914 temporary or short-term violation of the rules was acceptable so long as central banks maintained an unwavering commitment to currency stability and convertibility, whereas after the war this commitment, for a variety of reasons, became less secure. As Eichengreen (1996, 32, 91) writes, 'The single-minded pursuit of exchange rate stability that characterized central bank policy before the war became a thing of the past'.

Of greater import, however, is whether sterilisation policies were really effective. Floyd (1985, 59–69) has argued that gold sterilisation is impracticable when capital is internationally mobile. 'Countries could not effectively sterilise the effects of gold flows on their money supplies, even though they may have thought they were so doing' (ibid., 69). In the case of the United States, the largest gold holder, there is some support for this contention since both Triffin (1946–47, 57) and Williams (1953, 396–8) denied the existence of sterilisation. The total money supply was expanded rapidly in 1920–24 when the US was gaining gold, and again in 1925–29 when it was not. France, the other large gold absorber, experienced its 'golden avalanche' later in the 1920s when the Bank of France's gold holdings rose sharply under the influence of a favourable balance of payments and the liquidation of foreign exchange balances (Wolfe 1957, 96; Wynne 1937, 484–90; Royal Institute of International Affairs 1932, 208–9; Eichengreen 1986b). Sterilisation of gold inflows was certainly more in evidence in the case of France, partly because her stringent banking laws (a response to the inflationary experience of the 1920s) prevented the Bank of France from engaging in open market operations. Although the Bank suspended its conversion operations after 1929, the commercial banks kept up the pressure so that France absorbed even more gold (Eichengreen 1986b, 79; League of Nations 1944, 69). But deficit countries, too, were guilty of impeding the adjustment process by the same means (Eichengreen 1990a, 84).

Gold stocks and gold supply
If the sterilisation argument is somewhat less than robust, perhaps of greater significance was the growing maldistribution of the world's mone-

tary reserves. Gold is the operative medium in this context since, although key currencies were used for reserve purposes to stretch existing gold stocks, it was gold that mattered when the going got rough. Many countries regarded the gold exchange standard as a temporary expedient anyway, and were anxious to build up their gold holdings with the aim of transferring to a fully convertible standard. Moreover, countries were only prepared to retain balances in a reserve currency so long as that currency remained sound. Once difficulties arose they would demand conversion of their non-metallic reserves.

Yet contrary to popular conception, there was only a relatively small shift in the degree of concentration of gold holdings, which had in fact been very unevenly distributed before 1914 (Drummond 1987, 17). The largest eight holders accounted for some 79 per cent of the world total in 1913 and 83 per cent by 1929. There was, however, some change in the balance of holders. The United States, France, Spain, Japan and the European neutrals absorbed an increasing share of the world's reserves, whereas India and Russia declined in importance. The share of the United States rose rapidly from just under one-quarter before the war to 46 per cent in 1924, after which it declined; France's stock changed little in the first part of the period but then increased rapidly after 1926 to reach 15.9 per cent in 1929, 23.9 per cent in 1931, and peaking at 27.4 per cent the following year. Thus by 1929 these two countries accounted for nearly 54 per cent of the official gold reserves, compared with 40.6 per cent in 1913, while Britain, Germany, Japan, Spain, Argentina and Italy were the next largest holders (Palyi 1972, 181; Davidson 1933, 33; Macmillan Committee 1931, 63–4).

At face value the changes in the concentration of gold reserves do not appear of great significance. However, what really mattered was that much of the gold was accruing to countries that did not really need it, either because their currencies were not used for reserve purposes (for example, Japan, France, Italy, Spain and the neutral countries), or because they had more than enough gold for meeting any contingencies. This situation arose in part through the failure of adjustment on the part of surplus countries (Fleisig 1975, 109–11). The prime example in the latter context is the United States. By the end of the decade her gold stocks amounted to some $4 billion, ample cover for her dollar liabilities (central bank holdings of dollar exchange) which were in the region of $0.6 billion. A wholesale liquidation of these balances together with a deterioration in the balance of payments would not have stretched her resources. Britain's position, on the other hand, was exactly the reverse. Central bank holdings of sterling currency in the late 1920s were nearly four times greater than the Bank of England's gold reserve which, unlike the American, was constantly under pressure (Triffin 1968, 31, 46–7). Britain, of course, could in theory call upon short-term assets abroad, although in practice these were liable to become locked in during a severe crisis, as in 1931. Thus Britain was clearly the weak link in the chain. She had the largest liabilities and the smallest gold reserve of any major country, with the added disadvantage that her external account was anything but strong. Thus any deterioration in the latter or loss of confidence in sterling for whatever reason inevitably brought pressure to bear on the reserves which could not easily be countered in the competitive scramble for gold of this period (see below). It is true, of course, that Britain had operated with a very small gold reserve before 1914 when it had constituted a mere 3.4 per cent of the world total as against nearly 7 per cent in 1929 (Palyi 1972, 181). But then conditions were much more favourable; Britain's liabilities were smaller, her quick assets could easily be recalled, the balance of payments was far stronger and, above all, confidence in sterling rarely wavered: as 'good as gold' was more than just a cliché.

It is convenient to take up at this point another issue which caused much concern to contemporaries, and that is the alleged growing world shortage of the precious metal gold. World gold supplies, it was argued by some contemporary and later writers, were insufficient to support the then current level of prices and activity (Cassel 1936; Kitchen 1932; League of Nations 1930b; Warren and Pearson 1933; Hicks 1950, 163; Rist 1953; Jacobsson 1958, 18–19), whereas others maintained that the real problem was that of a maldistribution of existing supplies (Berridge 1934; Mlynarski 1931, 68; League of Nations 1930–32; Hardy 1936; Palyi 1972, 123–32). Bordo and Ellison (1985) have modelled a situation demonstrating an inescapable tendency to long-run deflation under a gold supply resource constraint, which would inhibit the equilibrating mechanism of a monetary system based on gold. However, it is doubtful whether this constraint could be considered critical at the time in question. Although gold production increased less rapidly than before the war, rising by about 2.5 per cent per annum between 1913 and 1929 compared with 3.1 per cent in the half-century before 1914, centralised gold reserves grew by about twice that amount (5–6 per cent a year), largely as a result of the growing concentration of gold stocks within central banks and treasuries as gold coins and private hoards were withdrawn from circulation. By 1929, centralised reserves accounted for the bulk of the world's gold stock as against just over 50 per cent in 1913. Moreover, the gold stocks were stretched or used more effectively since they were supplemented by larger foreign exchange holdings which, according to some authorities, were as good as gold until 1930 (Gayer 1937, 96–7). The last point has somewhat dubious validity, however, since it is very unlikely that foreign exchange holdings were ever regarded as a viable alternative to gold, especially in the later 1920s when the scramble for gold set in. Moreover, the larger centralised holdings of gold were less significant than appears at first sight. Many countries had higher legal cover requirements for their domestic liabilities (normally notes and sight deposits) than they did before the war. Practice varied a great deal as to the composition of liabilities covered and the mix of gold and foreign exchange for that purpose, but by the end of the 1920s the majority of central banks had legal reserve ratios of 30–50 per cent, and many exceeded the legal cover requirements. The League of Nations (1944, 94–6, 215; 1932, 200; Balderston 1995, 181) estimated that up to one-half of the gold and foreign exchange reserves of monetary authorities was earmarked as cover, thereby reducing the amount of gold available for the international currency function.

Although the trends are somewhat conflicting, there do not seem to be strong grounds for arguing that an absolute gold shortage was a major problem in the later 1920s, nor did the position change dramatically for the worse in the crucial years 1929–31 (Royal Institute of International Affairs 1933, 48). Some recent writers (Cooper 1992; Bernanke and James 1991, 246–7) do attach greater importance to the deflationary impact of the gold supply issue and the cover requirements but the arguments are not fully convincing. The large contraction in the value of world trade cannot be attributed to the attrition of international reserves which declined only modestly between 1929 and 1933 (Fleisig 1975, 108). Furthermore, the volume and percentage of central bank short-term liabilities backed by gold was as good as, if not better, than before the war, and if gold's international function had been constrained by shortage, the cover ratios could have been reduced to provide more liquidity for external needs (Eichengreen 1989, 273). After all, their existence was probably of no great consequence in the final analysis, for as Nurkse explained in his League of Nations' report (1944, 96) 'a paper currency in normal times gains little if anything by having a legal "backing" of gold and foreign exchange assets; while in abnormal times the cover regulations have usually had to be suspended, repealed or relaxed in any case'.

Thus gold shortage was not a factor in the collapse of the gold standard. Maldistribution of reserves may have a little more claim to fame in this respect, especially the concentration of holdings in France and the United States, which were occasioned partly by special factors such as debts, reparations and tariffs (Royal Institute of International Affairs 1933, 48).

Commitment to the standard

Modern writers have placed considerable emphasis on the degree of commitment as an element in the successful operation of the classical gold standard. At least as far as the core countries were concerned there was an unwavering commitment to maintain gold convertibility at all costs, although the unwritten contingent rule did allow for occasional lapses in emergencies provided there was certainty of a return to convertibility once the crisis had passed (see Bordo and Kydland 1995; McKinnon 1993; Giovannini 1993; Eichengreen 1992a). By maintaining this commitment, gold standard countries were rewarded, so to speak, with a 'good house-keeping seal of approval' for financial rectitude (low fiscal deficits, stable money growth and low inflation), even though this may have reduced the rate of growth slightly in the long run (Bordo and Rockoff 1996, 416). The success of the system depended, of course, on a wide range of other factors, including the relative ease with which adjustments could be made, but the steadfast commitment to maintain the system through adherence to unwritten rules, even though there were occasional lapses, inter-bank cooperation and the powerful influence of the Bank of England, were also important considerations. The whole process was also facilitated by the fact that the costs involved could to some extent be shifted elsewhere, either on to the domestic economy or from core countries to the periphery.

The inference is that the postwar gold standard was less successful because the commitment mechanism was constrained (Bordo and Schwartz 1996, 12; Redmond 1992, 359). Some authors, basing their case on the relative stability of the sterling/dollar exchange rate, have questioned the shift in the degree of commitment between the prewar and postwar regimes (Hallwood et al. 1996; Officer 1996b), but circumstantial evidence would suggest that there was some weakening. The more unstable economic and political conditions after the war helped to bring this about. For one thing, the contingent escape clause became largely inoperative. As Bordo and Schwartz (1996, 18) note, to have invoked it would have created destabilising capital flows; indeed, one can even go further and suggest that had a reserve currency resorted to it the whole system would have been undermined, as it eventually was in 1931. Second, political factors intervened to weaken the commitment. The rise of mass democracy meant that henceforth domestic economic conditions could no longer be sacrificed on the altar of the exchanges. Policy therefore had to take more cognisance of internal economic conditions, whereas before 1914 these could conveniently be ignored (Dam 1982, 58). Redmond (1992, 359) argues that commitment to defend the system was lessened by domestic considerations which had the effect of 'jamming' the adjustment mechanism. For similar reasons the peripheral countries were less committed to maintaining the gold standard system, and several of them in fact abandoned it at an early date. Too much should not be read into this last point, however, since many of them had been on and off gold before 1914 (Nugent 1973).

But perhaps of greater significance in this context was the fact that almost from the beginning there were doubts about the new standard (Mouré 1992, 267). Many countries were far from enamoured by the exchange standard, including the United States and France, since it was regarded as a temporary expedient until full gold convertibility could be attained. The French, especially, were disenchanted with the new system – one reason why they were so anxious to build up their gold reserves in the later 1920s. Even Montagu Norman, in some ways the prime architect of the system, was becoming disillusioned with it by 1927, and confessed that he had been mistaken in assuming that restoration would provide the same smooth international and domestic adjustment as he imagined had been the case under the classical system (Sayers 1976a, 334; Dam 1982, 58). This view no doubt sprang partly from his unpleasant experiences in trying to maintain the new standard when the Bank was constantly 'under the harrow'. In fact on more than one occasion (August 1929 and again in March 1931) it was intimated that Britain might have to go off gold (Sayers 1976a, 225–34).

Thus despite the struggle to restore the gold standard, there was a less ardent commitment to retain the new system. Once the going got rough, countries were prepared to jettison it. Although it has sometimes been suggested that the commitment remained strong, at least in Britain, until quite late in the day – and the absence of gold point violations in the sterling/dollar rate from May 1925 through to June 1931 implies that speculators and arbitrageurs were reasonably sanguine on this score at least until July 1931 (Officer 1996a, 249–50, 275) – one has the sneaking suspicion that people in high places felt that the gold standard's days were numbered well before the final collapse.

Management of the gold standard and international cooperation
The traditional view that the classical gold standard was an automatic, self-equilibrating mechanism, requiring little if any management or international collaboration among central bankers, can no longer be sustained (Bordo 1981; Cooper 1987). But nor was it a fully managed system in the way that later international monetary systems were to become. Probably the best way to describe it would be an informal, and intermittently managed, system. Three issues are relevant in this context: (1) the day-to-day management of the system; (2) the role of London; and (3) the extent of international cooperation. We can then see how the interwar system differed.

The notion that the classical gold standard was an automatically adjusting system that required little in the way of management has long since been discredited. In fact, even before the war, Viner (1932, 12, 17) had noted that the idyllic picture sometimes portrayed of the gold standard in its heyday was based largely on conjectural history. It required, he argued, constant management and unremitting attention to keep it in being, which inevitably entailed frequent discretionary intervention (Fremling 1986, 39).

Since the main central banks, and especially the Bank of England, were heavily committed to maintaining the gold standard, it followed that movements in gold reserves very much determined day-to-day management. The main weapons used to deal with gold flows were the discount rate and operations in the gold market. The Bank of England's chief policy objective was to safeguard the gold reserves, and its main weapon of defence, at least by the 1880s when the Bank had more or less established its supremacy in the market (Sayers 1957, 12), was use of the Bank rate. Until then the Bank, as did some of the continental central banks, made greater use of the gold devices which were later abandoned as the Bank's monetary management became more effective in the money market (Scammell 1965, 37, 41). Thus when its reserves fell, through either an internal or an external drain, the discount rate was raised to attract funds back. Conversely, an influx of gold and exchange reserves would prompt a lowering of the rate (Pippinger 1984).

Contrary to popular conception, the Bank was in fact sensitive to the domestic ramifications of its external policy, but by a fortuitous set of circumstances the clash between domestic and external stability rarely became the central issue that it was to be after the war. This was because the reserves tended to move inversely with the business cycle so that discount rate changes tended to be countercyclical – rising during booms and falling in recessions, although with some lagged reaction, thereby acting in a partially stabilising manner. There was a similar correspondence between discount rate changes and business reference cycles in other major countries, especially France (Morgenstern 1959, 397–8). The British experience was especially fortuitous since the balance of payments tended to improve in booms and deteriorate in slumps, which should have occasioned the reverse pattern of discount rate changes. However, the Bank's reserves varied inversely with the cycle because of internal drains of reserves in the upswing and external drains associated with British lending abroad which exceeded the current account surplus (Meyer and Lewis 1949; Mintz 1959).

There is a broad presentiment that fixed exchange rate regimes tend to be associated with some form of hegemonic leadership (Llewellyn and Presley 1995, 259). That is, fixed rate regimes are basically asymmetric, with the dominant leader providing the anchor for the system and the participant players having to accommodate their monetary policy to that of the centre country (Giovannini 1989, 14). This interpretation became fashionable following Keynes's view that London's financial strength and influence on credit conditions throughout the world was so profound that 'the Bank of England could almost have claimed to be the conductor of the international orchestra' (Keynes 1930, 306–7). The strength of London internationally, sterling's importance as a key reserve currency, and the near substitutability of sterling and gold gave the Bank of England 'not only the role of regulator of the British monetary system, but in great part, that of the regulator of the gold standard and the international payments system' (Scammell 1965, 13; Bordo 1984).

The thesis has its attractions since it would help to explain why the system seemed to work so well before the war, and so badly afterwards (Eichengreen 1987, 26; 1989, 287). There are, however, some difficulties in accepting the extreme version of the hegemonic theory. Viner (1945, 63–4) first raised doubts about London's unique role. He argued that the Bank of England had neither the resources, the powers, the will, nor the intellectual capability to manage the international monetary system, and he doubted whether London played a stabilising role in the world economy. More recent scholars have also expressed healthy scepticism of Britain's hegemonic role. McCloskey and Zelcher (1976, 6) demoted the Bank to the 'second violinist' at best, and possibly no more than a triangle player in the world orchestra, while Walter (1991, 92) maintains that Britain had little to do with the emergence of the international gold standard, and made only a small contribution to its management.

As Tullio and Wolters's (1996) careful study demonstrates, the truth probably lies somewhere in between. London was neither a conductor nor a triangle player, but the most influential member of the system. The gold standard, they argue, was essentially a multipolar affair, in which Berlin and Paris were important players who could sometimes call the tune, and throw the burden of adjustment on to London. It is true that Britain was often regarded as a lender of last resort in times of difficulty, but there were also occasions when the tables were turned and London had to call upon other centres for assistance. The Bank of England then became a borrower of last resort under collective leadership, or rather mutual cooperation in an emergency. Thus in the Baring crisis of 1890 and again in the financial crisis of 1907, the Bank of France came to the rescue of its English counterpart (Eichengreen 1990b, 97: 1995, 9). Even some of the smaller financial centres (Amsterdam, Vienna and St Petersburg) could occasionally influence the London discount rate. In other words, the Bank of England was often the follower rather than the leader in discount rate changes, although when it came to the crunch, London probably had the edge on the continental centres. The important thing to bear in mind is that there was greater symmetry in the system than implied by Keynes and some later writers.

The latter interpretation does raise some doubts, however, about the stress laid by several writers on the importance of central bank cooperation in the success of the classical gold standard. Scammell (1965, 34) saw the gold standard as a quasi-organisational system 'being operated by a team of central bankers co-operating under the leadership of the Bank of England on behalf of the world business community'. Similarly, in a series of separate studies Eichengreen (1985a, 1985b, 1992b) has emphasised the same point. But international cooperation seems to have been at best sporadic and intermittent, scarcely sufficient one would think to explain the system's success (Eichengreen 1985a, 16–17). One can point to occasions on which mutual cooperation took place, but it was far from being the universal norm. In fact Flandreau (1997, 737, 761) rejects the very notion that it was the key to exchange stability in the prewar era. Cooperation, he says, was the exception rather than the rule: 'what has been interpreted as cooperation was the product of the selfish interest of central banks: they helped each other only when this provided a direct benefit to them, instead of mutually adjusting towards some cooperative equilibrium as hypothesized by the cooperation view'. Admittedly Flandreau's analysis is somewhat selective, concentrating heavily on Anglo-French relationships, but it does raise serious question marks about the significance of central bank cooperation both in regard to the success of and the subsequent collapse of the gold standard.

Management postwar
It is clear that the classical gold standard required a certain amount of management and international cooperation among the financial centres. But much of the control was informal and London's role was influential rather than dominant. Postwar, the change was one of degree rather than substance. Greater intervention was required simply because the postwar standard was much more difficult to manage due to the vastly altered conditions under which it operated. Beth Simmons (1994, 28–31) stresses especially the way in which the drastic socio-political changes that had occurred since 1914 made it more difficult to resolve internal and external conflicts, which in turn reduced the credibility that governments would be prepared to defend the standard when it came to the crunch. The increased measure of uncertainty meant that holdings of foreign funds became extremely unstable: 'The turmoil of domestic politics gave holders of liquid capital ample incentive to destabilise the interwar gold standard' (ibid., 28).

The situation was aggravated by Britain's weakened position and the limits to international cooperation. While one may legitimately question the hegemonic capacity of London in the prewar period, there was no doubt that sterling did provide a sheet anchor for the gold standard which it could no longer do postwar. Sterling could not assume its former role because of Britain's loss of economic power, while the emergence of New York and Paris as rival financial centres weakened London's position even further. These two centres competed with London for the employment of funds, the flow of which 'ceased to be under any single, centralised control' (Nevin 1955, 15).

Fragmentation of financial control was not in itself fatal to the post-war gold standard. But more than ever before, as the Genoa Conference of 1922 recognised, concerted and coordinated action among the main financial centres was vital if the system was to work satisfactorily (Strakosch 1937, 162). The need for cooperation was especially important given sterling's weakened position, which required the support of New York and Paris in times of strain. The alternative was for one of the two centres to assume the leadership in managing the system. In the event, neither of these conditions was satisfied.

The need for more cooperative action to stabilise the system has been stressed on several occasions (Broadberry 1989, 64; Eichengreen 1985b, 170). In fact, cooperation among the major monetary centres was more in evidence than before the war (Walter 1991, 134). The problem was that it did not always work smoothly. Norman and Strong worked in close harmony for much of the time, while even the Bank of France was prepared to toe the line on occasions. Unfortunately collaboration was not free from friction and policy coordination was often difficult to achieve unless it suited the national interests of the parties concerned. Part of the problem arose from the fact that the major banks were dominated by powerful and idiosyncratic governors (Norman, Strong, Emile Moreau and Hjalmar Schacht). In part it was practical, especially on the French side which explains why France was an unwilling partner. The French belief that the Anglo-Saxons had cheated France over Germany and international security, and the fear that they were about to dominate the international monetary system, left its mark on the Bank of France. The Governor, Emile Moreau, was suspicious of Norman's alliance with Strong and also of his pro-German leanings. Since French interests could very easily be threatened by such a strong team, Moreau felt no great urge to work with the system. The strength of the French currency and balance of payments following the stabilisation of the franc allowed France to follow a largely independent line. Thus, as seen earlier, France liquidated her foreign exchange holdings in the later 1920s, a policy which put upward pressure on interest rates and threatened the stability of the system (Strange 1971, 51–4, 82; Eichengreen 1984, 82). In all fairness, the Bank of France (although not the commercial banks) did relax its policy after 1929 and it did not contribute to the pressure on London in the summer of 1931 (Wolfe 1957, 97–9).

The emergence of the Bank of France as a rival financial centre certainly threw an apple of discord into inter-bank cooperation. It offered a serious challenge to both the Bank of England and the Federal Reserve of New York, and helped to split the unity of leadership which had hitherto existed between London and New York, a situation not helped by the death of Strong in October 1928. His successor, George Harrison, was much less internationally minded. Coincidentally, this was the very time when Anglo-American relations in general were at their lowest ebb of the century (Young 1997, 95). Meyer (1970, 14, 138–9) sees this as a crucial factor in determining subsequent events:

> not only were there fundamental differences between the Bank of England and the Bank of France, but the unity of outlook on the part of the Bank of England and the Federal Reserve Bank of New York began to break down. Thus, the original unity of leadership disappeared, and at the same time no one of the three was strong enough alone to be accepted without question by the others as the leader.

Whether a more favourable political climate would have made much difference to the situation is to be doubted since the real challenge to effective international monetary cooperation lay elsewhere. Once currency stabilisation had been achieved, the main task was that of defending the new rates of exchange and to do this central banks required complete freedom of action in monetary policy. This they never had since domestic needs came increasingly into focus during the course of the decade, partly because of the unemployment problem and the increasing interest of treasuries in economic affairs. Thus it became increasingly difficult for central banks to target monetary policy unremittingly to satisfy external objectives, unless these happened to coincide with domestic requirements. In 1924 and again in 1927 the Federal Reserve was able to offer support for sterling because both conditions coincided, but in the boom of 1928–29, when sterling came under pressure, the Board gave priority to domestic needs. Similarly, the Bank of England, whose Governor for all his doubts about the gold standard was primarily concerned with safeguarding the pound, was not totally unmindful of the domestic consequences of monetary policy, although usually only after prodding from the Treasury (Williams 1959, 39–40, 51). In May 1927, for example, when Moreau requested the Bank of England to raise its discount rate to check the influx of sterling into Paris, Norman refused to oblige for fear of causing a riot (Clarke 1967, 29–30). In fact there were only rare occasions, 1919–20 for example, when external and domestic requirements coincided and the Bank was able to pursue a policy which met both (Aldcroft 1970, 44). Thus the conflict between the two was much greater than before the war and central bankers everywhere were forced to give greater consideration to national interests.

That France and the United States in particular followed policies which were inconsistent with good gold-standard practice is not altogether surprising, in that neither country had the experience or the institutions that Britain had in the heyday of the gold standard. They were not prepared to shore up a system which they had never created in the first place and which they had never fully supported. Neither country was equipped to take on the role of leader. The French certainly were not, while even the United States, despite all its economic strength, was neither psychologically attuned nor institutionally equipped to take up the burden. The American financial structure was far too immature and inexperienced, with many features of the rural frontier society still present (Walter 1991, 137; Arrighi 1994, 271–3).

There is no doubt that cooperative efforts in the international monetary arena were wholly inadequate to sustain the gold standard (Bloomfield 1968, 31; Clarke 1967, 27). Central banks, constrained by national policies, political rivalries, mutual distrust and conceptual differences regarding central bank practice, lacked the power, the understanding and sometimes the will required for more effective cooperation to make a success of the new international monetary system. In the words of Mouré (1992, 278), 'the gold exchange standard did not command sufficient support to attract the continuous cooperation advocated by the Genoa resolutions.' That it was found wanting in the crisis of 1931 is therefore scarcely surprising. But whether more substantive international management could have saved the situation, as some writers seem to imply (Eichengreen 1985b, 1990b, 1992b; Clarke 1967), is another matter. If the system was structurally flawed, as Cooper (1992, 2127) suggests, then it is doubtful whether any amount of international cooperation would have made much difference to the final outcome, short of possibly postponing it temporarily (Walter 1991, 145; Clarke 1967, 227). Although it should be noted that Cooper's notion that insufficiency of gold supplies was the main problem is not one we can confirm. More important were the underlying disequilibria and institutional changes of the 1920s which made the system much harder to operate (Bloomfield 1968). And if coordination, or lack of it, were to blame, it might be more appropriate to shift the blame to the haphazard and uncoordinated way in which stabilisation was effected in the first place (Traynor 1949, 160). But when all is said and done, the scale of events in the 1931 crisis was such that, with the best will in the world, effective international cooperation would probably have proved impossible (Balderston 1995, 183).

Convergence and harmony in policy and development
It has been argued that the prewar gold standard worked, at least for the core countries, largely because it was never subject to serious strain (Ford

1989, 226). Indeed, any system of fixed exchange rates will only operate smoothly so long as the countries which adhere to it are in fundamental equilibrium, that is, a convergence of real variables (Schwartz 1984, 18). It follows, therefore, that any severe disparities in costs and prices and in growth performance between countries will require some adjustment in order to preserve existing parities intact. If these are not effected then there is a very strong possibility that exchange rates will have to be adjusted, or even more extreme, that the system of fixed rates will disintegrate altogether. Fortunately for the classical standard, exchange rate stability was rarely threatened by serious disequilibrium of this sort, partly because national rates of monetary and credit expansion among the main gold-standard countries were harmonised in such a way as to prevent serious divergence across countries in rates of inflation, growth rates and external balances. Of course, the commitment to the gold-standard mechanism may well have behoved countries to adopt money and credit policies which did not jeopardise that convergence, but experience in non-core countries suggests that not all countries were prepared to toe the line to gain the coveted good housekeeping seal of approval. Many less-developed countries were not averse to forsaking the fixed rate system in order to reap the benefits of a depreciated currency (Nugent 1973, 1130).

On the other hand, an alternative scenario would be that the gold-standard system was not the real stabiliser of the international economic system; rather it can be argued that the gold standard itself was stabilised by the convergence of real economic forces and the absence of serious impediments to the working of market forces. There can be no doubt that the classical gold standard operated in an exceptionally favourable environment. Growth was steady if unspectacular, factor mobility across countries was free of impediments, trade flows faced few restrictions apart from tariffs which were fairly modest by later standards, there was a high degree of flexibility in prices and wages, little restriction on the activities of economic agents and generally very limited government interference in economic affairs. Furthermore, the world economy was more closely integrated than either before or since, with a close harmony between the core industrial countries and the primary producing periphery (Kemp 1962, 150; Ford 1989, 215). The political climate was also remarkably benign for most of the period with no major wars to cause serious disturbances to the system. Crises did occur from time to time but these were less severe than those of the postwar period and could relatively easily be accommodated (Bayoumi and Eichengreen 1996, 175). This conjuncture of favourable circumstances may have been weakening in the decade or so before the war – de Cecco (1984, 127–8) reckons that the system was becoming shaky – but it was never seriously threatened (Foreman-Peck 1983, 174).

Einzig (1935, 99) argued that prewar economic stability was not the result of the monetary system but rather the reverse, that the fundamental equilibrium in political and economic conditions was the key to the success of the international monetary structure. Basically the same point was later made by Triffin (1968, 14):

> [The] residual harmonisation of national monetary and credit policies depended far less on *ex post* corrective action, requiring an extreme flexibility downward as well as upward, of national price and wage levels, than on an *ex ante* avoidance of substantial disparities in cost competitiveness and in the monetary policies that would allow them to develop.

This interpretation (although compare Foreman-Peck 1983, 183) makes sense in the light of the much more hostile economic climate after the war, when structural and policy factors made it impossible to secure residual harmonisation or convergence in real variables among countries on gold. The increasing restrictions on trade and monetary transactions and on factor flows, the greater inflexibility in price systems, together with the structural distortions caused by war, especially the debt problems, and the emergence of more independent monetary policies, made adjustment increasingly difficult at a time when it was most required because of the distortions caused by the stabilisation process itself (Hill 1956). Thus relatively rapid adjustment to disturbances, which had characterised the prewar system, was no longer possible. Condliffe (1941, 102–3) even reckoned that the attempt to recreate the gold-standard system was a futile effort since the requisite conditions for its successful operation were no longer present. More recently, Floyd (1985, Chapter 5) has argued that exchange rate adjustment was determined by the shift in the equilibrium real price ratio between countries. The large relative price variability since 1914 could not be accommodated within the restored gold-standard system and so 'it broke down because of structural changes in international relative prices. Countries chose to abandon fixed exchange rates rather than let their nominal price levels adjust in response to changes in the real value of their goods relative to foreign goods in world markets' (ibid., 59). According to this scenario therefore, the absence of fundamental stability was crucial to the failure of the postwar gold standard.

Disintegration of the gold standard

De Cecco (1984, 127–8) reckoned that the gold standard was rotten even before 1914 and that it was already on its way to extinction. If so, we feel that this was even more the case with the restored standard, given its inherent weaknesses, and that it was only a matter of time before it collapsed. After all, even Montagu Norman was having doubts about its survival in the later 1920s when the Bank of England was struggling to defend the pound. No doubt the new system might have been able to totter along for several more years had there been no shocks to the system and had American lending been able to paper over the cracks in the international economy. But such speculations must remain academic since no sooner had the new system been set in place than pressures developed which drove the final nails into the coffin.

The first of these predate the famous crisis of 1931. As Williams (1963, 101) noted some years ago, the dramatic events of the spring and summer of 1931 represented the culmination of a prolonged increase in the demand for liquidity which began as far back as the middle of 1928. These early signs of strain were first apparent in some countries along the periphery which experienced falling incomes as a result of weakness in primary product prices at a time when international lending (primarily American) was beginning to decline. Consequently, these debtor countries soon ran into balance of payments problems since previously they had been dependent on capital imports and the maintenance of export prices to square their external accounts. Thus they were forced to repay, rather than fund, earlier borrowings at a time when their foreign exchange earnings were dwindling. Since accommodation from creditor countries was not readily forthcoming, the only way to balance the accounts in the short term was to draw upon their reserves. Several debtor countries experienced a steady drain of gold from late 1928 onwards. Total South American gold stocks for example, declined from $927 million at the end of 1928 to $558 million by the end of 1930; Asia's fell from $738 million to $601 million and those of Oceania fell by no less than 60 per cent between 1929 and 1930 (Williams 1962–63, 518). Some countries, notably Argentina, Brazil and Australia, used up most of their gold reserves in the process (Smith 1934, 43; Timoshenko 1933, 76–8). Rather than face the full force of the deflationary measures required to restore external equilibrium under the existing exchange rates, several countries took the plunge by breaking the link with gold and letting their currencies depreciate. The departure was started by Uruguay in May 1929, then Argentina and Brazil at the end of that year, followed by Peru, Bolivia, Australia and New Zealand early in 1930, while the Venezuelan bolivar started to fluctuate in September 1930 and the Mexican and Chilean pesos were quoted below par in August 1931 (League of Nations 1937a, 11). Canada also suspended gold exports in January 1929, but the Canadian dollar did not depreciate until late in 1931 (Bordo and Redish 1990, 358, 378). Thus the first cracks in the gold-standard system had been made.

The crisis along the periphery might have been eased had creditor countries been more willing to assist debtor nations before the international depression and financial crisis raised the issue of world liquidity to a completely different order of magnitude. Unfortunately the two strongest creditors, the United States and France, were unwilling to make sufficient funds available either on a long-term or short-term basis in 1929. In fact, they added to the pressure on the one other possible source of funds, that is London, since for much of that year funds were leaving London for New York (attracted by the stock market boom and interest rate differentials) and Paris which was in the process of liquidating sterling balances. Thus both countries were substantial gold importers in 1929, while Britain lost substantial reserves, especially in the third quarter of that year and so was in no position to provide relief to debtor countries (League of Nations 1931, 228–9).

A partial revival of American foreign lending in the first half of 1930 did provide a measure of relief but it proved a false dawn. The sharp decline in economic activity not only in the core countries but worldwide soon began to undermine confidence which resulted in a renewed scramble for liquidity. Thus, after the middle of 1930, creditor countries became increasingly reluctant to increase financial commitments to debtor nations. Although the final crisis was not played out until the spring and summer of 1931, it is evident that the international financial situation was becoming increasingly precarious well before the collapse of the Credit-Anstalt triggered off repercussions throughout Europe. In fact there was a steady contraction of credits and withdrawal of funds from abroad as the deepening business depression further eroded confidence and gave rise to bankruptcies and bank failures. Banking crises in the two main creditor countries in 1930–31 also intensified the demand for liquidity, which led to the withdrawal of funds from Central and Eastern Europe. The financial structure in Central and Eastern Europe, and especially in Austria, was known to be precarious, partly because of injudicious banking practices and the widespread foreign ownership of national bank deposits; while according to James (1992, 607–8), uncertainty about public sector deficits also played an important role in undermining stability in the international financial system. Thus through 1930–31 the international financial situation was steadily deteriorating and debtor countries in particular were losing reserves at an accelerating rate as they were finding it impossible to finance their overall deficits by borrowing or expanding exchange earnings, while even deflation proved to be no panacea, at least in the short term, to the liquidity problem.

The situation was brought to a head by the failure of the Credit-Anstalt in May 1931, which rocked the whole economic and financial structure of the continent and had severe repercussions on the banking systems of Germany and Eastern Europe (Schubert 1991, 4; Saint-Etienne 1984,

16–17). It alerted creditors to the inherent dangers in countries dependent on short-term credits from abroad and the implications that this might have for currency convertibility, especially in countries which had experienced serious inflation in the previous decade (Balderston 1994, 64; Eichengreen and Portes 1987, 25–7; Schubert 1991, 170). It led to severe pressure on many continental banks resulting in large-scale withdrawals of short-term funds, both by nationals and foreigners, and the loss of reserves from Germany and Eastern Europe through the summer of 1931 until brought to a halt by the imposition of exchange control (Ellis 1941, 74: James 1984, 84; 1986, 398; Ranki 1985, 71; Saint-Etienne 1984, 17; Nötel 1986, 227). Some 30 per cent of the foreign short-term assets located in Germany, for example, were withdrawn in the months through to the introduction of exchange control in the middle of July (Fleisig 1975, 148). The gold and foreign exchange reserves of 18 European debtor countries fell by nearly one-half between 1928 and 1931, with most of the loss taking place in 1930–31 (League of Nations 1944, 40–41).

By the summer of 1931, the scramble for liquidity had reached panic proportions and the heat switched to London, which bore the brunt of the crisis. The rapid withdrawal of sterling balances and loss of reserves between July and September were largely occasioned by the continental financial crisis which raised doubts about Britain's financial viability (Hamilton 1988, 74). Britain's financial position was known to be precarious in more ways than one. The balance of payments had deteriorated steadily since 1929, her short-term asset/liability ratio made her vulnerable to any loss of confidence abroad, as the Macmillan Committee emphasised in its report published on 13 July, while the unsound state of the public finances was laid bare by the May Committee which reported at the end of the same month. Views differ as to the weight attached to these factors but the overall effect could not be in doubt, namely loss of confidence in Britain's ability to weather the storm (see Moggridge 1970, 832–9; Cairncross and Eichengreen 1983, 75–83; James 1992, 607, 612). Despite lines of credit totalling some £130 million from the United States and France at the end of July and the end of August, pressure on the reserves continued, with Holland, Switzerland, Belgium and France draining gold from London (Hurst 1932, 638). The final blow came on the days following the alleged naval mutiny at Invergordon (15 September) when some £43 million in gold and foreign exchange was withdrawn from the London money market, making a total of nearly £200 million in the two months since the middle of July (Clarke 1967, 216). By the Saturday (19 September) all the credits from America and France had been exhausted and the Bank's holdings of gold had been reduced to the equivalent of the obligations under the credits (Clay 1957,

398). This proved to be the final straw for the authorities and on the Sunday evening it was announced that Britain would officially leave the gold standard on the following day. This effectively marked the end of the postwar gold standard, since many other countries followed suit.

Although the crisis has been much debated, it is worth clarifying Britain's position in the fateful months of that summer. It is clear that Britain could not have saved the gold standard single-handedly, although it has been argued that appropriate policies by the four major powers to alleviate the depression could have done the trick (Foreman-Peck et al. 1996, 240–41). Her much weakened position after the war, her slender reserves and large liabilities rendered her extremely vulnerable to any shock (Moggridge 1981, 69). There was no problem as long as confidence in sterling remained firm and no severe strains were placed on the currency. But events after 1929–30 rapidly undermined confidence, and fears arose as to the liquidity of financial institutions and the convertibility of currencies. It is possible that the adoption of a tariff in 1930 or earlier might have saved the day, according to Foreman-Peck's (Foreman-Peck et al. 1997) calculations, but by the summer of 1931, when the Bank was well and truly under the harrow, that option had been closed. Once London became the focal point of the pressure it was found impossible to marshal sufficient resistance (Feinstein et al. 1995, 41). There were three possible solutions – allowing the reserves to deplete, calling in short-term assets, and further borrowing – but each entailed difficulties. The drain in gold reserves simply tended to depress confidence in sterling further and there was obviously a limit to how far the authorities were prepared to continue this strategy. In any case, the Bank's reserves were only sufficient to offset a small part of her potential liabilities, while special measures to release additional reserves in support of the currency were more likely to aggravate the market's growing unease about sterling's continued convertibility. The second course of action, realising short-term assets abroad, was easier said than done. Many of them were located in European financial centres which in themselves were in an illiquid state. Short-term assets in Germany alone amounted to £70 million and most of these were effectively frozen either by exchange control or by voluntary agreement (James 1986, 398). Total short-term assets in Europe as a whole were a good deal larger but most of them were irretrievable (Williams 1962–63, 524).

The third possible solution was to secure assistance from abroad to tide over the crisis. This was done late in July and again in August, when two lines of credit were raised in New York and Paris. But the rescue operation was too little and too late, reflecting partly the limited scope of international cooperation in a time of emergency. Dam (1982, 67) reckons that the resort to borrowing was interpreted as a sign of weakness, and in any case the effect of the assistance was muted by the fact that it was made in two separate tranches, the second of which was not arranged until the first had been exhausted (Clarke 1967, 204). 'It was this inability to either retain previously invested funds in London or to attract further investment by foreigners that was the root cause of London's short-term difficulties' (Williams 1962–63, 522).

Did the Bank really do all it could to defend the gold standard? One can detect an element of drift and despair during the crucial period, although in all fairness the sequence of events was on such a scale and moved so fast as to overwhelm central bankers (Hurst 1932, 659). On the other hand, it may seem curious, as Williams (1962–63) notes, that the Bank of England made little use of its traditional discount rate weapon to defend the position, with the Bank rate on the night of the abandonment of gold still at 4.5 per cent, where it had been since 30 July (it was raised to 6 per cent on the following day, 21 September). But whether higher interest rates would have attracted more funds to London or prevented some from leaving is another matter. Clarke (1967, 204) believes sterling was beyond salvation whatever tactics had been employed. Furthermore, in the critical situation of the time, raising the Bank rate might have been the cue for a further loss of confidence in the currency. Yet why the Bank failed to resort to its traditional weapon is not altogether clear. One possibility is the awareness that higher interest rates would aggravate the already difficult domestic situation and so prevent the Bank from taking a stronger line (Morton 1943, 44). More telling is Balderston's suggestion that when the chips were down there were few people in authority willing to defend the gold standard to the bitter end. 'When push came to shove, the gold standard fell' (Balderston 1995, 183; Schuker 1988, 55). Palyi (1972, 266–77) on the other hand, reckons that more could have been done to save the situation had the Deputy Governor of the Bank and Treasury officials not dithered so much and eventually lost their nerve. One curious point is why they could not have held out a little longer until Norman, who had been away ill for most of the crisis, returned to the UK on 23 September (Clay 1957, 399; Boyle 1967, 268–9).

So much for Britain's role in the crisis. Once she had left the gold standard, a large number of other countries followed her example. By the end of 1932 the only major countries still on gold were the United States, France, Belgium, Switzerland and the Netherlands. This general exodus was partly conditioned by the extent of the depreciation of the pound (Gilbert 1939, 88–90, 103), but in some cases it was also precipitated by the fact that speculative pressure was switched to countries still on gold, for example Sweden and Japan (Jonung 1981, 298–9; Yamamura 1972, 202–3). There was also an important practical consideration involved.

Once several countries had departed it put greater strain on those countries still defending gold parities. As Oye (1986, 182) observed: 'Because the only path to sustaining gold pars involved trekking through the deflationary swamps mutual cooperation in defence of these parities became less attractive than mutual defection.'

The American dollar held out somewhat longer but it was only a matter of time before it succumbed. Technically there was no great urgency to defect given the strength of the external account and the large gold stocks, although it should be noted that before the relief afforded by the Glass–Steagall Act of February 1932, the free gold reserve for international use was quite small and nearly prompted an early departure (Kindleberger 1973, 184–5). The real problem was that once Britain and a host of other countries had abandoned the gold standard, doubts were raised about the inviolability of countries remaining on gold even though they acknowledged their commitment to do so. The dollar soon became the focus of attention and in the six weeks to the end of October 1931 the United States lost $727 million of its gold holdings, mostly to France, Belgium, Switzerland and the Netherlands (Hamilton 1988, 74–5). This served to drain off bank reserves and forced a further contraction of money and credit, as the Federal Reserve allowed the money base to contract for fear of being forced off gold. As a result, there was a new wave of bank failures in response to the Federal Reserve's restrictive policy. The gold flow abated for a short time towards the end of the year, but a new wave of gold losses hit the country in the first half of the following year, amounting to some $550 million, again principally to the same countries, followed in turn by another wave of bank failures. Despite a more liberal stance by the Fed the process was repeated in 1932–33, with the most severe banking crisis occurring in February–March (Chandler 1970, 104; Fearon 1987, 109–17; League of Nations 1933, 235–41).

The Federal Reserve has been heavily criticised for its restrictive monetary strategy in the years 1929–32, when the money supply declined by about one-quarter. Clearly its policy only served to aggravate the depression forces and undermined confidence in the economy. However, the Fed was in something of a cleft stick as far as monetary policy was concerned. If it expanded the monetary base to assist the banking system, it raised expectations of devaluation and so put pressure on the currency and the reserves; on the other hand, if it did nothing, which initially was the policy favoured, there was the danger of even more bank failures and further deflation which could also put pressure on the currency and raise the spectre of devaluation (Hallwood et al. 1997, 191–3). In other words, international forces made the position increasingly untenable and eventually domestic needs won the battle. President Roosevelt realised, after prodding by an inner group of advisers, that it was impossible to hold on to the gold standard and at the same time raise domestic prices to encourage economic recovery (Mitchell 1947, 136). And so, on 20 April 1933 the US was taken off gold and by the end of that year only a handful of hard-core gold bloc countries in Europe remained faithful to the gold standard (see Chapter 3).

The gold standard and the transmission of depression

While the gold standard is not generally accredited with having caused the depression, it has nevertheless been seen as an important factor in the transmission of deflationary forces internationally once the initial downturn was under way, thereby intensifying the slump. As Temin (1993, 92) writes: 'The single best predictor of how severe the Depression was in different countries is how long they stayed on gold. The gold standard was a Midas touch that paralysed the world economy.'

If monetary shocks were the main source of cyclical fluctuations in this period, then the gold standard provided the mechanism by which deflationary forces were transmitted from one country to another (Meltzer 1976; Huffman and Lothian 1984, 456). The close links forged by the fixed exchange rates of the gold exchange standard ensured that the decline would be worldwide since, as Friedman and Schwartz (1963, 359) pointed out, 'no major contraction involving a substantial fall in prices could develop in one country without those links enforcing its transmission and spread to other countries'. Countries on gold reacted to balance of payments deficits and unbalanced budgets with deflationary policies in an effort to regain equilibrium, which of course only served to aggravate the downturn. The gold standard itself also became increasingly vulnerable, not only because there was a limit to which countries were prepared to go in deflating their domestic economies to maintain the fixed exchange rate system, but also because the international monetary system was much more sensitive to disturbances than it had been before the war since 'it raised the ratio of claims on the relevant high-powered money – in this case, ultimately, gold – to the amount of high-powered money available to meet those claims' (ibid.).

Two other important adverse effects can be detected. The banking crises of the early 1930s were exacerbated by deflation and the collapse of incomes, and by the constraints imposed on central bank policy by adherence to the gold-standard regime. Bernanke and James (1991, 243, 253, 270) found a strong link between the gold standard and the severity of depression which helped to precipitate banking panics, while the latter, through feedback effects, aggravated the crisis, especially in the United

States. Second, the volatility of short-term capital movements between countries, which undoubtedly contributed to the crisis, was made worse by the growing doubts as to the continued commitment to the existing monetary system (Hamilton 1988, 87).

In support of this interpretation, the proponents of the thesis make the following points. First, that countries not on the gold standard, for example Spain (flexible exchange rate) and China (on a silver standard), escaped the depression (Temin 1993, 92; Choudhri and Kochin 1980, 569). In the former case this is not strictly true (see Chapter 3), but China on a silver standard, equivalent to floating *vis-à-vis* gold, was more or less insulated from depression, at least that is until the general abandonment of the gold standard (Foreman-Peck 1983, 248; Friedman and Schwartz 1963, 361–2). Second, early floaters gained advantage in trade competitiveness and freedom to manoeuvre in monetary and fiscal policy, while the general departure from gold has been seen as important to recovery (see Chapter 3).

However, while it is generally agreed that the gold-standard regime acted as a restrictive force and inhibited monetary expansion, it does not automatically follow that an alternative monetary regime, that is floating, would have insulated the international economy from the cyclical and monetary disturbances that occurred at this time. Fleisig (1975, 114–18, 165) questions whether, if a system of flexible exchange rates had been in place at the time, it would have made much difference to the outcome. In his view the roots of the international depression are to be located in the decline in American foreign lending and the subsequent tightening of the world monetary situation. Theoretical support for this view has been given by Dornbusch (1976a, 272–3; 1983, 24) and others by demonstrating that real business cycle disturbances will tend to spill over from one country to another whatever the format of the exchange rate regime. 'Flexible rates leave us with as much interdependence, or even more, as there is under a fixed rate regime' (Dornbusch 1983, 4). What the exchange rate regime does is to determine the nature of the spillover effects, that is, whether they take the form of a reduction in employment and output with unchanged competitiveness (fixed rate regime) or whether the effects show up principally in changes in inflation and real incomes, but with less significant changes in employment (flexible rate systems). Under the latter regime the countries which gain will be those with the least real wage rigidity. Not that an earlier abandonment of gold by the major countries would not have improved the situation, although not by all that much according to Foreman-Peck's (Foreman-Peck et al. 1992, 691) calculations.

In other words, it is difficult, if not impossible, to avoid the influence of real disturbances by the choice of exchange rate regime. Experience throughout the twentieth century indicates that cyclical fluctuations are just as easily transmitted under any regime, but that the nature of the impact will be governed by the type of regime in operation. This does not, of course, necessarily invalidate the argument that the removal of the fixed exchange rate regime in the 1930s provided a release from the deflationary constraints of the gold-standard system (see Chapter 3).

Final comment

For the reasons outlined in the chapter, the restored gold standard was found wanting and it probably would have disintegrated of its own accord had its demise not been precipitated by the shocks imparted by the great depression and the accompanying financial crisis. The early departures foreshadowed what was to come once the standard became untenable in the face of the alternative of internal compression. Britain's departure was undoubtedly spurred on by the continental financial crisis and it effectively signalled the end of the system, since so many other currencies surrendered in its wake.

It is difficult to pinpoint one fact above all others which was instrumental to the collapse. Most of the issues discussed above had some part to play, and in some ways it was these which in the final analysis had an important bearing on the growing disillusionment and hence reduced commitment to the gold exchange standard, especially when its retention implied an economic strategy which exacerbated rather than alleviated depression and unemployment (Oye 1986, 182). The responses to the collapse of the international monetary system differed considerably and they form the subject of the next chapter.

3 Life after gold: currency regimes of the 1930s

Whatever the merits or otherwise of the postwar international gold standard, the fact is that it did not work as well as it had done before 1914. Its inherent defects, coupled with the pressures generated by the great depression, ultimately undermined the restored standard. The almost universal disintegration of the international gold standard in the early 1930s ushered in a period of currency chaos not dissimilar to that of the first half of the 1920s. Exchange rates were extremely volatile and there were fears at the time that exchange rate instability would hamper the recovery of international trade and lead to a renewed burst of inflation. The devaluation of the dollar and the failure to establish even a modicum of international cooperation on monetary matters at the World Economic Conference of 1933 appeared to bode ill for the future.

However, the year 1933 probably marked the nadir of exchange rate turbulence. From thereon, currency systems began to settle down, although not through a restoration of the gold standard, much as some nations might have wished for such an outcome, nor could it be attributed to the resumption of hegemonic leadership by one nation. In fact, asymmetric managed currency systems became the order of the day, and although this still left scope for haphazard and unpredictable changes in exchange rates in a world beset by nationalistic forces, they did ensure a more orderly pattern of exchange rates in the latter half of the 1930s (Yeager 1976, 374).

Three factors were largely responsible for the rescue from continued currency chaos. First, a determination on the part of many countries to avoid undue instability in the exchanges even if this meant resorting to controls or administrative management; second, the emergence of fairly distinct, although loosely drawn, currency areas or blocs following the general collapse of gold, which provided a fragmented form of asymmetric leadership; and third, despite the fiasco of the World Economic Conference, a gradual resumption of international monetary cooperation during the course of the 1930s.

It is a mistake, therefore, to regard the 1930s as a period of unrelieved currency turmoil. Indeed, by the middle of the decade the degree of currency volatility was remarkably small, and the pattern of exchange relationships among the chief currencies not practising exchange control was very similar to that prevailing in 1930 (ibid.). Moreover, for many countries the abandonment of gold followed by currency depreciation was a blessing in disguise since it relieved the external constraint on domestic economic management and eased the path of recovery from the depression.

The flight from gold and currency devaluation
Most of the countries which re-established the gold standard in the 1920s eventually abandoned it in the early 1930s. Altogether, 59 countries went off gold between 1929 and 1936 (Kemmerer 1944, 120). Although there were some early departures along the periphery, principally in Latin America (Argentina, Brazil, Paraguay, Venezuela, Uruguay, Mexico, and Australia and New Zealand), it was Britain's departure in September 1931 that effectively signalled the end of the old monetary regime. However, it was the size of the sterling depreciation rather than the shock of Britain's giving up gold that pulled many other currencies with it (Gilbert 1939, 88–90, 103). A large number of countries quickly followed Britain's lead by going off gold and depreciating their currencies, including nearly all the British colonies, Egypt, Norway, Sweden, Denmark, Finland, Portugal and Japan (Hawtrey 1939, 166; Hauser 1973, 73). By early 1933, when the United States also capitulated, there was only a small group of countries which retained their faith in gold. They included Belgium, Czechoslovakia, France, Italy, Luxembourg, the Netherlands, Poland and Switzerland, a group which became known as the gold bloc. Even these countries were eventually forced to succumb to the pressure of events, and by the autumn of 1936 they, too, had all given up the gold standard. Certain other currencies, especially those of Central and Eastern Europe, also retained nominal official parities by means of exchange control.

The abandonment of gold was accompanied by a wave of exchange depreciation which affected most currencies except those where official parities were maintained by the means of exchange control, principally those in Central and Eastern Europe, although even here there was resort to various forms of concealed depreciation. Many countries also instituted exchange control, at least temporarily, following the abandonment of gold. By the mid-1930s, the League of Nations (1937b, 15) recorded 34 countries in which some form of exchange control was in force.

The extent of the currency depreciation varied considerably, ranging from the official nominal parities maintained in exchange control countries to 90 per cent in the case of the Bolivian free rate (ibid.). But as can be seen from Table 3.1, many of the devaluations fell within the range 40–50 per cent by the mid-1930s. However, these new valuations were the outcome of a period of severe currency turmoil as exchange rates adjusted to the new conditions. Fluctuations were widest at the initial stage of depreciation of each currency, after which they tended to subside significantly (League of Nations 1937a, 32). As might be expected therefore, the most intense phase of currency depreciation occurred between the latter half of 1931 and the end of 1933, the period when the majority of countries broke the link with gold and when, for the most part, currencies were allowed to fluctuate fairly freely. Beth Simmons (1994, 109) maintains that the 1930s were as turbulent for currencies as they were in the stabilisation period of 1923–26, and provide a sharp contrast with the near stability recorded in the period of the restored gold standard (1927–31). From a sample of mainly European countries, although also including the United States, Canada and Japan, she calculates that between 1932 and 1939, depreciations averaged about 5.6 per cent a year, as against 6 per cent for the years 1923–26.

However, the comparison may do injustice to the element of instability in this decade, even though it was influenced by a further bout of currency disturbance when the gold bloc countries left the gold standard in the mid-1930s. First, the comparison is made with the period 1923–26, when countries were either in the process of stabilising or had already stabilised their currencies. Second, her calculations exclude Germany for obvious reasons. Third, the years prior to this, 1918–22, when most exchanges fluctuated freely, no doubt witnessed even greater rates of exchange depreciation and volatility. Finally, exchange rate variability, as measured by the standard error, was far higher in the years 1923–26 than it was in the 1930s. In fact as far as the major European currencies were concerned, both nominal and real rates of exchange were more volatile under the managed float of the early 1930s than they had been under the restored gold standard, as one might expect, but they were not as unstable as they had been in the early 1920s (Eichengreen 1988a, 366–8). Drummond (1981, 253–4) feels that it is a mistake to view the 1930s as a decade of disorder: it was, he says, no more disorderly than the 1920s, and far less so than the 1970s.

In fact, what is perhaps most remarkable given the unsettled conditions of the early 1930s, is the speed with which currencies stabilised once the

Table 3.1 Exchange rates and exchange control in the 1930s

Country	Official suspension of gold standard	Introduction of exchange control	Depreciation or devaluation in relation to gold	Extent of depreciation by early 1935 (%)	Introduction of new gold parity
Albania	–	–	–	–	–
Argentina	17–12–29	13–10–31	11–29	54	–
Australia	17–12–29	–	3–30	52	–
Austria	5–4–33	9–10–31	12–31; 4–34	22	30–4–34*
Belgium	30–3–35	18–3–35	3–35	28	31–3–36*
Bolivia	25–9–31	3–10–31	3–30	59	–
Brazil	–	18–5–31	12–29	59	–
Bulgaria	–	1918	–	–	–
Canada	19–10–31	–	12–31	40	–
Chile	20–4–32	30–7–31	4–32	75	–
China	–	9–9–34	–	50	–
Colombia	25–9–31	25–9–31	1–32	61	–
Costa Rica	–	16–1–32	1–32	44	–
Cuba	21–11–33	2–6–34	4–33	–	22–5–34*
Czechoslovkia	–	2–10–31	2–34; 10–36	16	17–2–34; 9–10–36
Danzig	–	12–6–35	5–35	0	2–5–35
Denmark	29–9–31	18–11–31	9–31	52	–
Ecuador	8–2–32	2–5–32	6–32	73	19–12–35*
Egypt	21–9–31	–	9–31	–	–
Estonia	28–6–33	18–11–31	6–33	42	–
Finland	12–10–31	–	10–31	50	–
France	–	–	9–36	0	1–10–36*
Germany	–	13–7–31	–	–	–
Greece	26–4–32	28–9–31	4–32	57	–
Guatemala	–	–	4–33	–	–
Honduras	–	27–3–34	4–33	–	–
Hong Kong	–	9–11–35	–	–	–
Hungary	–	17–7–31	–	–	–
India	21–9–31	–	9–31	40	–
Iran	–	25–2–30	–	57	–
Irish Free State	26–9–31	–	9–31	41	–
Italy	–	26–5–34	3–34; 10–36	4	8–10–36*
Japan	13–12–31	1–7–32	12–31	66	–
Latvia	28–9–36	8–10–31	9–36	–	–
Lithuania	–	1–10–35	–	–	–
Luxembourg	–	18–3–35	3–35	0	1–4–35
Malaya	21–9–31	–	9–31	40	–
Mexico	25–7–31	–	8–31	67	–
Netherlands	27–9–36	–	9–36	0	–
New Zealand	21–9–31	–	4–30	52	–
Nicaragua	13–11–31	13–11–31	1–32	46	–

Table 3.1 (continued)

Country	Official suspension of gold standard	Introduction of exchange control	Depreciation or devaluation in relation to gold	Extent of depreciation by early 1935 (%)	Introduction of new gold parity
Norway	28–9–31	–	9–31	46	–
Palestine	21–9–31	–	9–31	–	–
Panama	–	–	4–33	–	–
Paraguay	–	20–8–32	11–29	–	–
Peru	14–5–32	–	5–32	63	–
Philippines	–	–	4–33	–	–
Poland	–	26–4–36	–	–	–
Portugal	31–12–31	21–10–22	10–31	42	–
Romania	–	18–5–32	7–35	0	–
Salvador, El	9–10–31	20–8–33	10–31	52	–
Siam	11–5–32	–	6–32	40	–
South Africa	28–12–32	–	1–33	41	–
Spain	–	18–5–31	1920	45	–
Sweden	29–9–31	–	9–31	44	–
Switzerland	–	–	9–36	0	27–9–36*
Turkey	–	26–2–30	1915	–	–
UK	21–9–31	–	9–31	41	–
USA	20–4–33	6–3–33	4–33	41	31–1–34*
Uruguay	20–12–29	7–9–31	4–29	54	–
USSR	–	–	4–36	–	1–4–36*
Venezuela	–	12–12–36	9–30	19	–
Yugoslavia	–	7–10–31	7–32	23	–

Note: *Provisional parity.

Sources: Bank for International Settlements (1935, 9); League of Nations (1937a, 111–13).

main devaluations had taken place, and the way in which traditional currency relationships were restored. Table 3.2 provides data on monthly fluctuations in exchange rates for a selection of countries which had abandoned their former parities. As early as March 1934, *The Economist* (1934, 685–6) had commented on the comparative stability of the major currencies of the world other than the dollar, and by the latter half of that year the volatility of currencies was already quite modest and it continued to decline in subsequent years. A comparative calculation on a daily basis for a small number of key countries shows a similar trend (Table 3.3). Only with the departure of the gold bloc currencies later in 1936 was there a renewed burst of currency instability, although it was of fairly modest dimensions compared with that of the early 1930s.

Table 3.2 Range of fluctuation of gold value of selected currencies, 1931–1937 (percentage by which the highest monthly average exceeded the lowest during each half year period shown)

	1931b	1932a	1932b	1933a	1933b	1934a	1934b	1935a	1935b	1936a	1936b	1937a
United States	–	–	–	22.5	16.6	6.6	1.4	0.6	0.6	1.4	0.8	–
Mexico	63.3	46.1	16.2	33.6	17.8	6.7	1.2	1.1	0.7	1.4	0.7	–
Austria	18.5	5.5	1.9	9.9	1.9	1.6	0.8	1.8	0.5	0.3	1.5	0.1
Yugoslavia	–	–	24.3	1.2	1.3	2.3	0.6	0.6	0.2	0.1	0.8	0.2
Canada	20.6	5.6	5.3	19.4	8.5	5.9	1.3	1.8	0.7	1.1	0.7	0.2
China	14.6	9.7	10.9	6.6	7.0	11.5	5.4	17.3	30.8	1.3	3.2	0.4
Japan	13.6	18.8	33.1	3.9	12.2	7.0	4.4	3.8	1.8	2.2	3.9	0.4
United Kingdom	44.0	9.4	8.3	2.3	6.2	6.3	2.7	3.5	0.7	1.7	3.6	0.6
Portugal	36.8	6.9	6.9	3.4	1.8	6.8	3.0	3.5	0.4	1.3	3.4	0.4
New Zealand	44.0	9.3	8.3	9.1	6.0	6.3	2.9	3.5	0.7	1.8	3.5	0.6
Siam	–	34.0	6.9	2.3	6.1	6.3	2.6	3.5	1.3	1.7	3.6	0.6
Denmark	43.5	8.6	12.8	13.1	6.1	6.4	2.6	3.5	0.7	1.7	3.6	0.6
Sweden	43.3	6.2	4.6	6.1	6.1	6.4	2.5	3.5	0.7	1.7	3.6	0.6
Norway	44.3	8.5	5.4	3.1	6.3	6.2	2.5	3.4	0.6	1.7	3.6	0.6
Finland	49.1	14.8	8.0	4.0	5.8	6.8	2.5	3.4	0.6	1.5	3.5	0.6
South Africa	–	–	–	4.1	6.1	6.2	2.5	3.5	0.8	1.7	3.6	0.6
Greece	–	103.3	17.9	5.0	0.5	0.7	1.0	0.6	0.3	0.9	5.9	0.6
Australia	38.9	9.2	8.4	2.2	6.0	6.7	3.2	3.5	0.7	1.9	3.5	0.7
Peru	2.2	31.0	26.5	21.7	10.5	4.0	2.2	3.9	5.0	0.7	2.5	0.7
Estonia	–	–	–	6.3	4.6	6.5	2.5	3.4	0.7	2.2	3.5	0.8
Chile	–	–	–	15.7	6.9	8.2	6.9	1.5	6.6	4.5	0.8	–

Source: League of Nations (1937a, 32).

*Table 3.3 Yearly range of quotations of certain currencies in Switzerland,
1931–1936 (daily figures, maximum as percentage of minimum)*

	1931	1932	1933	1934	1935	1936*
United States	1.6	2.0	70.4	9.8	3.4	2.6
Sweden	51.3	19.1	17.2	13.1	6.5	3.3
United Kingdom	51.2	19.5	14.9	13.1	6.7	3.4
Norway	43.0	26.3	16.1	13.0	6.6	3.4
Denmark	53.4	26.3	28.0	12.8	7.0	3.4
Austria	21.8	18.2	14.8	2.8	5.1	3.8
Japan	42.7	84.8	24.4	17.0	6.5	4.4

Note: *Nine months.

Source: League of Nations (1937a, 33).

There was, therefore, a gradual approximation to exchange rate stability in the years after 1933. The great majority of important trading currencies moved into a fairly close relationship with sterling, the dollar and the franc. Since these leading currencies were relatively stable it made for a much more tranquil situation in exchange markets generally. The main exceptions were the free rates in some South American countries and the fluctuations in the unofficial rates of countries maintaining nominal parities through exchange control (League of Nations 1937b, 18). By the mid-1930s, daily and weekly fluctuations of the major rates were almost back to the range of the old gold parity points, with significant movements occurring only at times of major policy changes, as, for example, the devaluation of the French franc in September 1936 (Sayers 1976b, 475–83).

While it would be highly misleading to suggest that currency fluctuations were of minor importance in the 1930s, or that all exchange rates were in equilibrium after 1933 (which was far from the case as we shall see), it is plausible to argue that currency movements became far more orderly than many contemporary accounts suggest once the dust had settled from the wholesale abandonment of gold. It is true that the Bank for International Settlements was still complaining about the adverse effects of currency instability in its fifth report covering the year to the end of March 1935 (Bank for International Settlements 1935, 5), but by that time currency variability had been reduced to quite small proportions, and the Bank was obviously harking back nostalgically to the golden days. Nor would it be correct to argue that competitive depreciations were a special feature of this period. In fact, the majority of devaluations were once-and-for-all events, most of which followed the leaders – Britain in 1931, the United States in 1933, and France in 1936. Hawtrey (1939,

240) thought the competitive depreciation argument was ill-founded and, as Simmons (1994, 110) notes more recently, none of the three major powers devalued simultaneously.

In fact, despite the inauspicious outcome of the World Economic Conference regarding currency issues, most countries hankered after exchange stability and eschewed free floating. For a time some countries cherished the belief that it would be possible to restore some form of the gold standard, although this became increasingly unlikely as time wore on. As the League of Nations (1944, 122) later reported: 'one of the facts that stands out from this experience [currency volatility of the early 1930s] is that monetary authorities in most countries had little or no desire for freely floating exchanges'. The experience of the early 1920s, while perhaps not the most appropriate for judging the merits or otherwise of free floating, had been more than enough for most contemporaries, associated as it was with severe inflation, budgetary deficits and delayed trade recovery. This was one of the main reasons why France and her faithful disciples clung to the gold standard until well into the 1930s. The French, especially, were obsessed with the fear of inflation and believed that monetary and exchange stability were crucial to economic recovery (Jackson 1985, 220–21; Mouré 1991, 4). At the time of extreme currency instability it seemed a logical move, but it subsequently proved a fatal policy error as far as their domestic economies were concerned.

What the gold bloc countries failed to appreciate was that there was an alternative to gold: that currency chaos was not, as Hawtrey (1939, 243–4) explained, necessarily a product of breaking the link with a metallic standard and moving to a managed paper system. Nor did they fully appreciate the determination of most countries to avoid large fluctuations in their exchange rates wherever possible, even though the international climate for formal stabilisation was far from ideal. On the abandonment of gold the exchanges were initially allowed to fluctuate fairly freely, but this gave rise to large and unpredictable fluctuations which were regarded as being inimical to trade and industry, apart from the inflationary implications of uncontrolled depreciation. Two factors in particular were instrumental in bringing some order to the exchanges following the turbulence of the early 1930s. One was the active intervention of monetary authorities to dampen excessive fluctuations by administrative control; the second was the emergence of currency blocs which permitted a degree of leadership under asymmetric management. A third, although less important, factor was gradual improvement in the climate for international cooperation, once the shock of the débâcle of the World Economic Conference had passed.

Currency blocs: the sterling area

Out of the wreckage of the currency turmoil of the 1930s there emerged several distinct currency areas or blocs. The three most important were the sterling area, the gold bloc, and the exchange control or Reichsmark bloc. One can also identify a dollar zone, associated primarily with Latin American countries, and possibly a yen bloc, covering a significant part of Asia. Most of them were loosely drawn and none of them had any formal organisation with executive power over currency activities. Classification of countries is also sometimes difficult because of changes in regime structure over time. Nevertheless, there was undoubtedly a measure of informal leadership exercised by the dominant country which encouraged the members to link their currencies to and track the currency of the leader. Einzig (1937, 309) reckoned that as a result of these arrangements 'there was *de facto* stability practically all over the civilised world' by the end of 1936.

The largest of these systems was the sterling area. It was a very diffuse and informal grouping of countries which kept their currencies pegged to sterling, invoiced the bulk of their trade in sterling and held most, if not all, their official external reserves in sterling. The early members included the British Dominions and crown colonies (apart from Canada, Newfoundland and Hong Kong), Ireland, Portugal, Egypt and Iraq, to be joined later by the Scandinavian countries, Estonia, Latvia, Lithuania, Iran and Finland. Several other countries, including Argentina, Brazil, Bolivia, Greece, Japan, Siam, Yugoslavia and the Straits Settlements, also maintained a stable link with sterling for several years, although they were never regarded strictly as formal members of the area since from time to time they practised exchange control and the use of multiple exchange rates (Cairncross and Eichengreen 1983, 23–4; de Vegh 1939, 8–10).

The emergence of the sterling area was a logical outcome of Britain's departure from gold. Many members of the group had strong commercial links with Britain, especially the imperial countries, and these were to become even stronger during the course of the decade. In the past they had relied heavily on Britain for people and capital, much of their trade had been financed through the City and they had held their reserves in the London money market. Thus they were bound together by 'interests and historical habits as much as by formal rules and obligations' (Llewellyn and Presley 1995, 268). The system was extremely flexible since there were no formal constitution or terms of agreement so that members could join or leave at will. The only exception to this generalisation was the monetary resolution adopted by the Ottawa Conference in the summer of 1932 which decreed that the general aim of monetary policy throughout the area should be that of ensuring the stability of sterling prices. The chief

factor binding them together was the belief that it was in their best interests to maintain their currencies at a fixed rate with sterling (Scammell
1961, 246). Compared with the alternatives available at the time, the sterling option seemed the most attractive (Bareau 1945, 131–6).

Despite its informality, the sterling area has been seen as much more
than a holding operation in response to the crisis of the early 1930s. The
French, and to a lesser extent the Americans, suspected that it was a new
version of imperialism designed to bolster Britain's waning pre-eminence in
international affairs, and specifically in international finance (Strange 1971,
50–52). There is some substance in this view which Cain (1996, 337–8) has
recently forcibly emphasised. He argues that the main objective of British
international economic policy (under the aegis of the Treasury and the
Bank of England) was to safeguard the sterling area and to foster its extension in an effort to salvage as much as possible from the wreckage of 1931
and restore Britain's former international financial supremacy (compare
Williamson 1992, 499). It is in this context that the Ottawa agreements for
preferential trade among imperial countries and the monetary prescriptions laid down at the negotiations take on special significance, since it was
essential for the survival of stable exchange rates that members follow consistent policies and maintain some form of monetary discipline. A year
later, on 24 July 1933, the British Empire Currency Declaration reaffirmed
the Ottawa commitment to avoid undue fluctuations in the purchasing
power of gold and to encourage non-imperial countries to join the sterling
'club' so as to widen the area over which exchange stability could be
secured (Clavin 1996, 136–7). Several countries, notably Sweden and
Denmark, were attracted by the prospect of exchange stability and
promptly joined the scheme. Meanwhile, Montagu Norman, on behalf of
the Bank of England, was busily trying to equip Commonwealth countries
with the requisite local machinery and financial organisation to protect
and strengthen the sterling system (Strange 1971, 55). Cassel's view that the
Bank of England never endorsed the sterling bloc programme seems somewhat at odds with Norman's imperial endeavour (Cassel 1936, 205). That
the policy misfired in the case of Canada, whose divergent commercial
interests led her to gravitate to the dollar zone, should not be construed as
a failure of the overall strategy (compare Cain 1996, 338).

In essence, therefore, the sterling area was tantamount to a fixed
exchange rate system similar to that of the gold exchange standard, the
main difference being that it was sterling not gold that was the medium of
account for settling imbalances among members. For the most part,
exchange rates of the members remained remarkably stable and changes in
sterling parities were something of a rarity despite the fact that they could
be made at will. The success of the system owed much to the fact that ster-

ling still retained much of its former status as an international currency in this period and, as in the nineteenth century, its stability in value and wide acceptability as a means of payment made it the most sought after currency. Although it lost some 40 per cent of its former value relative to gold countries, most of the depreciation had taken place by the end of 1931. Thereafter, it retained a fairly stable value relative to other currencies which had followed it and so members of the sterling bloc were happy to keep a large part of their reserves in sterling (Scammell 1961, 248). Drummond (1981, 19–20, 253–4) notes that a large part of the trading world enjoyed reasonably stable exchange rates in the 1930s and this he attributes to the management of the sterling system, although it was probably less successful in restoring equilibrium between costs and prices (Cassel 1936, 204). Only in the early 1930s and again late on in the decade was there really serious disorder in the foreign exchanges.

The gold bloc
The spate of devaluations and exchange restrictions of the early 1930s left those countries still on the gold standard in a somewhat exposed position. When it became apparent, pending the breakup of the World Economic Conference in July 1933, that an early resumption of the gold standard was out of the question, the governments of Belgium, France, Holland, Italy, Luxembourg, Poland and Switzerland issued a joint declaration on 3 July confirming 'their intention to maintain the free functioning of the gold standard in their respective countries at the existing gold parities and within the framework of existing monetary laws. They ask their central banks to keep in close touch to give the maximum efficacy to this declaration'. A few days later, the governors of the respective banks met at the Bank of France to review the practical measures required to give effect to this resolution and to protect their currencies from exchange speculation (Bank for International Settlements 1934, 13).

It may seem anomalous that a small group of countries whose trading links and interests were both relatively weak and divergent, should seek to maintain a gold regime in the face of abandonment elsewhere. It is true that several of the countries in question (France, Belgium, Holland and Switzerland) were in a relatively strong position, with gold reserves at their highest ever recorded (Yeager 1976, 357). Questions of prestige and fear of inflation also played an important role since, apart from Holland and Switzerland, these countries had all suffered severely from inflationary pressures and currency depreciation in the first half of the 1920s. According to Einzig (1937, 69) the Dutch Prime Minister, Dr Hendrikus Colijn, 'regarded it as a matter of prestige to outbid any country in the civic virtues of deflation'. The French, for their part, were obsessed about the inflationary implications of devaluation which rekindled memories of the disastrous experience of the franc in the 1920s. Devaluation was also seen to be socially disruptive and there was little popular support for it. Moreover, France was initially in a very strong financial position and experienced a belated depression, although she did have a chronic budgetary problem. Hence there was little obvious pressure to resort to devaluation (Jackson 1985, 220–21; Mouré 1991, 4; Schwarz 1993, 100–111).

Exchange rate stability within the gold bloc was purchased at a price. Because the currencies of gold members became overvalued relative to those which had devalued it was necessary to resort to domestic deflation to maintain international competitiveness. Throughout most of the first half of the 1930s, deflationary policies, together with defensive trade measures, were pursued relentlessly, although occasionally interspersed with reflationary measures especially in France, with the result that recovery from depression was delayed (Hogg 1987, 208–9; Asselain and Plessis 1995, 202–11). But such draconian domestic measures were insufficient to offset the hefty overvaluation of their currencies or prevent periodic pressures on their exchange rates and external accounts. Within the gold bloc itself there was very little in the way of mutual assistance between members, since each country was intent on husbanding its resources for the defence of its own currency. Thus what was hoped originally would develop into a monetary and economic union eventually became 'a small group of members who watched each other jealously, half hoping and half fearing that their fellow-members would be the first to devalue'. (Einzig 1937, 241).

In fact it was the smaller countries that were in the weakest position; their currencies were frequently subject to speculation as gold losses mounted. However, for most countries it was the intolerable internal compression required to compensate for overvalued currencies, rather than sheer inability to defend the old rates, that eventually forced them to abandon gold (Simmons 1994, 253). By early 1935, the end was in sight for the gold bloc. Belgium and Luxembourg were forced to devalue in March 1935, Italy withdrew from the gold bloc in the same year because of surreptitious devaluation of the lira and the introduction of exchange controls in the previous year, while Poland ceased to be a member from early 1936, because of the introduction of exchange controls. These departures put even further pressures on the remaining members. The French situation was also exacerbated by the inflationary policies of Léon Blum's Popular Front government in the summer of 1936 with the result that the franc became even more overvalued (Patat and Lutfalla 1990, 82). The pressure was reflected in a flight of capital and a hefty discount on the pegged rate which eventually forced the French to give up the struggle on 26 September 1936. The franc was devalued by some

30 per cent, although even this still left it overvalued so that it continued to come under pressure in later years. Within hours of the French announcement the remaining members of the gold bloc followed suit.

Although the gold bloc helped to maintain currency stability while it lasted, it turned out to be a costly exercise. It did little to promote intra-bloc trade or closer economic cooperation among its members. Its demise was followed by another period of currency uncertainty as the French franc adjusted to the new situation. Most of the countries involved per-formed poorly in the 1930s when set against their sterling area counterparts. The only worthwhile thing to emerge from the wreckage was the controversial Tripartite Agreement between France, America and Britain pertaining to cooperation on currency matters (see below).

Exchange control countries
Whereas many western countries removed the constraint of the 'golden fetters' by coming off gold and devaluing their currencies so as to allow more room for manoeuvre in domestic economic policy, this option was not followed by most countries in Central and Eastern Europe. They attempted to maintain their former parities by restrictive external policy rather than outright internal compression. Tariff levels were raised sharply between 1929 and 1931, and these were accompanied by extensive quantitative controls on imports and exchange control (Condliffe 1941, 103; Pollard 1981, 302). By the end of 1931 Austria, Germany, Bulgaria, Czechoslovakia, Hungary, Yugoslavia, Greece and Turkey had all imposed exchange control and Romania followed suit in May 1932. Only Poland resisted until the spring of 1936, by adhering to the gold bloc (League of Nations 1933, 222–3; 1937a, 11; 1942, 70).

Several factors explain this course of action. In virtually every case the imposition of exchange control originated as a result of exchange and balance of payments pressures as a result of the crisis of the early 1930s (League of Nations 1938a, 22; 1943b, 10). Trade balances had been gen-erally unfavourable before 1929 and they were considerably worsened by rapidly falling commodity export prices and unfavourable terms of trade thereafter (Ranki 1983c, 51–2). Rising protection in western countries, especially on agricultural products, did not help matters as far as many of Europe's primary producers were concerned. In addition, the sharp rever-sal of capital imports and the very limited international reserves held by these countries meant that import surpluses could no longer be financed and hence imports had to be reduced at all costs. Protection of domestic industry and agriculture also became an important concern in a world awash with goods. Initially, however, there were even more pressing motives for the introduction of exchange control and the defence of currencies. One was the desire to check capital outflows, especially in the financial panic of 1931. A second important consideration was the reluctance to relinquish former currency parities, grounded in the belief that depreciating currencies were bad for inflation; most of the countries in question had bitter memories of their disastrous experience in the previous decade. Currency depreciation also raised the burden of debt service costs, and in any case there was a belief that debt servicing should be maintained if at all possible in order to demonstrate financial soundness. Exchange control would facilitate the collection of foreign exchange for that purpose (League of Nations 1943b, 9–11; 1944, 162–7).

The initial results of trade restriction and exchange control were reasonably promising. Capital flows were staunched, trade balances generally improved and exchange rates remained fairly stable. In so far as exchange control was used as an instrument of commercial policy it did allow greater latitude in the use of macroeconomic policy for domestic purposes. However, longer term the costs probably outweighed the benefits. Exchange control tended to raise domestic prices and rendered exporting more difficult in so far as it maintained fictitious currency values. One estimate suggests that in 1934, East European currencies were overvalued relative to the pound and the dollar by as much as 60 per cent (Nötel 1986, 229). Moreover, following the imposition of exchange control, the trade shares of these countries fell sharply and remained below the level of 1929 throughout the 1930s (League of Nations 1938a, 30; Harris 1936, 101–2). In this respect they fared worse than the gold bloc countries. Most contemporary studies concluded that exchange control countries experienced a lower level of output and trade than countries with depreciated currencies (Heuser 1939, 230; Harris 1936, 103; Ellis 1939, 1941, 152), a finding confirmed by more recent scholarship (Eichengreen 1992c, 351; 1992b, 233).

Recognition of the perverse effects of maintaining official parities was manifest in the efforts made to relax or modify the control system. Most countries, apart from Poland, eventually introduced a measure of devaluation in a concealed form. This was done principally by the provision of export bonuses or currency premia or through the use of multiple exchange rates, which meant that exporters received more domestic currency for their exports than they would have been entitled to under the official rates. The terms of the premia varied a great deal from country to country, ranging between 20 and 50 per cent. Such sub-species of currency created by means of multiple exchange rates were also used by a number of Latin American countries (Einzig 1970, 257). However, even with this relief the currencies still remained overvalued relative to those of free market economies (Lampe and Jackson 1982, 464–5; Ranki 1983a, 90; Royal Institute of International Affairs 1936, 85–9; League of Nations 1938a, 5; 1944, 171).

By the end of the 1930s, a substantial proportion of international trade – possibly as much as 30 per cent – was subject to exchange control in one form or another. Because exchange control required a high degree of state interference and control of economic activity, the countries which practised it tended to trade more among themselves and less with those countries having free exchange markets. However, the closer affinity among exchange control countries which developed in Central and Eastern Europe was predicated on two factors: the need for primary producers to find an outlet for their exports and Nazi Germany's quest to secure access to the resources of its eastern hinterland without having to use scarce foreign exchange.

Clearing agreements became one of the principal instruments by which Germany sought to extend its control over the trade and payments of the region. Clearing agreements entailed the bilateral balancing of claims between exchange control countries, thereby minimising the need for free foreign exchange. Following the launch of Schacht's New Plan in 1934, by which foreign trade transactions were brought under centralised control and exchange control became a specific instrument of trade policy, Germany concluded a series of bilateral clearing agreements with both European and non-European countries (principally Latin American). By 1937, when some 12 per cent of world trade passed through clearings, more than 50 per cent of the trade of Germany, Hungary, the Balkans, Greece and Turkey, was subject to clearing agreements (League of Nations 1939, 186–7; 1942, 70–72; 1944, 182–3).

There is continuing debate as to who gained from the whole exercise. There is no doubt that trade among the Reichsmark bloc members increased significantly, although most of this was due to the trading links with the centre country, since Eastern Europe's share of world trade declined. As a result, Germany gained an increasing foothold in the trade of Eastern Europe, especially in Hungary and the Balkans. Yet despite the closer relations of the group, Germany still depended on the rest of Europe for some 40 per cent of her import requirements by the end of the decade (Griffiths 1989, 27; League of Nations 1939, 186; Hiden 1977, 173; Kaiser 1980, 325–6).

Conventional wisdom asserts that Germany exploited the region for its own benefit to gain access to food and raw materials on favourable terms, and in so doing piled up large import surpluses with these countries, the Reichsmark balances from which could only be used to purchase German goods. Indirectly, therefore, it could be argued that Germany was rearming at the expense of weaker nations. Furthermore, Germany has been accused of dumping large quantities of unwanted goods, such as aspirins and cuckoo-clocks, on her hapless eastern neighbours (Einzig 1938, 26).

On the reverse side of the coin, one should note that the eastern countries were able to find a market for their primary products at reasonably favourable prices, and that they received more than ephemeral goods in return. Exports to other exchange control countries, especially those to Germany, generally fetched higher prices than those to non-exchange control countries (League of Nations 1938a, 34). Moreover, they were able to acquire a large part of their machinery and arms supplies from Germany, as well as a variety of consumer goods (Basch 1944, 179; Momtchiloff 1944, 56, appendices 1–4; Rothschild 1974, 22). Nor did Germany use her potential monopsonist power as exploitatively as many contemporaries alleged. German purchases helped to raise the export prices and incomes of these countries and Germany did not take undue advantage of her position to turn the terms of trade in her favour (Bonnell 1940, 131; Kaiser 1980, 160; Royal Institute of International Affairs 1939, 119). In actual fact, Germany's import prices rose faster than her export prices and on average she paid some 30 per cent above world prices for her imports from South-east Europe (Neal 1979, 392–5; James 1993, 86). Abelshauser (1995, 409–10) reckons that Schacht's attempt at the economic penetration of South-east Europe was something of a failure largely because payment in blocked marks involved considerable extra costs.

In the light of later events, the revisionist judgement may be somewhat academic. Trade relationships with Germany could be very unpredictable and the large unrequited balances, although reduced in time, left many countries highly vulnerable to political and economic pressures, especially when market conditions deteriorated, as they did later in the decade (Friedman 1976). Germany felt no compunction about terminating agreed purchase contracts when it suited her purpose, as happened in the case of the contract for the bumper Yugoslav plum harvest in September 1939 (Hoptner 1962, 103). On a more serious note, Germany undoubtedly used her trade connections with South-east Europe for political gain. Political agents, in the guise of commercial travellers and business representatives, were widely employed throughout the region to spread the Nazi gospel. In one case, the Germans set up a soya-bean factory in Romania which employed no less than 3000 commercial agents in this capacity (Jones 1937, 64, 82). These disguised agents were thick on the ground in the region by the end of the decade and the countries in question realised only too late in the day that economic dependence was but a prelude to political control (Munk 1940, 151).

Exchange stabilisation funds

After the collapse of the gold standard, many countries established more formal mechanisms for managing their exchange rates. The first of what became known as exchange stabilisation funds was announced in the British budget of April 1932 – the Exchange Equalisation Account (EEA) which began operations in the June of that year. It was followed by similar institutions in many other countries including the United States (January 1934), Belgium (March 1935), Canada (July 1935), the Netherlands and Switzerland (September 1936), France (October 1936), as well as in Argentina, Colombia, Czechoslovakia, Latvia, Mexico, Spain and Japan (League of Nations 1937a, 57). These arrangements were essentially a more elaborate extension of classical central banking practice, whereby specifically constituted funds held assets in gold and national currencies which they deployed in an attempt to insulate their domestic economies from excessive fluctuations in exchange rates caused by speculative activity and volatile capital movements (Condliffe 1941, 237).

It is difficult to make broad generalisations about the nature and working of these funds since no two were alike in terms of assets held, their working practices or their underlying purposes, while for the most part their activities were kept highly secret. However, we do know that one of the chief aims of the funds was to try to smooth out fluctuations in exchange rates caused by erratic capital movements and the activities of speculators which, it was widely believed at the time, had caused so much disruption in the early 1930s. Active intervention in exchange markets, it was thought, would help to stabilise exchange rates for the benefit of recovery (League of Nations 1944, 143; Bloomfield 1944, 69–87). Smoothing operations apart, a second important objective in some cases was that of establishing and defending what was thought to be an appropriate exchange rate in the light of the requirements of domestic economic policy.

In the latter respect the British EEA provides a fine illustration since one of the main reasons for its creation was the authorities' belief that the pound, which had begun to rise from the low level of \$3.24 recorded in early December 1931, should be kept down so as to aid recovery, raise the price level and make cheap money effective. There was considerable debate as to the most appropriate target rate but eventually a value of \$3.40–\$3.50 was selected, adjusted to \$4.50–\$4.60 following the dollar devaluation in the spring of 1933 (Howson 1975, 83–6; 1980a, 54; Howson and Winch 1977, 104–5).

Howson (1976, 249–51, 1980a, 55–6) maintains that domestic objectives were of paramount importance in setting the exchange rate target in the 1930s. This was interpreted as being the lowest possible value for sterling which was consistent with the exchange rate priorities of Britain's main trading competitors. Repegging the exchange rate was consistently ruled out on the ground that this would limit the authorities' room for manoeuvre on the domestic policy front to the detriment of economic recovery. While this interpretation is no doubt consistent with the policy statements made at the time, it is somewhat at odds with the actual course of events. Although the EEA concentrated much of its interventionist operations on the sterling–dollar rate, it did find difficulty in preventing the pound from rising in the early years. But, in any case, its activities in this area may have been somewhat academic since, according to Drummond (1981, 256), the United States effectively took control of the sterling–dollar rate in 1933, which meant in practice that the British authorities were only free to prevent the pound falling below what the Americans deemed to be the most appropriate rate from their own domestic point of view (Pumphrey 1942, 808, 816).

Moreover, bilateral rates, even one as important as the sterling–dollar, give a somewhat one-sided view of a country's overall exchange rate position. In actual fact, the pound's effective rate (measured against a basket of 28 currencies) appreciated continuously between 1932 and 1939, which hardly squares with the Treasury's stated intention of capping sterling (Redmond 1980, 88–9; 1988, 293). One reason for this seeming paradox may lie in the limited resources of the EEA in the face of large capital inflows, especially during the golden avalanche arising from the flight from the French franc in 1936–37, when the Account almost ran out of sterling reserves so that it could do little more than dampen the upward pressure on the exchange rate.

Whether the EEA made for greater stability in exchange rates overall is a moot point. Howson (1980b, 56) reckons that the EEA's management of sterling made it a more stable currency than would otherwise have been the case. However, since the bulk of its operations were confined to the sterling–dollar market, one doubts whether it could have had much effect on other rates. The relative stability of the sterling–dollar rate after the middle of 1933 suggests that the EEA had some success in this quarter, although it can be argued that US intervention, and the more stable economic conditions and policies in the respective countries, were more important to the outcome (Broadberry 1987, 74; Whitaker and Hudgins 1977, 1478). Nevertheless, Whitaker and Hudgins (1977, 1483–4) do detect a modest contribution to the stabilisation of inter-month variations in the sterling–dollar rate and they suggest that the EEA may also have been successful in combating irrational speculation in the exchanges following disturbances such as the Belgium and French devaluations, and Hitler's entry into the Rhineland during the period 1935–37.

In contrast to the virtually clean floating of currencies in the postwar years, currencies were extensively managed in the 1930s by new and more formal mechanisms. Howson (1980a, 59) describes the British float as being very dirty. Because of the secrecy shrouding the operation of the stabilisation funds, it is very difficult to determine just how effective they were. Although the scale and scope of their operations were constrained by their limited asset base, they probably made a modest contribution to the stabilisation of the exchanges, while their very presence may have helped to curb the volatility of markets. Bloomfield (1944, 59, 85) believed they exerted a sobering influence on exchange markets by discouraging undue speculation and limiting the impact of short-term capital movements (compare Bareau 1938; Marjolin 1938; Pumphrey 1942). They may even have averted the danger of competitive depreciations, especially in the later 1930s when coordinated operations of the exchange stabilisation funds took place within the framework of the Tripartite Agreement.

International monetary cooperation

Much has been written about the lack of international monetary cooperation and economic leadership in the crisis of the early 1930s and the implications this had for the subsequent turn of events. It is true that at the peak of the crisis international economic management, both by bankers and statesmen, was found to be wanting, hence the failure to save the gold standard. However, two points are worth considering. First, the failure can be seen as something of a blessing in disguise given that the gold standard in its restored form had outlived its usefulness. As noted in the previous chapter, it was far from being an equilibrium system, and it became even less so once the dramatic fall in the general price level distorted the original structure of exchange rates even further. Thus to have held on to the gold standard with its rigid parities would no doubt have entailed even greater distress and economic hardship in the 1930s. The Royal Institute of International Affairs (1933, 78) correctly summed up the situation as follows:

> The gold standard tends to be a fair-weather standard, especially helpful to trade and industry in time of prosperity. On the other hand, in abnormal periods it often serves to intensify depression rather than to relieve it. This must to some extent be the effect of any international standard, and is not a peculiarity of the gold standard.

The second thing to bear in mind is that international cooperation did not collapse completely in the 1930s. The failure of inter-bank cooperation in the financial crisis of 1931 followed by the collapse of the World Economic Conference nearly two years later may have seemed like the end of an era, but in actual fact this was not the case.

What complicated the situation was the fact that whereas before 1914 and for most of the 1920s, inter-bank cooperation, acting largely independently of governments, had predominated, in the 1930s national domestic policies determined by politicians intervened to weaken the power of central banks. Clavin (1992, 282, 310–11) has demonstrated how the priority of national economic policies effectively scuppered cooperative bank efforts for the World Economic Conference of the summer of 1933. Despite the massive gathering (65 nations and about one thousand delegates) the proceedings were dominated by the United States, Britain and France, whose politicians were activated largely by their own country's domestic interests rather than by the longer-term issues of international monetary cooperation (Einzig 1933, 4–5). Initially there had been high hopes of a successful outcome. Of the three major issues on the agenda – currency stabilisation, public works and anti-depression monetary policy – each of the three major powers were in favour of at least two of the proposals, and were not implacably opposed to the third. Unfortunately, the prospects of securing unanimity on all three issues deteriorated during the first two weeks of the proceedings due to the increasing intransigence of each country to their least-favoured issue – the French over Anglo-American monetary policy, the United States on the question of currency stabilisation, and the British attitude to public works and tariff policies (Hauser 1973, 209, 215; Cassel 1936, 141; Traynor 1949, 122, 151). Clavin (1991, 519–20, 525) also reckons that Britain further muddied the waters by raising the war debt issue, which incensed the Americans. Thus relations among the major states had already turned sour long before President Roosevelt finally killed the proceedings early in July by rejecting any proposal for joint currency stabilisation of the key currencies.

If economic nationalism determined the outcome of the London Conference (Einzig 1933, 4–5), one may recall that the Genoa Conference of 1922 failed largely for similar reasons, but this did not prevent central bankers from cooperating throughout most of the 1920s (Clarke 1973, 2–3). But of course the political threat to the banks' independence had increased in the meantime which meant that central bankers felt they required the support of their governments. 'The clearest lesson of all', writes Patricia Clavin (1992, 311) 'was that central bankers needed unequivocal support on a domestic and international level before collaboration stood any chance of success'. This observation may, however, belie what was actually happening in the banking world.

Although collaboration at the political level was for the time being put into cold storage, central bankers continued to cooperate in a modest way, and indeed they were instrumental in exerting some influence on governments with regard to currency matters (Sayers 1976b, 458–9, 463–6). A year before the eventful crisis of 1931, the Bank for International Settlements (BIS), located in Basle, had been set up. The main pretext for its establishment was for purposes of dealing with the reparations issue, and in particular the task of administering the Young loan to Germany under the revised reparations plan of 1929. Although personally he did not participate directly in its creation, Norman's conception, which he had long cherished, was a sort of bankers' club to provide a permanent channel of communication between central banks (Einzig 1932, 97–9). It was largely a private institution whose membership consisted of most of the main European central banks, the only non-European members being Japan and the United States (Schloss 1958, 40; Simmons 1993, 403).

Although one of the objectives of the BIS was to provide the means for inter-bank financial assistance, which were developed quite extensively later in the 1930s, it did not have the resources or the power to deal effectively with the crisis of the early 1930s (Schloss 1958, 136–9; Dam 1982, 70; Foreman-Peck 1991, 14–15). However, it very soon became an important forum for inter-bank cooperation and the exchange of views on currency and monetary matters. Following the collapse of the gold standard, the Bank became a consistent advocate of currency stabilisation and a return to the gold standard and it frequently urged governments to make a move in that direction. 'That move means the return to an international monetary system based on gold, which remains the best available monetary mechanism, – and as a condition thereof, a stabilisation of the world's leading currencies' (Bank for International Settlements 1935, 70). While the Bank failed in its ultimate objective, the influential tone of its respected annual reports has perhaps been too little appreciated. Most governments were fully aware of the need to achieve some form of currency stability after the débâcle of the early 1930s, even though this might fall short of a full restoration of the gold standard. And although the London Conference foundered on that very issue, it did not spell the end of efforts to bring order to the exchange markets. The regional approach to stabilisation may have had its drawbacks in that the exchange rates between the major currencies were more volatile than previously, but at least it provided a degree of stability of currencies within the different exchange zones. More significantly, by the middle of the decade there was a move to secure the alignment of some of the major currencies in the controversial and much-debated Tripartite Agreement of September 1936.

Although the untimely demise of the World Economic Conference put paid to any immediate formal stabilisation between the major currencies, the central bankers of both Britain and France did not abandon the idea entirely and a few years later the US government also became an enthusiastic supporter (Leith-Ross 1968, 170). However, the factor which occasioned the negotiation of the Tripartite Agreement (TA) between the three countries was the need to provide some form of *de facto* stabilisation to facilitate the devaluation of the French franc and prevent an outbreak of disorderly exchange rate policies as a result of the French action (Einzig, 1937, 209; Sayers 1976b, 456–7, 475–80). Thus on 26 September 1936, through a series of bilateral agreements, the governments of Britain, France and the United States undertook to refrain from competitive devaluations and to do their best to defend their currencies around the then existing levels. Belgium, Switzerland and Holland also subsequently participated. The participants agreed to cooperate to this end on a day-to-day basis so as to 'maintain the greatest possible equilibrium in the system of international exchange and to avoid to the utmost extent the creation of any disturbance of that system . . . by monetary creation' (League of Nations 1937b, 26). Despite the grandiose pronouncements, it was a very loose and informal arrangement. There was no rigid commitment to maintain exchange rates at any specific level and each country reserved the right to change the international value of its currency at a moment's notice (the 24-hour rule). What this meant in practice was that the signatories were not prepared to defend international currency stability at the expense of their domestic economies (Einzig 1937, 223).

Much was expected of the new agreement and some contemporaries saw it as the beginning of a new era in international monetary relations. The League of Nations (1937b, 8) was very optimistic and saw it as the nucleus of a restored but more flexible international monetary standard. This view was somewhat wide of the mark, however, since it is doubtful whether the TA can be seen as a real precursor of postwar monetary institutions (see Feinstein et al. 1995, 67). In fact, the TA has in general had rather a bad press, no doubt because of its somewhat provisional and flimsy character, negotiated by governments who were not fully committed to international monetary cooperation at all costs.

On the other hand, it is easy to be critical of an agreement drawn up at a very difficult time internationally, and when, for national reasons, there was still widespread aversion to any long-term commitment to fixed exchange rates. After all, as Clarke (1977, 57) points out, the TA did demonstrate a willingness to collaborate on exchange rate policy after several rather barren years. Moreover, it also marked the final usurpation of the position of the central banks in international exchange matters since the TA was negotiated by governments and not by bankers (Dam 1982, 53).

It is difficult to discover any very positive impact of the TA on the exchange rates of the participating countries. Clarke (1977, 57) noted that in the six months immediately following the TA the sterling–dollar rate was far more stable than it had been in 1934 and 1935. But further out the outlook was less promising. Drummond's careful analysis of the period 1936–39 led him to conclude that exchange rates were no more tranquil than they had been in 1931–36 (Drummond 1979, 1, 32). Both sterling and the franc were subject to bouts of weakness and strength during these years, which to a large extent reflected the extent of intervention by the respective authorities to manage their exchange rates, rather than the benefits arising from international cooperation under the new arrangements. In practice there was relatively little systematic cooperation, there was no pooling of reserves and little in the way of mutual assistance among the members. In fact the degree of consultation and cooperation was little better than it had been prior to the TA, which had taken place intermittently between central banks and Treasuries (Drummond 1981, 249). The authorities tended to manage the exchanges in their own interests and did not feel unduly constrained to consult their partners about their intended actions. Moreover, in the immediate prewar period it seems to have been of little help in securing inter-allied cooperation on financial preparations for war, since the United States forced Britain to reduce its war chest reserves which precipitated a sharp fall in the pound (Parker 1983, 261–76).

On a more positive note, it can be argued that, although the TA did not produce exchange stability, it was probably instrumental in preventing the devaluation of the franc from sparking off a wave of competitive devaluations and international monetary conflict (Oye 1986, 197). It has also been noted that the TA helped to moderate the initial depreciation of the franc, while at the same time it served to strengthen the dollar as the anchor currency of the international monetary system (Clavin 1996, 189; Cleveland 1976, 56). Technical cooperation within the framework of the TA also helped to stave off disaster in the later slide of the French franc in mid-1937 and again in May 1938 (Sayers 1976b, 482–3). On the other hand, it is worth stressing again that when the exchanges were relatively stable as in the winter of 1936–37, this probably owed more to the domestic management of exchange rates rather than to any specific benefits flowing from the TA. At the time, the French authorities were supporting a weak franc by using their gold reserves, while the British were buying gold in order to cap sterling (Drummond 1979, 7). However, the suggestion that the TA was largely responsible for international recovery from depression because it permitted an expansion of the world's monetary base, appears somewhat far-fetched for reasons other than technical ones (Cleveland 1976, 51). The fact is that considerable recovery had already taken place before the TA was negotiated, while defence needs were probably the key factor prolonging the recovery from 1937 onwards.

Exchange rates and economy recovery

By 1935, Europe 'had descended to a historical nadir in trade and commercial policy' (Friedman 1974, 32). The value of European exports and imports were some two-thirds less than they had been at the peak of 1929, while trade volumes (constant prices) were some one-third lower. Almost every conceivable form of trade and payments restriction was being used apart from blockade. Not surprisingly, therefore, trade volumes failed to regain former levels even by the end of the decade, despite the fact that world output of primary products and manufactured goods had made modest progress since 1929.

On the surface, therefore, it would seem that the external side and commercial policy had little to contribute to recovery in the 1930s. It is true that the beginnings of recovery can be detected late in 1932 and that these coincided with the wave of devaluations and trade and payments restrictions following the financial crisis of the previous year. But it would be rash to draw positive conclusions from these two events. In any case, it was not until well into 1933 that recovery took a firm hold on a wider front and even then the process was by no means rapid and universal. Several countries, notably France and Czechoslovakia, continued to experience further declines in economic activity, while in the United States the recovery was slow and patchy, due partly to that country's late departure from gold (Temin and Wigmore 1990). During the next two years the momentum gained increasing strength, with the result that by the middle of the decade many countries were recording at least modest gains in the level of activity above the previous cyclical peak of 1929. Recovery was temporarily interrupted in 1937–38 when several countries experienced a mild recession, but this was soon reversed as a result of defence requirements.

The data in Tables 3.4 and 3.5 compare the recovery experience of countries classified under different regimes. It should be pointed out that the classification of countries is sometimes somewhat arbitrary because of the overlapping of regimes and changes in regime structure through time. Greece is a prime example. It introduced exchange control in September 1931 and suspended convertibility in April 1932, which was followed by a large depreciation of the drachma (nearly 60 per cent by the end of that year). In June 1933, Greece joined the gold bloc and pegged its currency to the Swiss franc, but when the gold bloc finally disintegrated (September 1936) she joined the sterling area and pegged the drachma to sterling (Lazaretou 1996, 664–7). The League of Nations (1939, 186) also classed Greece as belonging to the German economic bloc by the later 1930s.

Table 3.4 Fluctuations in GDP/GNP and exports, 1929–1937/38

	Gross domestic product			Export volume		
	1929–32/33	*1932/33–37/38*	*1929–37/38*	*1929–32*	*1932–37*	*1929–37*
Exchange control						
Austria	–22.5	25.8	–2.5	–43.9	35.3	–24.1
Bulgaria	–7.1	63.3	51.8	–	–	–
Czechoslovakia	–12.9	13.1	–1.5	–	–	–
Germany	–23.5	63.7	25.2	–40.5	15.2	–31.5
Greece	36.7	25.4	71.4	–	–	–
Hungary	–3.7	18.0	13.6	–	–	–
Italy	–5.5[1]	21.7	15.0	–42.1	3.9	–39.8
Romania	–5.2	22.7	16.3	–	–	–
Spain	–5.3[1]	–9.4[2]	–14.2[3]	–	–	–
Yugoslavia	–9.4	24.5	12.7			
Gold bloc						
Belgium	–7.1	9.8	2.0	–31.4	51.4	3.8
France	–14.7	13.5	–3.1	–41.5	–2.3	–42.9
Netherlands	–7.6	14.2	5.5	–33.4	31.8	–12.2
Switzerland	–8.0	14.4	5.2	–50.1	39.4	–30.4
Poland	–20.7	40.8	14.9	–	–	–
Sterling bloc						
Australia	–5.8	27.5	20.1	31.8	1.1	33.2
Denmark	4.3	16.9	21.9	20.1	–10.6	7.3
Finland	–4.0	46.9	41.1	–	–	–
Ireland	–4.3	2.4	–2.0	–	–	–
Norway	–1.0[1]	32.5	31.2	2.6	36.1	39.6
Portugal	13.3	14.4	29.7	–	–	–
Sweden	–4.3	31.4	25.8	–37.0	60.8	1.3
United Kingdom	–5.1	24.7	18.4	–37.6	28.8	–19.7
Other countries						
Japan	–6.5[1]	47.0	37.4	1.3	145.7	149.1
United States	–29.6	39.7	–1.7	–48.6	54.5	–20.5
Canada	–29.5	41.5	–0.3	–32.0	53.7	4.4
USSR	20.5	40.7	69.6	–	–	–

Notes:
1. 1929–31.
2. 1931–40.
3. 1929–40.
Italy was originally in the gold bloc but imposed exchange control in May 1934 and devalued October 1936.
Greece and Turkey, along with Bulgaria, Hungary, Romania and Yugoslavia, formed part of the Reichsmark bloc.
Japan devalued early and the United States late.

Sources: Bairoch (1976, 295); Maddison (1991, 316–18; 1995, 148–50); Nunes, Mata and Valério (1989, 293–5); Spulber (1966, 58); Prados de la Escosura (1993); Hjerppe (1996, 93).

Table 3.5 Fluctuations in industrial/manufac-
turing production, 1929–1937/38

	1929–32	1932 –37/38	1929 –37/38
Exchange control			
Austria	–34.3	53.9	1.0
Bulgaria	8.9	25.6	36.9
Czechoslovakia	–39.8	60.0	–3.7
Germany	–40.8	122.2	31.6
Greece	0.9	60.0	61.5
Hungary	–19.8	64.2	31.7
Italy	–22.7	48.5	14.8
Romania	–18.2	63.4	33.6
Spain	–15.7	–19.7[1]	–32.3[2]
Yugoslavia	–17.1	63.8	35.7
Gold bloc			
Belgium	–27.1	42.3	3.7
France	–25.6	20.0	–10.7
Luxembourg	–32.0	40.2	–4.7
Netherlands	–9.8	35.1	22.0
Poland	–38.6	99.6	22.5
Switzerland	–20.8	29.8	2.8
Sterling bloc			
Australia	–	–	–
Denmark	–5.6	47.1	38.9
Finland	–15.0	89.4	60.9
Ireland	–9.0	54.0	40.3
Norway	–18.2[3]	58.7[4]	29.9
Portugal	33.0	9.8	46.0
Sweden	–10.8	72.4	53.8
United Kingdom	–11.4	52.9	35.4
Other countries			
Japan	–3.3[3]	100.0[4]	93.3
United States	–44.7	86.8	3.3
Canada	–32.3	68.3	14.0
World	–29.3	80.6	27.7

Notes:
1. 1933–40.
2. 1929–40.
3. 1929–31.
4. 1931–37.

Sources: OEEC (1960, 9); League of Nations (1936, Table 107); United Nations (1949, Table 36); Berend and Ranki (1974b, 298–300); Mitchell (1975, 357); Freris (1986, 90); David (1996); Lains and Reis (1991); Prados de la Escosura (1993); Hjerppe (1996, 128); Pryor (1973, 203).

It can be seen that there was a great diversity of recovery experience among nations. Several countries made almost no headway at all from peak to peak of the cycle, 1929–37. These included Austria, Czechoslovakia, Spain, Belgium, France, the Netherlands, Switzerland, Ireland, Canada and the United States. Conversely, Bulgaria, Germany, Japan and most of the sterling bloc countries recorded substantial gains in output and industrial production. Three of the most successful countries were the USSR, Germany and Japan, but under regimes which imposed severe social costs on the population.

Generally speaking, those countries which left the gold standard and devalued their currencies fared better than those countries which clung to gold until the mid-1930s and were forced to deflate their economies to compensate for overvalued exchange rates. Leaving gold and devaluing removed constraints on both the domestic and external fronts. International competitiveness improved with benefits to the external account, prices firmed upwards, investment opportunities became more attractive (partly through import substitution), while there was more scope to relax the macroeconomic stance, that is, monetary and fiscal policy. The advantages accruing to countries which jettisoned gold were fully recognised by contemporary economists (Gregory 1936, 218–22; Rist 1936, 223–43; Hawtrey 1939, 227–32, 243–4) and the League of Nations (1936, 56) and more recently several writers have written extensively on this issue (see, for example, Eichengreen 1988b, 1991, 1992b, 1992c; Eichengreen and Sachs 1985; Cooper 1992; Campa 1990; Kitson and Michie 1994). Countries which devalued early and by a large amount tended to experience the strongest recoveries: that is, Denmark, Norway, Sweden, Finland, Great Britain and Greece (Haavisto and Jonung 1995, 264–5). It is particularly noteworthy that the last-mentioned country had the largest devaluation in Europe and the fastest rate of growth between 1929 and 1937 (Mazower 1991a, 225–6; 1991b, 250–53). While much of this improvement could be attributed to import substitution through a combination of import restrictions, devaluation and exchange control, it should also be noted that a good part of it had already taken place before Greece suspended the gold standard in April 1932. Overall, however, it would be true to say that countries with depreciated currencies performed much better than either gold bloc or exchange control countries. The former saw their industrial production rise on average by some 27 per cent between 1929 and 1936, whereas the gold bloc and exchange control countries experienced declines in industrial activity (Eichengreen 1992b, 351). Some contemporary scholars (Harris 1936, 103; Ellis 1939, 1941, 152) concluded that exchange control countries tended to experience a worse trade and income performance than either gold or paper currency countries, but recent research suggests that it was the gold bloc group that fared the worst.

The gold bloc group was in a very invidious position. Adherence to the former gold parity rates made it difficult to adopt any sort of reflationary action to promote recovery, since in order to maintain the old parities in the face of depreciation elsewhere, deflationary policies were unavoidable because of the continued pressure on the balance of payments and the exchange rate (Condliffe 1941, 235). Adjustment was effected, albeit not always very successfully, by compressing the internal price level, import controls, export subsidies and high interest rates, which in turn put pressure on state finances (League of Nations 1936, 56). In the final analysis, such policies proved intolerable because of the disastrous effects on domestic economies, quite apart from the fact that they proved largely ineffective in restoring equilibrium. Thus the gold bloc began to crumble in 1935 and broke up altogether in the following autumn, with France, the Netherlands and Switzerland the last to go as international pressure on their exchanges led to capital flight (League of Nations 1937a, 26–8). The gold bloc in fact paid a high price for its faithful attachment to gold. Industrial production declined on average by some 14 per cent between 1929 and 1936 and by the end of the decade, output and production levels were little better than they had been in 1929 (Siegenthaler 1976, 531; David 1995, 1996; Griffiths 1987; Eichengreen 1992b, 351).

There were, however, a number of notable exceptions to the general pattern, so that one has to be cautious about attributing too much importance to the influence of devaluation. The experience of the exchange control countries was far from uniform despite their weak trade performance. Austria and Czechoslovakia did very badly but Germany and several East European countries, especially Bulgaria, performed quite strongly despite their overvalued currencies. Of course, much depended on the extent of the overvaluation and the use which was made of special rates for exporters and export subsidies, as well as the benefits arising from trade links with Germany. In the latter case, the economic strategy suppressed the normal working of the labour market and established a highly regulated regime to prevent short-circuiting of the economy, and by this means was able to achieve strong growth, although at social costs unacceptable to liberal economies (James 1993, 92).

Similarly, one can argue that the experience of Ireland, Canada and the United States does little to support the devaluation thesis. America, it is true, was a relatively late devaluer, but Canada and Ireland were not. The Canadian case is a little unusual, however, in that although the gold standard was relinquished *de facto* early in 1929 the Canadian dollar did not depreciate until late in 1931; subsequently its depreciation against the American dollar was only about half that of the pound sterling, but by late 1933 the traditional relationship between the three currencies was restored. Against competitive raw material producing countries, the Canadian dollar tended to appreciate (Fishlow 1985, 428). In other words, Canada did not benefit initially from her early departure from gold through reflation and currency depreciation (Bordo and Redish 1990, 358, 378). On the other hand, the Baltic states did quite well even though Latvia and Lithuania were late devaluers (Royal Institute of International Affairs 1938, 187–8; Simutis 1942, 70–71). The British case is also worth reconsidering. Devaluation undoubtedly eased pressure on the external side in 1932 and allowed the authorities to loosen monetary policy. But the direct trade impact of devaluation was tempered by the fact that about one-half of Britain's trade was with countries whose currencies were linked with sterling (Kitson and Solomou 1990, 90–91), and by the fact that the effective sterling exchange strengthened during the 1930s. Thus the overall comparative advantage of devaluation in terms of export and import prices was quite modest. In fact, Kitson and Solomou (ibid., 63) see the tariff as being more important than devaluation in explaining manufacturing import substitution. The role of the tariff in the recovery process has been a source of debate for some years now and the arguments for and against are neatly summarised by Routh (1993, 272).

Finally, Spain and Portugal provide interesting case studies of substantial devaluations which had very little impact. Portugal had come through the depression quite strongly, with positive gains in output and industrial production. The gold standard was abandoned and the currency devalued at the end of 1931, but after 1932 the economy remained rather flat, and then subsequently felt the backwash of the Spanish Civil War. Thus industrial production charted an erratic course and actually fell slightly between 1932 and 1936, before rising sharply in 1937 and then falling back again (Nunes, Mata and Valério 1989; Lains and Reis 1991). Spain is a more exceptional case since she had by far the worst record in the 1930s, much of which could be attributed to the Civil War and its aftermath. It is sometimes argued that Spain avoided the worst effects of the depression because of her floating exchange rate (Temin 1993, 92; Choudhri and Kochin 1980, 569). This is not strictly correct. Although Spain initially fared better than many countries due to her depreciating currency, the early 1930s still saw a considerable decline in industrial activity, even though good weather favoured agricultural output (Payne 1968, 48; Lieberman 1995, 18; Mitchell 1975, 357). At the trough of 1933, industrial output was a fifth or more lower than in 1929, while trade volumes declined by one-quarter (Ranki 1985, 63; Prados de la Escosura 1993). Spain in fact lost much of the advantage of her flexible exchange rate with the imposition of exchange control in May 1931 and the subsequent widespread devaluation elsewhere later in the year. The depression was, of course, prolonged with the Civil War and the emergence of the Franco regime which erected an extensive system of bureaucratic controls that led to a seizing up of the economy. Hence there was no recovery in the 1930s and it was not until the 1950s that the 1929 levels of economic activity were finally regained (Payne 1968, 57; Lieberman 1995, 18; Prados de la Escosura 1993).

On a more general note, it is important to bear in mind that the benefits of devaluation were to some extent offset by the uncertainty created by the widespread exchange instability of the early 1930s, which merely served to complicate the economic situation. Fluctuating exchange rates, aggravated by speculative and non-economic capital movements, the prospects of competitive depreciation of currencies and restrictive measures of defence thrown up by this threat, together with renewed deflationary policy measures, banking crises and rigid exchange controls to protect weaker currencies, created a thoroughly unstable situation. These uncertainties were not only a serious impediment to early recovery, but they presented a constant threat of further deterioration. Contemporary accounts repeatedly stressed the gravity of the situation. The League of Nations in their world report for 1932–33 (League of Nations 1933, 15, 221) reckoned that exchange instability was the most destructive element resulting from the breakdown of the gold standard and it was seen as 'one of the principal causes of further economic deterioration in 1932 and figured prominently among the factors which limited and checked the revival of prices and productive activity in the third quarter of that year'. It was not until 1933–34 that there was a slow approximation towards exchange rate stability as the majority of trading currencies gradually moved into a more stable relationship with sterling, the dollar and the franc (League of Nations 1937b, 15–16). Yet even by the spring of 1935 the Bank for International Settlements (1935, 5) was complaining that the world still suffered 'without relief from the unrest and uncertainties caused by moving currencies' and that 'no fundamental, durable recovery can be hoped for unless and until a general stabilization at least of the leading currencies has been brought about'.

Although, as noted earlier, it is possible to exaggerate the currency turmoil of these years, there is no doubt that contemporary observers were very much concerned about the continued prospects of disorderly exchange markets. Second, while countries going off gold early secured temporary relief, the benefits reaped by the leaders soon evaporated as other countries followed suit. No doubt a coordinated programme of devaluation would have produced wider benefits than the sequential approach adopted at the time, but failing international action, the second-best solution was better than none at all. Third, trade expansion was certainly not the engine of recovery in the 1930s, even for those countries which devalued early. One or two countries, notably Finland and Norway, did quite well on the export front through the complete cycle, but for the most part exports failed to regain their previous cyclical peaks. As Solomou (1996, 121) notes, 'the exchange rate regime did not have a significant effect on the cyclical recovery path of exports', since both gold bloc and sterling countries had weak export performances. Moreover, although early devaluers gained an initial competitive edge, this was later eroded through higher inflation rates in devaluing countries and the capitulation of the gold bloc after 1935. One reason for the desultory export performance was, of course, the restrictive policies taken to protect external accounts despite some modest relaxation later in the decade. Protection, import quotas, exchange control and the drying-up of international investment all helped to depress economic intercourse, even though they may have helped domestic recovery through import substitution. To an increasing extent, also, the trade of the major European countries gravitated towards 'economic blocs', within the orbit of the UK, France, Belgium, the Netherlands and Italy and their dependent territories, Japan with Korea, Formosa. Kwantung and Manchuria, and Germany with South-eastern Europe and, to a lesser extent, Latin America. One feature of the latter was the increasing importance of bilateral clearing agreements which had been unknown in 1929. By 1937 they accounted for about 12 per cent of world trade, although in the case of the Reichsmark bloc countries of Germany, Bulgaria, Greece, Turkey, Hungary, Romania and Yugoslavia the proportion of trade passing through clearing agreements exceeded 50 per cent (League of Nations 1938a, 172–3; 1939, 186–9).

Although an increasing proportion of world trade took place within the trading blocs or zones, the overall effect was not especially beneficial except in the case of sterling area countries. In most of the other blocs the impact was adverse both for intra-bloc trade as well as for trade with the rest of the world (see Eichengreen and Irwin 1995, 21–2). This negative outcome was not simply a function of the existence of trading blocs *per se*, but more the result of the network of restrictions on intercourse to prop up overvalued currencies.

Overall, therefore, currency changes of the 1930s did not generate trade-induced recovery. Those that devalued early secured an initial advantage, but more important in the longer term was the fact that devaluation, along with defensive commercial measures, provided greater protection for the external account. This in turn allowed greater flexibility in domestic economic policy, especially in breaking the constraint on monetary policy (Kitson and Michie 1994, 94). At the same time it helped to raise the general price level and encouraged import substitution, both of which were conducive to investment and economic recovery.

The 1930s in retrospect

Contrary to popular conception, the currency experience of the 1930s may be seen in a more favourable light. After the initial disturbances following the general abandonment of gold, the exchanges were far less volatile than they had been in the first half of the 1920s. Moreover, the exchange regime of this period probably had more credibility than the restored gold standard of the later 1920s since few people had much confidence in its long-term sustainability. The managed system of the 1930s certainly provided more flexibility than the former gold standard, while it avoided the worst excesses of the free floating era after the war. Foreman-Peck's judgement seems basically sound: 'The managed float of the 1930s gave the international economy rather more stability than it had in the 1970s and almost as much as in the (later?) 1920s' (Foreman-Peck 1983, 255).

The chief advantage of the regime of the 1930s is that it allowed countries much more room for manoeuvre in domestic policy once the restraint of fixed exchange rates had been removed. It is true that currency depreciation was not the only factor making for recovery but it certainly eased the process. What is perhaps most remarkable, given the general turmoil of the early 1930s, is the relative degree of stability in the exchanges for much of the decade and the speed with which realignment took place once the gold standard had been jettisoned. No doubt recovery and the more stable economic conditions after 1933 assisted the process, but important also were the role of the new currency zones or blocs, the more energetic management of currencies through official intervention and the groping towards a measure of international cooperation among the key currency countries. The system was by no means perfect and in the later 1930s there were renewed currency scares as the international political situation deteriorated. But in the difficult circumstances of the time, and against the background of the poor track record of the previous decade, the system was far from being an utter disaster. The experience also demonstrates that asymmetric management can provide a passable alternative to hegemonic rule.

However, the experience of the 1930s cannot readily provide a guide to the merits of floating or fixed exchange rates since they were neither one nor the other. Exchange rates were extensively managed, although in a flexible manner, and free floating was the exception rather than the rule (Yeager 1976, 375–6). On the other hand, one lesson emerges quite clearly, namely that abandoning metallic standards does not necessarily lead to chaos, as Hawtrey (1939, 243–4) made plain at the time:

If inconvertible paper currencies have often led to disaster in the past, that is because they have usually originated from some overwhelming financial strain due to war, revolution or an economic catastrophe. The very purpose of forsaking a metallic standard has been to alleviate the financial strain by a depreciation of the currency unit, and more or less considerable depreciation has accordingly occurred. But experience has shown again and again that, the emergency once past, the currency can go on not merely for years but for generations without serious disturbances in its value. Such disturbances, when they occur, are usually traceable to another emergency of the same kind as that which originally led to the suspension of the metallic standard. And the new emergency, like the old, had it supervened upon a metallic standard, might have been expected to cause suspension and depreciation.

4 The Bretton Woods era

From conference proceedings, monographs, articles and textbooks, the impact of the Bretton Woods regime forged at New Hampshire in 1944 has pervaded academic discussion long after generalised fixed rates collapsed in the early 1970s. Indeed, when the fiftieth anniversary of Bretton Woods was marked with a deluge of literature in 1994, it appeared that the regime had even surpassed the gold standard in supplying as many citations as praises. For one historian, Bretton Woods had become 'the most revered name in international monetary history, perhaps in economic history' (de Vries 1996, 128). However, despite the acclamation by de Vries, it is important to bear three points in mind about Bretton Woods from the outset.

First, while the life of the Bretton Woods System is traditionally given as between 1944 and 1971, the system functioned in essence only between 1959 and 1968. From 1946 through to January 1959, exchange rates were supported by stabilisation loans, the European Recovery Programme and by regional payments and arrangements such as the European Payments Union. Only in 1959, when West European currencies were made fully convertible, was the system put into operation, and it was during the 1960s when it broke down. From 1968, the life of the 'adjustable peg' hung on a thread down to its fatal demise in 1971.

Second, compared with the interwar years, the quarter of a century following the Articles of Agreement was a period of greater economic stability, but care needs to be taken in apportioning the contribution played by the international monetary system. For instance, Maddison (1991, 168) does not single out the importance of Bretton Woods *per se*, but cites the liberalisation of international trade as a contributory factor to the Golden Age. The move towards convertibility in the 1950s undoubtedly aided this liberalisation but it is impossible to quantify precisely the contribution of Bretton Woods in this process. Moreover, for many of the West European countries, the 1950s were a decade of faster growth than the 1960s and this occurred without the Bretton Woods system operating in full.

Third, by the 1960s the exchange rate regime was suffering from a repetition of the interwar problems of confidence, liquidity and adjustment (Machlup 1964). While many of the Bretton Woods members dared not risk a return to the impasse of the 1930s, non-cooperation between members began under the fixed rates of the mid-1960s and not during the floating era of the 1970s.

Nevertheless, it is true that the Bretton Woods system should largely be seen as a triumph of international coordination following the disharmony of the interwar years and in what follows, we trace the development of the Bretton Woods system and its impact on member countries.

The Bretton Woods Agreement and the first ten years

As we have seen, the exchange rate regimes of the interwar years were fragmentary and piecemeal in nature. To recapitulate, during the 1920s, there were three pervasive problems. First, limited economic cooperation among the major powers and the marked rivalry between the key financial centres of London, Paris and New York meant that there was no country which could, or was willing to orchestrate the system. Second, the increasing restrictions on trade, payments and resource flows together with less flexibility in domestic price systems, made it more difficult for adjustments to take place. Finally, cost and price relationships between countries had been so distorted by the first world war and the subsequent violent inflation in Europe that it was extremely difficult to determine equilibrium exchange rates in such volatile conditions. In the 1930s these problems had manifested to such an extent that competitive devaluations, capital controls and nationalistic economic policies were pandemic.

According to Ruggie (1991, 203) the international economic institutions of the postwar period were built on a historic political compromise: 'Unlike the economic nationalism of the thirties, the international economic order would be multilateral in character; but unlike the liberalism of the gold standard and free trade, its multilateralism would be predicated upon domestic interventionism'. Essentially then, the new international institutions which were established in the first 15 years after 1944 sought to establish international commitment and coordination. The list of institutions included the International Monetary Fund and International Bank for Reconstruction and Development (World Bank) which both emerged from the Bretton Woods negotiations in 1944; the General Agreement on Tariffs and Trade (GATT) in 1947; the European Payments Union (1950); the European Coal and Steel Community (1952), the European Economic Community (1957) and the European Free Trade Association (1959).

As far as international monetary cooperation was concerned, apart from the Genoa Conference of 1922, there had not been any attempt made during the interwar years to view the international monetary system as a whole. Clearly, those who were charged with designing a new international monetary order in the postwar world had an unenviable and complicated task. Not only did they have to take into account all of the problems of the interwar years, but the architects had to understand the perceived weaknesses and strengths of the gold standard if they were to design a monetary system which could stand the test of time. If this responsibility was not Herculean enough, an enormous amount of visionary insight was also needed to ascertain how the world economy was going to evolve in the future and how this would shape the monetary regime.

One of the most undesirable consequences of the gold standard, seen from the perspective of the 1940s, was that when a country had a balance of payments deficit it was required to reduce its domestic money base. Keynes in particular wished to avoid the deflation associated with this adjustment mechanism which would produce a decline in national income and a rise in unemployment. Indeed, in Keynes's original plan for an international currency union, those countries with a balance of payments surplus would be penalised.

The discussions which formed the Bretton Woods agreement in July 1944 were essentially Anglo-American in origin but the regime that eventually evolved was more influenced by American considerations than the British input (Scammel 1975). Although the currency union plan put forward by Keynes was rejected, Bretton Woods nevertheless established the International Monetary Fund (IMF). Broadly speaking, its Articles of Agreement contained three main features.

First, every member of the Fund had to establish a par value for its currency and to maintain it within a 1 per cent margin on either side of the declared par value. Although currencies were treated equally in the articles, Article IV defined the linchpin of the system as either gold or the US dollar (the fixed price of gold was $35 per ounce). As the US was the only country that pegged its currency in terms of gold, all other countries would fix their parities in terms of dollars and would intervene to monitor their exchange rates within 1 per cent of parity with the dollar. In the event of a 'fundamental disequilibrium' with the balance of payments, the parity could be changed only if the IMF member had consulted with other members (Article IV, Section 5). The phrase 'fundamental disequilibrium' was never defined, and later proved to be a source of contention among some members. The escape clause differed from that of the gold standard because countries were not expected at a later date to return their currencies to the original parity.

Second, under Article VIII, members were expected to make their currencies convertible for current account transactions but were allowed a three-year transitional period to achieve this (Article XIV). Capital controls were allowed (Article VI, Section 3) and members had to avoid discriminatory currency and multiple currency arrangements.

Finally, the Fund could help finance members with short- or medium-term payments difficulties and issue sanctions against countries with large surpluses. The rights of members to draw on the Fund, along with their contributions and voting powers, were based on members' quotas. Each quota was decided by the world share the member country had according to national income, international trade and international reserves. The quota would be paid by gold or US dollars (25 per cent) and the member's own currency (75 per cent). While members could draw on their quotas at will, stringent conditions were attached to further borrowing beyond the existing allotments. At the outset, the total fund was set at $8.8 billion and could be raised every five years by a majority vote. For those countries which ran a large surplus, the Fund was able to invoke the scarce currency clause (Article VII). Members would then have to adopt exchange controls on imports and other current account purchases from the surplus country.

As numerous writers have pointed out, the architects never made it clear how the system was supposed to work, and the practical evolution of the international monetary system post-1944 was different to the theory. However, it was understood that as the existing gold stock was too low to sustain the growing demand for international liquidity it would make sense to have key currencies (that is, the dollar and sterling) which could be used in lieu of gold to settle international transactions. At the beginning of the preconvertiblity period, sterling was the dominant currency in world reserves but was eclipsed by the dollar at the end of the 1950s. In short, it is simply impossible to answer Bordo's (1993) counter-factual of how the real Bretton Woods system would have worked if it had not developed into a gold–dollar standard.

With the benefit of hindsight, the initial par values established in October 1945 were unrealistic for several countries, as some contemporaries realised (Mikesell 1947; Samuelson 1948). The IMF devoted much time and effort into investigating the current and future economic status of every member but did not establish equilibrium exchange rates. To have constructed a world system of equilibrium rates at once would have been an enormous task and, given the degree of structural change taking place in the world economy, it was far better to adjust parities in the light of new developments. Unfortunately, as Scammell (1975, 143) has suggested, by adopting a passive attitude towards exchange rates from the beginning, the Fund allowed the initiative in exchange rate policy to pass back to its members. The actions of three countries in particular (France, the UK and Canada) marred the prestige of the Fund. Each of these actions will be considered in turn.

In January 1948, France devalued the franc and replaced the existing par value with a system of multiple exchange rates. The justification for such a move was to economise on scarce hard currency, with France argu-ing that if it had to continue with the existing regime further devaluation would be required. The IMF did not really object to the devaluation but issued a statement announcing that the move to a new multiple currency *coupled* to the devaluation was unacceptable and that France was ineligi-ble to use the Fund's resources (IMF 1948, 37). Thus although the IMF was powerless to stop the implementation of the new regime, it could at least censure France under Article IV, Section 6. While France ended the multiple system in October 1948, 12 other members had exchange rate problems simultaneously, with several other countries proposing to adopt multiple rates (Horsefield 1969, 206–9).

The decision by the UK to devalue on 17 September 1949, which trig-gered 31 worldwide devaluations, also called into question the power of the IMF to deter a major power from pursuing domestic considerations. The official history of the IMF in this period suggests that the Board was 'fully prepared' for the devaluation (ibid., 239) but this differs from the opinion of most commentators who believe that the UK gave the IMF 'hardly more than mere notification' of the decision (Yeager 1976, 445). Moreover, the size of the devaluation at over 30 per cent also caused con-sternation for the IMF. The UK justified this measure by claiming that the loss of gold from its reserves was dramatic and that providing other countries did not devalue equally, the competitiveness of British goods in non-dollar markets would be increased.

Prior to the British devaluation, the French and Italians had argued that the value of sterling was unfairly high, yet both countries were quick to follow the lead of the UK. France was adamant that the British had chosen a 'trade war rate' (Tew 1970, 237) and devalued three days later. *In toto*, the devaluing countries accounted for two-thirds of world trade while among the other major world powers, the US and Japan did not alter their parities. Yet although the international chain reaction to the British decision in 1949 was similar to the British devaluation in 1931, the economic background was entirely different. Moreover, the process in 1949 was facilitated by an international institution which at least encour-aged the formulation of devaluation proposals and contrasted sharply to the haphazard, disorderly and unilateral decisions taken after 1931.

During the devaluations of 1949, Canada also adjusted its parity from $1.00 to $0.909, but within a year, prompted by a massive capital inflow from the US, it decided to float the Canadian dollar. The IMF made an unsuccessful attempt to persuade the Canadian authorities to absorb the additions to its reserves by open market operations and to control the capital inflows. In the light of the Canadian decision, discussions at the IMF centred around the problem of trying to stop generalised float-ing while recognising that there were occasions when a member country might have to resort to fluctuating rates (IMF 1951, 36–41). Following the float in October 1950, Canadian exchange rate fluctuations were mild and orderly through to May 1961 (Wonnacott 1972). The float of the Canadian dollar also allowed Canada to accept Article VIII on convertibility in March 1952, some six years earlier than many other members.

Canada's tranquil experience with floating rates did much to attract supporters of floating rates, while the IMF's hostility towards flexible rates appeared unreasonable. For a while Britain flirted with the idea of floating under ROBOT (Cairncross and Watts 1989, 302–22) and Otmar Emminger of the German Bundesbank suggested floating the Deutschmark within a 6 per cent band following 'hot money' inflows from France in 1956. Simultaneously, the IMF was under increasing criticism from the European press, who claimed that the institution had failed to attract members to use its lending facilities. Ironically, within a short space of time of the criticisms appearing in the *Financial Times* and *Le Monde*, both France and Britain had applied to the Fund for financial assistance (James 1996, 102–3). The cause of Britain's application was to prevent a further slide of sterling in the wake of the Suez crisis. Moreover, the discussions over floating remained purely academic as Britain's crucial support in the debate was lost and Britain used the standby arrangement as a way of increasing its reserves in the run-up to convertibility.

As already suggested, the run-up to convertibility in Western Europe was a slow process. Britain's earliest attempt in July 1947 was aborted after just six weeks and she was forced to reintroduce exchange controls. Given the shortage of international reserves generally, Western European nations had to continue with exchange controls and introduced bilateral payments agreements. Thus the major problem facing all European nations in the first stage of recovery was a shortage of dollars. The interim solution to this shortage was a combination of World Bank loans in 1947–48 and aid by the United Nations Relief and Reconstruction Agency between 1945 and 1947. The more far-reaching American solution was the Marshall Plan.

While American political considerations might have belied the decision to grant this money to Europe, at least the hard currency which was provided through the Marshall Plan secured domestic political stability and fostered the expansion of European economies. As a condition to receiving aid, the Plan stipulated that recipients would have to liberalise trade and payments. In April 1948, the Organization for European Economic Cooperation (OEEC) was formed to administer the money. The amount each country received was dependent upon the size of its current account deficit. On this basis approximately $13 billion was distributed in grants and loans to Western Europe between 1948 and 1952 and $1.2 billion to Japan (Killick 1997, 91).

In order to facilitate the payments, the European Payments Union (EPU) was formed to act as a clearing system (Tew 1988, 38–43). Historians have widely viewed the EPU as having played an integral part in helping Western Europe achieve a more open system of trade and exchange payments (Block 1977). Recent work by Kaplan and Schleiminger (1989), however, has suggested that this was not a view shared by many American bankers in the US Treasury Department or the IMF, who considered the EPU an unnecessary barrier to the early restoration of a multilateral system of European payments. Indeed, as James (1996, 76–7) has suggested, the EPU was fundamentally at odds with the philosophy of Bretton Woods: the IMF wanted to restore convertibility and end discrimination while the EPU was discriminating against the dollar as a way of restoring a limited convertibility. By the mid-1950s, there were two different convertible areas separated by exchange controls: a soft currency bloc based on sterling and the EPU and a hard currency bloc, based on the dollar.

The two-stage French devaluation of 1957 and 1958 accompanied by economic measures (the Reuff Plan) was the prelude for French convertibility in December 1958. The problem with the French economy was that, despite excellent growth rates from the early 1950s, inflation was rising and there was a persistent current account deficit. Huge private hoards of gold were held by the public out of the fear of inflation, so the government was financing its deficit in an inflationary way. Jacques Reuff, appointed by the government to examine France's economic situation, concluded that the widespread system of indexation and subsidies should be abolished and that the economy should be fully opened to foreign competition. To reduce the budget deficit further, the Reuff Committee also recommended increased excise and income tax rates. Finally, the franc was devalued by 15 per cent to bring French prices into line with its competitors. The introduction of a more realistic exchange rate (an 'offensive' devaluation) coupled to a shift into the tradable sector provided the French economy with a much-needed fillip. Although the competitive advantage of devaluation had been eroded by 1963 as a result of domestic inflation, the structure of industry had changed enormously (Boltho 1996).

The success of the French experience encouraged Spain to stabilise its economy in a similar fashion in 1959 and to allow external convertibility (Fuentes Quintana 1984). Among the other industrial nations, the move to convertibility was swift, and only Japan delayed until 1964 for political and economic reasons. Following the French devaluation of the late-1950s and the implementation of widespread convertibility, there were few changes in members' parities until 1967. Unfortunately, the stability in parities masked a number of flaws with the Bretton Woods system which were to emerge in the post-convertibility era with a vengeance.

The decline of Bretton Woods

For the industrial countries, the decade following convertibility is traditionally portrayed as the apogee of the Bretton Woods system, with widespread exchange rate stability and cooperation among member states accompanied by high rates of economic growth. However, the rate of growth of GDP for the European members of the Organisation for Economic Cooperation and Development (OECD) fell in every cycle from the early 1950s and was accompanied in the 1960s by higher rates of inflation and unemployment. This period was also punctuated by a number of problems with the international monetary regime.

First, by the 1950s the Bretton Woods system had effectively evolved into a fixed exchange rate gold–dollar standard so that during the 1960s, the monetary authorities were more unwilling to accept changes in parities. The IMF was cautious about giving countries the option to alter exchange rates and after 1964, its *Annual Report* did not mention the possibility of parity changes. As John Williamson (1977, 6) noted, this meant that exchange rate changes were 'relegated to the status of confessions that the adjustment process had failed'.

Second, some countries had an inappropriate mixture of monetary and fiscal policy which prevented short-run internal balance while others failed to maintain even a medium-run external balance until they were forced to devalue as a result of a fundamental disequilibrium.

Third, despite efforts at international coordination throughout the OECD, the Economic Policy Committee was only able to delay and not prevent the manifestation of tensions within the system. The first stage of this perseveration culminated in the ending of the gold pool in March 1968 and ended with generalised floating in 1973.

Finally, from 1958 there was a constant fear that the ratio of dollar liabilities to gold would increase to a level that could cause a loss of confidence in the dollar and to a run on gold.

In short, in the decade after convertibility the international monetary system exhibited all the problems of the interwar years: adjustment, liquidity and confidence. The system did not have a sufficient adjustment mechanism, so payments imbalances became widespread, which then threatened the stability of exchange rates. The only way to maintain exchange rate stability was by injecting extra liquidity into the system. Unlike the 1930s, however, the most serious problem which threatened to engulf the international community by the end of the 1960s was inflation.

No industrial country was immune to exchange rate and balance of payments problems (Table 4.1). In particular, an examination of the experiences of the UK, Germany and America highlights the flaws in the system and shows what was going wrong with the Bretton Woods regime during the 1960s.

Table 4.1 The collapse of the Bretton Woods system

1958		1969	
Dec.	Fourteen European countries start convertibility of their currencies for current account transactions	July	SDR amendments are in force
1961		Aug.	French franc is devalued from 0.18 grams of gold per franc to 0.16 grams
Mar.	Basle Agreement among central banks to hold each other's currency and to lend to each other	Sep.	Deutschmark floats
Oct.	Establishment of the London Gold Pool	Oct.	Deutschmark is revalued from $0.25 to $0.273
1962		1970	
Jan.–Mar.	Start of persistent French gold purchases from the United States	Jan.	First SDR allocation
Feb.	Beginning of the swap facilities to provide reciprocal lines of credit among central banks	1971	
Oct.	Beginning of the GAB (General Agreements to Borrow)	Jan.	Second SDR allocation
1963		May	Deutschmark and the Dutch guilder float
Oct.	Start of technical studies and discussions that would lead to the establishment of the special drawing right (SDR)	Aug.	United States suspends convertibility of the dollar into gold for official transactions, suspends the use of swaps, and imposes price controls and a 10 per cent import surcharge; all countries with major currencies except France start to float, impose exchange controls, and undertake major interventions to buy dollars
1965			
Feb.	President de Gaulle and Giscard d'Estaing propose a return to the gold standard	Dec.	In the Smithsonian Agreement, the G10 realign currency exchange rates in a revised fixed rate system; the United States agrees to devalue the dollar to $38.00 per ounce of gold; average devaluation of the dollar against other currencies is 10 per cent; dollar convertibility into gold by the United States was not restored, and the US made no commitment to support the dollar
1967			
Oct.	End of persistent French gold purchases from the United States		
Nov.	The United Kingdom devalues the pound sterling from $2.80 to $2.40	1972	
1968		June	Pound sterling starts to float against the dollar
Mar.	Gold Pool interventions end; the two-tiered market for gold begins	1973	
May	SDR amendments are sent to IMF members for approval	Feb.	Dollar devalued to $42.22 per ounce of gold; all major currencies therefore revalued against the gold dollar by 10 per cent
June	Exchange pressure on the French franc because of internal political crisis	Mar.	After massive interventions by foreign exchange authorities, the system of fixed exchange rates collapsed into generalized floating
Nov.	Exchange crisis closes markets in France, Germany, and the United Kingdom		

Source: Garber (1993, 465–6).

In the case of the UK, one economic historian has recently suggested that after the 1949 devaluation sterling became:

> the emblem of Britain's world status in the 1950s. To its adherents, it repre-sented not simply successful economic recovery from a victorious but immensely costly war, but restoration to a position of economic leadership which had been surrendered in 1931. (Alford 1996, 242)

However, this does tend to somewhat overstate the case because the 1949 devaluation did not herald a New Jerusalem. Even before convertibility, Britain's status as a key currency was under threat. Britain's share in the exports of all industrial countries declined between 1953 and 1959 while the share of the European Economic Community (EEC) countries increased markedly (Lamfalussy 1963). This deterioration in the UK's competitive position was due to slower productivity growth which in itself was a result of the failure to reform industrial relations and to increase product market competition (Bean and Crafts 1996). British macroeco-nomic policy, dominated by demand management (or 'fine-tuning'), was also damaging to economic growth, though. Inappropriate policy fre-quently led to the infamous 'stop–go' cycles of the 1950s and 1960s. For much of the period, demand was crudely encouraged by fiscal stimula-tion (for example, 1953, 1955, 1959, 1963) and the subsequent overheating was solved by a monetary contraction (for example, 1951, 1957, 1961, 1964, 1967) to cure the deficit on the balance of payments.

The slower rate of economic growth in the UK compared to its com-petitors and a higher underlying rate of inflation had threatened the pound several times in the late-1950s. By the early 1960s, the balance of payments had improved. Following an expansionary budget in 1964, sterling was again increasingly put under pressure as the current account steadily deteriorated. After taking office in October 1964, the Labour government refused to devalue. It is difficult to weigh up whether this decision was influenced more by economic analysis or political expediency. For domestic political reasons, Harold Wilson did not want his party to be known as the devaluation party, following the devaluations of 1931 and 1949. At a wider level, such an action would have shocked international opinion and displeased America as confi-dence in the dollar would inevitably have been shaken. The economic rationale also appeared sound: poor British export performance was a reflection of non-price competitiveness rather than a price disparity, so any short-term relief could be applied through mild deflation. Consequently, the subject of devaluation became known as 'the unmen-tionable' (Brandon 1966, 40–44).

As Cairncross notes, the unmentionable did not disappear as three sterling crises in as many years were inflicted upon the British economy (Cairncross 1995; 1997). The drain on reserves continued throughout 1967 and, with poor prospects for the balance of payments, the decision to devalue on 18 November was more or less inevitable.

The Treasury had been against devaluing when the Labour Party was returned to office, although it is doubtful whether these judgements did much to influence a prime minister who was already opposed to the issue (Cairncross 1995, 92). In a recently published confidential memo, which was written in December 1968 and sent to President-elect Richard Nixon, Milton Friedman criticised this decision:

> Harold Wilson exemplifies a wasted opportunity. If he had floated the pound on first gaining office, putting all the blame, as he could then have done, on the allegedly 'irresponsible' policies of the prior Tory regime, it is very likely that he would still be firmly in the saddle, and that the Labour Party would hold unquestioned political power. His failure to take this step forced on him one unpopular expedient after another – and did not even prevent later devaluation. He got the worst of all worlds – and so did Britain. (Friedman 1988, 430)

However, the British were able to avoid doing anything about the weakness of sterling as the US was willing to offer financial support. As James (1996, 187–8) notes, the US was concerned that if a reserve currency fell then other currencies would become more vulnerable to speculative attacks.

While the British were wrestling with (comparatively) lower rates of growth, balance of payments deficits and an overvalued currency, Germany had a different set of problems. The German economy had enjoyed good rates of growth in the 1950s although the rate had slowed by the 1960s. Economic growth continued to be export led, but the surplus on the balance of payments began to generate imported inflation. The German devaluation of 1949 was advantageous for exporters, and through the 1950s the balance of payments was in surplus. Although there was a big inflow of foreign exchange, the excessive increases in the money supply in the 1950s were offset by budget surpluses.

The trade surplus generated a binary divide in Germany between those who wanted to see it reduced (senior economic officials in the trade unions, political parties and research institutes) and those who argued that a revaluation would damage the economy (banking and industry). The latter were successful at limiting the amount of the revaluation in 1961 and 1969, in spite of the pressure from the international community. Consequently, Germany revalued by only 5 per cent in 1961 to DM 4.00. As a short-term measure this was effective, and by 1962 the trade balance was halved. Yet the DM remained undervalued: the current account was in surplus throughout the decade (with the exception of 1965) and between 1960 and 1970 the level of reserves had almost doubled. It was only in 1965 that the Bundesbank was able to raise interest rates to control inflation without worrying about imported inflation from capital inflows. To discourage foreign portfolio investments in Germany, the Bundesbank began to tax the capital earnings of non-residents.

Following a domestic recession in 1967, there were calls from the OECD's Working Party No. 3 for Germany to stimulate its economy and reduce its current account surplus. To the frustration of the Group of Ten (G10), the German coalition government ruled out a revaluation of the DM at the Bonn meeting in November 1968 and six months later issued a statement that the decision not to revalue was 'final, unequivocal and for eternity' (Solomon 1982, 162). After elections at the end of September 1969, the DM was briefly floated, but within a month a new parity had been established at DM 3.66. This revaluation of 9.3 per cent encouraged German officials into believing that the inflation rate would be cut. Unfortunately, worldwide inflation had strengthened by this date and overrode the beneficial effects of revaluation for the domestic economy.

Clearly, Germany's obvious preference for domestic stability at the expense of external stability (by ruling out more substantial revaluation) was at odds with the rules of the game in the Bretton Woods regime and appeared more in line with Japan's exchange rate policy from the mid-1960s (Horiuchi 1993). Yet in contrast to the UK, Germany was conducting internal economic policy with far more prudence. Throughout the debate on revaluation in the mid-1960s, Germany also felt aggrieved at what it saw as economic imperialism by the US.

US foreign policy was very active at the start of the postwar period and this has led critics to suggest that she wished to create a United States of Europe. It needs to be borne in mind, however, that Europe needed American aid and assistance and that the strengthening of the foreign economies was the *sine qua non* for the liberalisation of trade and a return to economic growth. Perversely, it was in breach of the Bretton Woods agreement that the US accepted the trade discrimination and monetary controls aimed at the dollar and dollar goods through the workings of the EPU.

In 1948, the US held about three-quarters of the world's monetary gold stock and as she lost gold in the following years the redistribution was seen as a desirable step towards convertibility. However, concern was being expressed during the 1950s about the size of the US balance of payments deficit. By 1958, the US had an official settlements deficit which, apart from the period 1968–69, lasted throughout the life of the

Table 4.2 *Treatment of disequilibria by pegging countries under the Bretton Woods regime*

Policy options open to authorities in the pegging countries	Strong currency *(Exchange rate would rise unduly above parity in the absence of official action)*	Weak currency *(Exchange rate would fall unduly below parity in the absence of official action)*
1. Intervention in the foreign exchange market	a. If the *dollar* was strong, its rise in the market was checked by the dollar sales of the weak-currency countries	a. If the *dollar* was weak, it was supported in the market by the strong-currency countries
	b. If any other currency was strong, its rise in the market was checked by dollar purchases by the strong-currency country	b. If any other currency was weak, it was supported by dollar sales by the weak-currency country
2. Exchange control or equivalent regulations	Controls on capital inflows	Control on capital outflows
3. Adjustment via fiscal and/or monetary policy	*Reflation*, e.g., tax cuts, lower interest rates	*Deflation*, e.g., a tough budget, higher interest rates
4. Change of parity	*Revaluation* (as with the DM in 1969)	*Devaluation* (as with the £ in 1967)

Source: Tew (1997, 166).

Bretton Woods system. The cause of the problem was that the trade and current account surpluses were not large enough to finance the capital outflow (comprising net private investment abroad and the military, travel and foreign aid spending). In 1959, the US balance on current account was negative for the first time since 1953 (although the current account then returned to surplus until 1970). Consequently, the world was relying on US official settlements deficits for the growth of reserves. This led to two criticisms of the system.

First, some European countries were unhappy with the asymmetry of a monetary system which allowed the US to run a deficit and lose reserves without ever having to change policy to stem this outflow. The official actions to operate this system were undertaken almost exclusively by other countries. The policy options are set out in Table 4.2.

All these options had side-effects which were either unwanted or unacceptable. The French were particularly resentful of US financial dominance and from 1965 began to convert outstanding dollar liabilities into gold. Germany and Japan, under more moderate leadership, realised that a confrontation with the US would be counterproductive. Such fissures only served to make the Bretton Woods mechanism more politically volatile.

Second, the deficit was seen as a problem because of the role of the dollar in providing liquidity to other countries. If the US deficits were erased, the world supply of reserves would not grow enough to satisfy the demand; if the deficit continued, instability would ensue as US liabilities increased relative to US reserve assets. This scenario was identified by Robert Triffin (1960) and encouraged economists to suggest ways of increasing liquidity in the system.

Although much is made of the fact that Triffin predicted the inevitable demise of the Bretton Woods system, he was wrong on two counts. First, although the gold–dollar ratio (liquidity ratio) fell during the 1960s, the accelerated decline from the mid-1960s was as a result of an increase in US dollar liabilities and the US gold stock continued to decline at the same rate as before (Table 4.3). Yet Triffin had suggested that the declining liquidity ratio would lead to a large-scale conversion of dollars into gold by the central banks and these conversions would reduce the outstanding dollar liabilities (De Grauwe 1996, 45).

From this conclusion Triffin made his second mistake, by claiming that the conversion would be deflationary as it would reduce the total amount of international reserves. This fear was also misplaced.

Throughout the 1960s, concerns grew about the impact that US foreign policy commitments were having on the balance of payments and the price of gold. A summary of actual and proposed measures to reduce the deficit is provided in Table 4.4. Many of the measures the US imple-

Table 4.3 Total international reserves, at end of selected years (US$ billion)

	1949	1958	1969	1972	1974	1980
Gold reserves*						
US	25	21	12	10	51	160
Other countries	8	17	27	29	139	420
Total	33	38	39	39	190	580
Total as percentage of year's world imports	55	38	15	10	24	30
Non-metallic reserves						
US liabilities	3	10	16	62	77	157
Other	10	10	24	59	99	257
Total	13	20	40	121	176	414
Total as percentage of year's world imports	22	20	16	31	22	22

Note: * Gold is valued at its official price of $35 an ounce in 1947, 1958, and 1969 and $38 in 1972; in 1974 and 1980 it is valued at market price.

Source: IMF (1976) and subsequent issues; IMF (1979, 1982).

mented antagonised international relations and did little to address the cause of the problem.

Even the establishment of the London Gold Pool in 1961, the expansion of the IMF's resources in 1960 and 1966 by increasing members' quotas, and finally the introduction of the special drawing right (SDR) in 1969, did little to halt the decline in the gold–dollar ratio. The major central banks did not convert their dollar holdings into gold and the congenital discipline of the gold–dollar standard was lost with inflation replacing the fear of deflation.

With the advantage of hindsight, it is unclear whether a significant growth in world reserves would have prevented the system from its ultimate collapse. While such a growth in aggregate reserve stocks would have been more readily acceptable in the hey-day of 1960s Keynesianism, the monetarist argument – that only a constancy of reserve stocks along with full convertibility could guarantee an inflation-free environment – was far more convincing. Indeed, the monetarist argument can go a long way in explaining the demise of the Bretton Woods system and ought to be considered at greater length here.

Up until the mid-1960s, the US enjoyed a combination of rapidly expanding output, falling unemployment and relative price stability. As the target rate of 4 per cent unemployment was reached, the economy

Table 4.4 Selected balance of payments measures (actual and proposed) for the United States, 1960–1967

1960	Expansion of Export–Import Bank lending and guarantees of non-commercial risks. Reduction in military dependents abroad (repealed in 1961)
	Reduction in defence and non-defence government purchases abroad
1961	Offsets for military expenditure in Europe and additional procurement at home
	Tying development aid to dollar purchases
	Increased taxes on foreign earnings of US corporations
	Reduced allowance for tourist purchases abroad from $500 to $100
	Treasury intervention in foreign exchange markets
	Repayment of German loans
1962	Expansion of earlier programmes
	Offset purchases by Germany and Italy
	Increased borrowing authority for the IMF
	Beginning of Federal Reserve 'swap' arrangements for currencies
	Treasury issues foreign denominated securities
1963	An interest equalisation tax of 1 per cent on foreign borrowers in US market. Additional tying of foreign aid to domestic purchases
1965	Interest equalisation tax on bank loans with duration of one year or more made to borrowers in developed countries (except Canada)
	Limits on growth of bank lending to foreigners
	Encourage private companies to increase exports and repatriate earnings. Guidelines for direct investment by non-financial corporations to limit growth of foreign direct investment
1967	Permit higher tax rates (up to 2 per cent) for interest equalisation tax
	Expansion of lending authority of Export–Import Bank

Source: Meltzer (1991, 62).

was given an additional stimulus in the form of a rapid increase in defence spending. Between 1965 and 1968, military spending rose by almost 60 per cent, largely as a result of the Vietnam war. According to Paul Volcker (Volcker and Gyohten 1992, 63) Vietnam marked America's 'imperial overstretch' and also the point at which fiscal policy became progressively looser.

Table 4.5 shows that the rise in US prices was fairly stable until the mid-1960s but in early 1965, wholesale prices began to increase rapidly. In 1966, the rate of wage growth outstripped the productivity trend and rising unit labour costs fuelled inflation further. As the corporate sector was not able to pass these costs on, profits were kept under pressure from the mid-1960s onwards. With an overvalued dollar, imports rose strongly between 1965 and 1969.

Table 4.5 Quarterly rates of change of consumer prices at annual rates (percentage per year)

Period[a]	CA[b]	FR	GE	IT	JA	NE	UK	US
1955I–58IV	2.02	5.37	2.05	2.01	0.88	3.32	3.75	2.04
1958IV–67IV	2.07	3.54	2.41	3.61	4.99	3.32	2.86	1.73
1967IV–73I	4.13	5.57	4.45	4.58	5.87	6.17	6.86	4.58
1973IV–76IV	8.85	10.68	4.89	16.09	13.19	8.92	16.36	7.95

Notes:
a. All rates are computed from the first quarter of each period to the quarter which ends the period. Periods mark changes in international monetary institutions.
b. The abbreviations for this and the following two tables are as follows: CA, Canada; FR, France; GE, Germany; IT, Italy; JA, Japan; NE, Netherlands; UK, United Kingdom; US, United States.

Source: Schwartz (1983, 20).

Even confidential US Treasury estimates suggested that by the beginning of the 1970s the dollar was 10–15 per cent overvalued but they refused to consider a dollar devaluation (Odell 1982, 252; Volcker and Gyohten 1992, 72). The rate of growth of the money supply increased continuously between 1961 and 1965. Despite a sharp drop in 1966, money supply growth after 1967 was considerably in excess of the growth rate in real GNP, although other industrial countries (except the UK) had a faster rate of money supply growth from the mid-1960s (Table 4.6). From the late-1960s, inflation began to accelerate again.

Even though the rate of US inflation was below that of the rest of the Group of Seven (G7) before 1968, Corden (1985, 87) has argued that this does not rule out the possibility that the US was exporting its inflation. Indeed, the US enjoyed a lower rate of inflation precisely because it was exporting a large part of its monetary and fiscal expansion via the fixed exchange rate! As Swoboda and Genberg (1982) have argued, the money growth in the US was the prime determinant of world money growth because of an asymmetrical relationship between the US and the rest of

Table 4.6 Quarterly rates of change of money^a at annual rates (percentage per year)

Period^b	CA	FR	GE	IT	JA	NE	UK	US
1955I–58IV	5.67	8.74	10.52	11.96	17.11	5.27	–0.46	3.34
1958IV–67IV	6.79	12.15	8.01	13.26	17.41	7.90	6.00	5.83
1967IV–73I	10.97	9.40	12.75	14.02	18.11	11.98	11.09	8.09
1973I–76IV	16.21	12.99	5.07	19.29	13.16	15.01	11.52	8.62

Notes:
a. Money is defined as currency plus adjusted demand and time deposits held by the public.
b. All rates of change computed from the first quarter of each sub-period to the quarter which ends the sub-period.

Source: Schwartz (1983, 20).

the world. Between 1960 and 1967, neither the supply of, nor demand for, dollars placed any significant pressure on reserve outflows from the US (Swoboda and Genberg 1993). By 1967, however, foreign demand for US dollars increased but the money supply grew only moderately. This lasted until 1969, when the income elasticity of demand for money became higher abroad and US monetary policy became more expansionary. By the late-1960s, the growth of the world's money supply was also fuelled by the development of the Eurodollar market (Figure 4.1; Swoboda 1968).

The increasing degree of capital mobility transformed the excess supply of dollars into a US payment deficit and an explosion of reserves elsewhere. As the dollar reserves of other countries accumulated in the late 1960s and early 1970s, it became more difficult to sterilise them, leading to increased domestic expansion, money supply growth and inflation (Table 4.7). Even if the US had followed a more moderate increase in its rate of monetary expansion, the rest of the world would have undoubtedly accelerated domestic credit creation which would still have resulted in (as) high world inflation. The only solution to prevent importing US inflation was for countries to float, which they did in 1973.

In broad terms, the end of the Bretton Woods adjustable peg system and the move to floating rates was a three-stage process. The first stage was the closing of the London Gold Pool by the Bank of England in March 1968. Sterling's devaluation and increasing gold scarcity triggered private speculators into buying gold in anticipation of a rise in its dollar price (Johnson 1968). The Gold Pool was replaced by a creation of a two-tier gold market – one for private gold traders, the other for official transactions. Private traders could continue to trade on the London gold market but there would not be an official price for gold. In the official

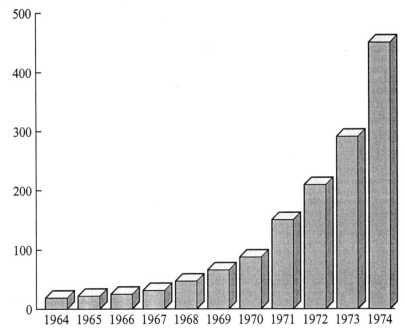

Source: BIS, various issues.

Figure 4.1 Growth of the Eurodollar market, 1964–1974 (gross deposits, US$ billions)

Table 4.7 Rates of growth of money, 1969–1971

Country	1969	1970	1971
United States	5.9	3.8	6.8
France	6.1	–1.3	13.7
Germany	8.2	6.4	12.0
Italy	15.0	21.7	22.9
Japan	18.4	18.3	25.5
Netherlands	9.4	10.6	16.7
United Kingdom	–0.3	6.8	12.9

Source: Meltzer (1991, 67).

tier, central banks would trade only among themselves at the official price of $35.00 an ounce.

Although the two-tier arrangement remained in place until November 1973, its immediate effect was far-reaching. The free market gold price went to $38 per ounce (suggesting that the market would have been happy to see a 10 to 15 per cent devaluation of the dollar) and for the rest of the year it fluctuated at between $38 and $43. While Solomon (1982, 123) claims that the establishment of the two-tier system 'did nothing to alter the US commitment to buy and sell gold in transactions with monetary authorities', the wider impact of the two-tier grouping was far-reaching as the link between the supply of dollars and a fixed market price of gold was severed. The ending of this link, which was one of the central tenets of the Bretton Woods negotiations, destroyed the system's defence against inflation. As we saw earlier, maintaining an official price for gold did not constrain worldwide monetary growth.

With hindsight, it was remarkable that the Bretton Woods system was actually surviving at the end of the 1960s although the *dies irae* was performed quite quickly in the early 1970s. The second stage in the process was the announcement by President Richard Nixon on 15 August 1971 to suspend the convertibility of the dollar into gold or other reserve assets. This decision had been planned in advance as it was feared that repeated demands for gold by France and Britain would generate a run against the remaining US gold reserve (Shultz and Dam 1977). Nixon also declared a 10 per cent surcharge on all imports to the United States, which would remain effective until America's trading partners agreed to revalue their currencies against the dollar.

In early December, Nixon agreed that the dollar should be devalued by repricing gold from $35 to $38 per ounce (Volcker and Gyohten 1992, 88–9). This agreement broke the impasse which had affected the G10 since Nixon had closed the gold window in August. A week before Christmas, the G10 met at the Smithsonian Institution in Washington, DC to agree a general realignment of exchange rates. At the start of the meeting, the combative US Treasury Secretary, John Connally, who had become increasingly frustrated at the tardiness of the G10, threatened generalised floating in lieu of any agreement.

In an atmosphere described by the German Minister, Karl Schiller, as 'carpet trading' (James 1996, 237), the discussions did produce a new set of exchange rates. The mark was revalued by 13.6 per cent against the dollar, the yen by 16.9 per cent, the pound and the French franc by 8.6 percent and most other European currencies by 7.5 to 11.6 per cent. The Canadian dollar continued to float. Bands on exchange rates were raised from 1 per cent to 2.25 per cent of central rates (the US had hoped for 3 per cent). In return, the US agreed to eliminate the 10 per cent surcharge on imports and the leading countries agreed to discuss reductions of trade barriers. For President Nixon, it was 'the most significant monetary agreement in the history of the world' (Dale 1971, 1), yet the deal lasted a mere 15 months.

The third and ultimately debilitating blow to the adjustable peg began in January 1973. On 11 January, the US announced the end of wage and price controls and flows out of the dollar began. Italy then introduced a two-tier exchange rate to discourage capital outflows, which prompted a flow of funds into Switzerland. The Swiss National Bank responded by ceasing intervening in the currency market, which effectively meant that the Swiss franc was now floating. In early February Paul Volcker, the US Treasury Under-Secretary for Monetary Affairs, was dispatched on a secret mission to Tokyo to put pressure on Japan to revalue the yen by at least 10 per cent against the dollar. The Japanese were unhappy with the American proposals but were told bluntly by the German finance minister that 'if you don't accept this, there will be economic war between the United States and Japan' (Volcker and Gyohten 1992, 130). In Bonn, Volcker proposed a 10 per cent dollar devaluation against the European currencies. The Bank of Japan closed its foreign exchange markets to allow the yen to appreciate and the European banks closed their foreign exchange markets to halt the inflow of dollars. Following these moves, the IMF effectively acknowledged that the game was over and issued a statement that 'if the crisis led to widespread floats, this should not be opposed' (James 1996, 242).

On 12 February, the dollar was devalued by 10 per cent (to $42.22 per ounce of gold) and the US authorities stated that they would not intervene to maintain the new price. Within weeks, there was a renewed flight from the dollar. This prompted further intervention from the central banks, mainly in the G10, which reached such a level that it was agreed among the European currencies that a joint float against the dollar and other currencies was necessary. From March 1973, floating had become widespread for the industrial nations (Table 4.8).

Table 4.8 The shift to floating rates

Country	Date float begins
British pound	June 1972
Canadian dollar	May 1970
Dollar floats	March 1973
Dutch guilder	May 1971
French franc	March 1973
German mark	May 1971
Italian lira	February 1973
Japanese yen	February 1973
Spanish peseta	January 1974
Swiss franc	January 1973

The developing countries

The developing nations were something of a residual under the Bretton Woods agreement and in 1944, few industrial nations had even considered that the poorer countries might wish to borrow from the IMF (James 1996, Ch. 5). By the late-1940s, a number of developing countries had adopted multiple exchange rate regimes, to the chagrin of the IMF. The Fund was unhappy at agreeing to these arrangement as it felt that exchange rate instability was caused by a loose monetary policy in these countries. *Per contra*, some economists even suggested mistakenly that in a number of developing countries 'a case could be made for making inflation an instrument of policy, rather than the control of inflation an object of policy' (Bruton 1961, 57). By the mid-1950s, the IMF had limited success in encouraging the developing countries to move away from inflation, exchange controls and multiple rates and towards trade liberalisation. Yet some countries that simplified their exchange rate arrangements in the 1950s (such as Chile) later reverted to a dual-rate system in the 1960s when exchange rate pressures mounted.

Edwards and Santaella (1993) have provided a detailed examination of 48 major devaluation episodes in the developing countries between 1954 and 1971, and have attempted to contrast devaluations undertaken within the context of an IMF programme to those without a formal IMF-sponsored programme (a unilateral devaluation). To classify whether or not the devaluations were either successful or unsuccessful, three key indicators were used: real exchange rates, net foreign assets of the monetary system and the current account as a percentage of GDP.

To focus on the real exchange rate as an indicator, Edwards and Santaella compiled data on the cumulative *ex post* elasticity of the real exchange rate. The data was computed in the form of an effectiveness index of nominal devaluations. This can be expressed as:

$$\text{Effectiveness Index}_k = \frac{R\hat{E}R_k}{\hat{E}_k}$$

where k refers to the number of years since the devaluation, $R\hat{E}R_k$ is the accumulated percentage change in the real exchange rate between the year prior to the devaluation and k years after the devaluation ($k = 0, 1, 2, 3$) and $\hat{E}_k$ is the accumulated percentage change in the nominal exchange rate during the same period. An index of the degree of erosion experienced by the *real* exchange rate during the three years after the devaluation can then be compiled. A value of one means that the nominal exchange rate adjustment has been fully transferred into a one-to-one real devaluation. A negative value would indicate that more than 100 per cent of the nominal devaluation has been eroded and at that particular point, the real exchange rate is below its value one year before the crisis.

From this, a devaluation episode was defined as 'unsuccessful' if in any of the three years after the devaluation the effectiveness index was less than 0.1 (in other words, more than 90 per cent of the real exchange rate effect of the devaluation had been eroded), or if, even when the effectiveness index was above 0.1, both the net foreign assets and the current account positions had worsened three years after the devaluation. The effective devaluations were subdivided into a 'successful' group and a 'limited success' group. Countries qualified for the former classification when the real exchange rate elasticity of the devaluation exceeded devaluation by 0.3 after three years and where the current account or net foreign assets displayed evidence of an improvement three years after the crisis. The rest of the countries were classified as having limited success. Table 4.9 reports the results of their finding.

Further analysis emphasised that the most effective devaluations were those accompanied by tighter macroeconomic policies. Those classified as a failure had more unstable political structures with a higher frequency of strikes and riots. A number of failure episodes were also followed by a coup attempt (Argentina, Colombia in 1965, Ecuador in 1961, Uruguay in 1963 and 1971, and Ghana in 1971). On average, the countries which requested IMF assistance experienced a quick and notable current account improvement, while most non-IMF devaluers saw little improvement even three years after the devaluation. Edwards and Santaella also found that IMF devaluers were more prone to inflationary pressures and that where crawling pegs were introduced, this further fuelled inflationary pressures.

The relationship between the international institutions and the developing countries did improve from the late-1950s, largely because it was accepted that the size and nature of the balance of payments difficulties were unlike those of the developed nations. These changes included an increase in size of small quotas to give small countries greater access to IMF credit; the introduction of the Compensatory Financing Facility (CFF) in 1963; and the introduction of the Buffer Stock Financing Facility (BSFF) in 1969.

As Bird argues (1990) argues, CFF was the most significant development as it provided temporary financial compensation against shortfalls in exports receipts and was the first formal institutional response to the demands of developing countries for international financial reform. The BSFF was more disappointing. It was used in 1971 to fund a stock of tin but was rendered ineffective following the currency instability of the early 1970s and the oil price hike in 1973.

Table 4.9   Successful and unsuccessful devaluation episodes for 48 developing countries, 1954–1971

Country	Year	Country	Year
A. Non-IMF devaluers		B. IMF devaluers	
1. Successful		1. Successful	
India	1966	Colombia	1967
Israel	1962	Ecuador	1970
Korea	1964	Ghana	1967
Malawi	1967	Mexico	1954
Sierra Leone	1967	Philippines	1962
Spain	1967	Philippines	1970
Turkey	1958	Spain	1959
Venezuela	1964	Turkey	1970
2. Limited success		2. Limited success	
Chile	1962	Colombia	1957
Israel	1967	Costa Rica	1961
Jamaica	1967	Egypt	1962
Korea	1960	Peru	1967
Nicaragua	1955	Tunisia	1964
Pakistan	1955	Zaire	1967
Sri Lanka	1967		
Trinidad–Tobago	1967		
3. Unsuccessful		3. Unsuccessful	
Argentina	1955	Argentina	1959
Argentina	1970	Argentina	1962
Colombia	1965	Brazil	1967
Ghana	1971	Colombia	1962
Israel	1971	Ecuador	1961
Uruguay	1959	Indonesia	1970
		Peru	1958
		Uruguay	1963
		Uruguay	1971
		Yugoslavia	1961
		Yugoslavia	1965
		Yugoslavia	1971

Source: Edwards and Santaella (1993, 438).

The regular meetings of the G10 industrial countries since 1962 (made up from Working Party No. 3, a subcommittee of the OECD's Economic Policy Committee) was also viewed unfavourably by the developing countries. In these meetings, important decisions were made which refined the operation of the international monetary system: increases in Fund quotas, the operation of the Gold Pool and the negotiation of the SDR. In response to the rich countries' club, the developing countries created the United Nations Conference on Trade and Development (UNCTAD) in 1964 which put forward an ill-fated series of proposals to reform the international monetary system in the interests of the developing countries (Hart, Kaldor and Tinbergen 1964).

The establishment of the SDR in 1969 was meant to establish a greater link between international liquidity and the developing countries but even here the developing countries remained excluded from the official financial debate. Indeed, in early versions of the scheme which were drawn up by the major industrial countries, developing countries were not included in SDR allocations and it was only senior management of the IMF which forced their inclusion. As the following chapter will show, it was not until the late 1970s that the IMF began to devote more attention to the problems of the developing countries.

Conclusion

McKinnon (1993) has suggested that a system of pegged but adjustable exchange rates should meet three needs. First, it should provide sufficient reserves and reserve credit to allow governments to keep their exchange rates pegged. Second, it should solve the 'nth country' problem that originates because a system covering n countries contains only $n - 1$ exchange rates, so that n countries cannot follow independent exchange rate policies, threatening a conflict in policy. Third, it should fix firmly the monetary policies of its members to prevent inflation or deflation.

Despite the teething problems in the 1940s and 1950s, the Bretton Woods system was able to meet the first requirement. Liquidity was facilitated through the IMF, which used the pool of national currencies provided by its member countries. Article IV also allowed for changes in the price of gold in terms of national currencies which would alter the value of the all gold reserves. In the late 1960s, the creation of the SDRs supplemented existing reserve assets. As we have seen, however, the growth in reserves took the form of dollar balances held by central banks.

In the Bretton Woods system the dollar was the nth currency. The US only rarely intervened in the foreign exchange market – usually the $n - 1$ foreign central banks intervened when necessary to adjust the system's $n - 1$ exchange rates, while the US was responsible in theory for maintaining the dollar price of gold. It was expected that the IMF would solve the nth currency problem by requiring countries to obtain approval before they changed their exchange rates, but this obligation was not taken seriously and industrial countries were able to follow their own exchange rate policies. Moreover, the US was reluctant to change the value of the dollar against other currencies and the burden of adjustment became asymmetrical.

Bretton Woods had been designed when the commitment to full employment was paramount and wildly fluctuating exchange rates had been a recent phenomenon. As Eichengreen and Kenen (1994, 34) note, the architects of the system aimed at conferring autonomy on national policies, not at imposing a common discipline. As we have seen, the US as the leading economy and nominal anchor of the system was able to force other countries to adjust. All the while the US could do this, the Bretton Woods met McKinnon's third requirement. By the mid-1960s, a combination of events forced many countries to question their commitment to the international monetary system. In the late 1960s, a continuing deficit on the US capital account and a dwindling trade surplus coupled with an increase in world liquidity transformed the dollar with its fixed parity from an undervalued currency to an overvalued one. The dollar shortage of the 1940s and 1950s became a dollar surplus problem by the end of the 1960s. Once a hegemon's trade and capital accounts are both negative, the international economic regime cannot last for long.

In some ways it is perhaps not surprising that it took so long for the system to finally dissolve. As Polak (1994, 21) has remarked, 'can one fault the official family (ministers, central bank governors, senior officials) for their unwillingness to administer euthanasia to a beloved system while there was still a glimmer of hope that it might survive?'. However, it is strange that in the quarter of a century since the end of generalised fixed rates, policymakers and politicians have sought to return to some variant of fixed rates by frequently assuming that the Bretton Woods system was a paragon of a rules-based system. Ultimately, fixed rates can only be successful if the nominal anchor to the system – the US in the Bretton Woods era – is able to maintain its commitment.

In the international monetary sphere, there were two responses to the breakdown of fixed rates. The first was a general move to floating exchange rates, followed in some areas by the creation of regional monetary arrangements. The next chapter considers the international monetary system in the aftermath of Bretton Woods, before the European regional arrangements are dealt with at length in Chapter 6.

5 The aftermath of Bretton Woods

The collapse of the fixed exchange rate was an inauspicious start to a decade which was characterised by a series of economic crises. The problems of the 1970s stretched far wider and lasted longer than contemporary commentators realised at the time and were part of a broader pattern of change following hard on the heels of the collapse of Bretton Woods. Indeed, the structural changes in the pattern of world payments; the increased international capital mobility and the substantial changes in the conduct of financial policy in major countries fed through into the 1980s and beyond.

Initially it was believed that the international monetary system would be reformed so that fixed rates would again become the natural order of things. Yet in essence, the era of managed floating has persisted since 1973 and while there have been regional currency groupings, for example, the European Monetary System (EMS), there has been no successful worldwide restoration of fixed rates. Moreover, while the global powers seemed unable or unwilling to agree in the 1970s on how they should act in a world without Bretton Woods, it was not until the 1980s that there was positive action on trade imbalances, macroeconomic coordination and exchange rate instability. By the late-1990s, exchange rates in the industrialised world were more stable but macroeconomic policy coordination had faltered. In the developing world and the post-socialist countries, debt overhang and acute balance of payments problems continues to have deleterious effects on economic performance.

Clearly, life after Bretton Woods has not been easy for the world economy but it would be unwise to ascribe these problems solely to the shift in exchange rate regime. Although the move to widespread floating in the 1970s was accompanied by inflation, this was not true from the 1980s when there was still an absence of fixed parities among the dollar, yen and Deutschmark (as the next chapter will argue, the managed system of the Exchange Rate Mechanism (ERM) survived for only 14 years in a world with open capital markets). Moreover, many of the developing countries which experienced huge economic problems were not on floating rates during the 1970s. Thus it is too simplistic and certainly naive to suggest that if only a fixed exchange rate system had been reintroduced, there would have been harmony among countries. This is simply not true and as the previous chapter argued, it is too elementary to assert that only good came from Bretton Woods.

These initial thoughts form the basis of a wide-ranging chapter which is sandwiched between the chapter on Bretton Woods and an account of the evolution of the EMS. This chapter will consider three main issues. First, it will discuss how the industrialised countries coped during the 1970s in a 'world without rules'. Second, the experience of the developing nations needs to be examined. Finally, it will examine the attempts made by the G7 to stabilise currencies in the 1980s and the move towards greater international economic cooperation.

Inflation, stagnation and exchange rate problems of the 1970s

With the benefit of a quarter of century of hindsight, it is difficult to imagine how the Bretton Woods system could have continued to survive in the turbulent world of the 1970s. At the time, the European countries seemed to share the view expressed most forcibly by France that floating should only be temporary, while the US took the lead in opposing the return to fixed rates (Tew 1988, 185). Eventually all the European countries softened their opposition to US enthusiasm for permanent floating, largely as a result of an improvement in the US balance of payments and the status of the dollar. Following France's agreement at Rambouillet in November 1975 not to insist on a re-establishment of a system of fixed but adjustable rates, the IMF Interim Committee in January 1976 was able to settle new rules for exchange rates. Ironically, the IMF had rejected floating as a viable option in 1972, but under the IMF Articles in 1976 which were implemented in April 1978, gold was formally removed from its central role in the IMF and IMF par value obligations were abolished.

It is difficult to generalise on the exchange rate policies of the industrial countries post-1973, but there were broadly two types of exchange rate policy. First, there were a number of EC countries floating jointly in the 'snake' (see Table 6.1), although membership vacillated during the course of the decade. By the end of the 1970s, membership of the snake comprised Germany, Benelux, Denmark and Norway. Second, there were a number of countries which managed the movement of the floating rate by aiming at a target rate related to trade competitiveness (Italy, the UK, the US, Canada, Switzerland and Japan).

After several years of floating it seemed that much of the original theoretical optimism on the merits of flexible exchange rates was misplaced. For instance, the instability in the real aggregates was accompanied by volatile nominal exchange rate movements post-1973. A study by the IMF (1984) concluded that short-term variability of nominal exchange rates for the seven major currencies (British pound, Canadian dollar, French franc, German Deutschmark, Japanese yen, Italian lira and US dollar) was about five times greater under floating rates than under fixed

Table 5.1 *Effective exchange rates (1970 = 100)*

	France	Germany	Italy	UK	Belgium	Denmark	Netherlands	Norway	Sweden
1971	98.5	103.7	98.9	100.2	100.3	99.4	101.1	99.4	99.9
1972	101.8	107.2	98.6	96.9	103.3	100.1	102.5	100.1	102.0
1973	106.4	119.4	68.8	87.7	104.4	106.6	105.8	104.9	103.8
1974	99.4	125.6	81.1	85.0	105.5	107.4	111.8	111.1	103.7
1975	109.4	127.7	77.9	78.5	106.6	111.3	113.6	114.6	109.0
1976	103.8	132.4	63.8	66.4	107.1	113.7	115.9	116.0	109.4
1977	98.4	143.2	58.7	63.1	111.9	114.0	121.6	116.7	106.1
1978	98.7	153.3	5.9	64.0	114.9	115.0	124.6	108.4	98.5
1979	100.4	162.4	54.7	68.9	116.8	114.9	127.0	107.4	100.6
1970–79*	–	5.5	–6.5	–4.0	1.7	1.6	2.7	0.8	–

Note: *Average annual percentage changes.

Source: IMF (1980).

rates. Table 5.1 shows that in Europe, Germany, Italy and the UK were affected by the greatest exchange rate vacillations. This was not what the proponents of floating rates had promised, but in their defence they could at least argue that exchange market uncertainty and exchange rate volatility was inevitable given the underlying international macroeconomic instabilities and the financial repercussions of OPEC I. Moreover, as Frenkel and Mussa (1980) note, while exchange rates were volatile, their volatility was less than that of stock prices in the 1970s.

The unexpected nature of exchange rate changes caught policymakers unaware during the first ten years of floating so that by the early 1980s, official intervention in exchange markets was substantially higher than that predicted by the advocates of floating rates. Thus currency market turbulence and exchange rate instability persisted even after floating was generalised with the markets exhibiting little social learning when new rules of the game had been established. It is also worth adding that the volatility of exchange rates was matched and influenced by the volatility of interest rates. Critics also argued that the widening of bid–ask spreads and increase of transaction costs and the failure of forward rates to predict future spot prices as well in the 1970s as in the 1960s was evidence that speculators destabilise foreign exchange markets. Let us not forget, however, that the most intense speculation during the last twenty years occurred under a fixed but adjustable peg when the Italian lira and British pound were forced out of the ERM in 1992.

It was the problem of rising inflation following OPEC I with the destabilizing influences for the international monetary and financial system which caused one of the biggest headaches for policymakers. As Triffin (1984, 13) has suggested, the combination of inflation and recession could be better described as 'infession' (inflation followed by recession) rather than 'stagflation' (which signifies stagnation followed by inflation). The higher inflation after 1973 begged the question as to whether floating rates were causing inflation. In the mid-1970s, international opinion was divided on this issue. US officials argued that the rate of domestic inflation was determined primarily by domestic monetary and fiscal policies and that the exchange rate played only a passive role in inflation (IMF 1976, 93). *Per contra*, European officials suggested that when a major currency depreciated, domestic prices for imports in the country experiencing the depreciation rose, along with wage costs, further fuelling internal inflation (ibid., 74; National Bank of Belgium 1977, xi–xii).

In the mid-1970s, the 'vicious circle' hypothesis was used to account for this pattern of events. This suggested that there would be a continuous and unavoidable cycle of domestic price increases and exchange depreciations which would become harder to stop. The converse thesis is the 'virtuous circle' hypothesis which is associated with exchange rate appreciation and price stability. When the vicious circle thesis was most popular among academics in the mid-1970s, there were marked disparities between those countries such as Japan and the Federal Republic of Germany and Switzerland who were in the virtuous club and the UK and Italy who were weaker and seemed trapped in a vicious circle. Subsequent analysis by academics on the strength of the vicious circle debate has been more muted, which Goldstein (1984) notes, because it is now recognised that inflation differentials are not the overriding determinant of exchange rate changes and because the theory has lost some of its appeal due to the changes in fortune between the formerly strong and weak currencies.

Yet it is worth looking in more detail at the empirical work by Braun (1976) and Sachs (1979) for the 1970s. The results of their research are reported in Table 5.2. Braun's data (column 8) shows that both Italy and the UK have experienced vicious circle problems, with widespread wage indexation policies in both countries. Sachs has calculated real wage resistance for the two years after the oil price increase of 1973–74 by comparing the actual and equilibrium wage rate. Columns 6 and 7 show the percentage of excess wages above their equilibrium level for 1975 and 1976. Braun's evidence suggests that indexation policies coupled to expansionary monetary policies were largely responsible for wage resistance in Italy and the UK. By 1976, only Italy and the UK showed signs of real wage resistance.

Table 5.2   Seven industrial countries: unemployment rates, excess wages and wage indexation in the 1970s

	Unemployment rate*					Excess wage Sachs (1979)		Wage indexation
	1972 (1)	1973 (2)	1974 (3)	1975 (4)	1976 (5)	1975 (6)	1976 (7)	Braun (1976) (8)
Canada	6.2	5.6	5.4	6.9	7.1	0.0	–2.0	Relatively unimportant
France	2.8	2.7	3.0	4.2	4.6	2.5	1.0	Prohibited
Germany, Fed. Rep.	0.8	0.8	1.7	3.7	3.6	7.5	3.5	Prohibited
Italy	6.7	6.5	5.9	6.3	6.7	21.0	17.0	High (almost 100% since 1975)
Japan	1.4	1.3	1.4	1.9	2.0	1.1	–5.1	Relatively unimportant
United Kingdom	4.2	3.2	2.8	4.7	6.4	13.8	11.5	High (1973–74 Stage II incomes policy encouraged cost-of-living adjustments)
United States	5.6	4.9	5.6	8.5	7.7	0.0	0.0	Relatively unimportant

Note: *Using US concepts.

Source: Bond (1980, 703).

There are two further sources of evidence which show how expansionary monetary policy was in some of the industrial countries in the early to mid-1970s and the policy response to the exogenous shocks of the period. From a strictly European perspective, Table 5.3 shows that total excess monetary growth increased by 6.0 per cent in the 1970s and was particularly high in Italy and the UK. This does seem to coincide with the 5.4 percentage point increase in the inflation rate between the 1950–69 period and the 1969–79 period and has led the monetarists to claim that this resulted in volatile exchange rates, as shown in Table 5.1 (Budd and Dicks 1982, 114).

Using a slightly different composition of industrial countries, Table 5.4 shows that while monetary policy was expansive across the board in 1972, it thereafter slowed significantly in Germany, Japan and the United States. Black's (1978) survey for the Council on Foreign Relations found that far from abusing its freedom from the external constraint, Germany used its monetary and fiscal policies to aim at a lower domestic inflation rate. Germany's success at achieving a current account surplus in 1974 placed further upward pressure on the Deutschmark (which made the external constraint more binding in those countries which were pegged to the Deutschmark). Equally, France, Sweden and the United States moved to a restrictive fiscal policy in 1973, while Italy and the UK, in particular,

Table 5.3   Changes between the fixed and floating exchange rate periods[1]
(differences in average annual percentage changes)

	$M1^2$	$M2^2$	GDP	Excess monetary growth[3]	Inflation[4]
France	−0.1	2.1	−1.3	3.4	4.0
Germany	−0.1	−3.1	−3.7	0.6	3.2
Italy	7.2	5.1	−2.3	7.7	9.0
United Kingdom	10.0	10.0	−0.6	10.6	9.0
Belgium	3.5	4.7	−0.3	5.0	4.9
Denmark	3.4	3.6	−1.4	5.0	4.8
Netherlands	4.2	5.0	−1.3	6.3	3.2
Norway	5.0	6.5	−1.1	7.6	4.2
Sweden	4.6	2.8	−2.0	4.8	4.6
Total	4.6	4.1	−1.9	6.0	5.4

Notes:
1. Defined as the years 1950–69 and 1969–79, respectively.
2. M1 and M2 stand for the narrow and broader definitions of the money supply, respectively.
3. Growth of M2, less growth of GDP.
4. Consumer prices.

Source: Budd and Dicks (1982, 114).

followed expansionary fiscal policies. Why did policymakers continue to allow excessive monetary growth and a loose fiscal policy to persist in this latter group of countries?

Initially, the Italian government responded to the oil shock by tightening interest rates, and then imposed credit ceilings on banks with the effect that the current account balance improved significantly between 1974 and 1975. However, the government was under pressure after OPEC I to ameliorate the effects of rising unemployment and the initial good intentions of the government came undone rapidly. The trade unions, in particular, were successful in their demands that the *scala mobile* should be made more generous, and in 1975 it was extended to provide on average 75 to 80 per cent cover against increases in the costs of living. This resulted in wage-push inflation which was further aggravated by the double-digit expansion of the money supply; according to Goodman (1992, 154), the Director General of the Treasury told the Governor of the Bank of Italy to open his window and 'throw out packets of 10,000 lira notes'. Such financial imprudence made Italy a major contender for IMF assistance in the early part of 1976.

*Table 5.4   Eight industrial countries' use of monetary and fiscal instruments, 1972–1976**

	1972	1973	1974	1975	1976
Canada					
Monetary	+	–	–/+	–	–
Fiscal	+	+	+	+	–
France					
Monetary	+	–	–	+	–
Fiscal	+	–	+/–	+	0
Germany, Fed. Rep.					
Monetary	+	–	–	+	+
Fiscal	+	–	+	+	–
Italy					
Monetary	+	0	0	0	–
Fiscal	+	+	0	+	–
Japan					
Monetary	+	–	–	+	+
Fiscal	+	+/0	0	+	+
Sweden					
Monetary	+	+	–	+	–
Fiscal	–	–	+	–	–
United Kingdom					
Monetary	+	0	0	0	–
Fiscal	+	+	+	+	0
United States					
Monetary	+	–	–	+	+
Fiscal	+	–	–	+	–

Note: * + = expansionary; – = contractionary; 0 = neutral.

Source: Black (1978).

The floating of the pound in 1972 had implications for the conduct of British economic policy in general and for monetary policy in particular. The monetarists argued that an excessive increase in the money supply would lead to a depreciation in the exchange rate and leave the UK economy with a higher price level (Johnson 1972). Yet the authorities showed little interest in controlling the money supply, as they increased the lending power of the banking system in the spring of 1971. Coupled to the freeing of the pound, two big constraints on monetary policy had been abolished within a very short time and these were reinforced by the relaxation of controls on commercial rents and property development. The combination of falling interest rates in 1971–72 with an expanding bank and property market, led to a boom in house and property prices and an emerging current account deficit. Notwithstanding the imposition of quantitative restrictions on the banking system via the Supplementary Special Deposit Scheme (the 'corset') in December 1973, the rise in world commodity prices in the same year and the quadrupling of oil prices in 1973–74 added to the upward trend in inflation in the UK. Although inflation had peaked by 1975, the authorities were concerned by three developments: the growth of the Public Sector Borrowing Requirement; the fall of sterling on the foreign exchanges and the high rate of inflation. By December 1976, the IMF had agreed to help overcome the UK's worsening financial difficulties on condition that monetary targets were reintroduced and adhered to (Oliver 1997).

From the evidence presented it is clear that in the 1970s, vicious circle experiences were a result of expansionary domestic money supplies. The advent of floating rates required greater internal discipline and those countries which successfully adjusted to the new external regime pursued sound domestic policies.

The developing world
For the developing nations, the breakup of Bretton Woods also marked the beginnings of a new era of problems in international finance. The mass of theoretical literature which blossomed in the wake of freely floating exchange rates was of little relevance for the bulk of the developing nations, as the majority of these countries continued with a fixed nominal exchange rate regime. Figure 5.1 provides a summary of exchange rate arrangements in developing countries for the period 1975–96. While few of these countries moved away from a predetermined nominal exchange rate regime in the first five years following the generalised float, quite a few had done so by the early 1980s.

The main problem for the developing nations was not so much exchange rate volatility as overvalued real exchange rates and inappropriate exchange rate policies which contributed to perennial economic underperformance and, in the case of several Latin American countries, to the debt crisis of the 1980s. It is true that where exchange rate adjustment was combined with political and economic reform, the results have been successful for the developing countries. Unfortunately, where developing countries have yet to undergo a process of structural reorganisation, they are condemned to pandemic economic problems.

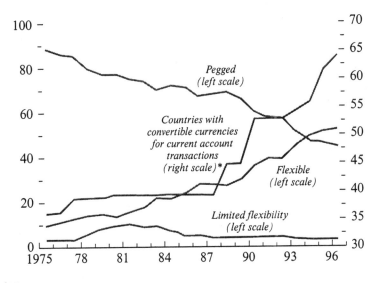

Notes:
The classification is based on officially reported exchange rate arrangements as of year-end. 'Pegged' regimes include exchange rate arrangements in which the currency is pegged to a single currency, to the SDR, or to a basket of currencies. 'Flexible' regimes consist of exchange rate arrangements in which the exchange rate is adjusted according to a set of indicators, following a managed float, or is independently floating. For some countries, the exchange rate may be classified as 'managed floating' or 'independently floating' but in fact is informally pegged. The difference between pegged and flexible regimes may therefore not be as significant as those indicated in the figure. The total number of countries included increases over time in keeping with increasing Fund membership.
*Percentage of developing countries that have accepted Article VIII of the IMF's Articles of Agreement; countries are weighted by their 1990–95 share of aggregate exports of all developing countries.

Source: IMF (1997, 78).

Figure 5.1 Developing countries' exchange rate arrangements, 1975–1996 (percentage of total number of countries)

Some authors have argued that the move to floating rates held out little attraction for the developing countries (Bird 1990). There was the fear that the uncertainty associated with flexible rates would impart a global anti-trade bias and that this uncertainty would be particularly acute for developing countries, given the lack of access to forward cover. Moreover, if groups of developing countries then decided to peg the value of their currencies to major world currencies, any variations in the value of these major currencies *vis-à-vis* each other could lead to disequilibrium in developing countries' real effective exchange rates. There was also the concern that where debt was denominated in currencies which appreciate, the real value of the debt would rise and debt management would become more of a problem. Finally, it was felt that currency misalignment associated with flexible exchange rates would have a deflationary and protectionist bias, adversely affecting developing countries.

By the end of the 1960s, even the Bretton Woods system was forcing a number of deficit countries to deflate and invoke trade restrictions. This could hardly be described as satisfactory. Yet following the move to generalised floating in the developed world in March 1973, a communiqué issued by a group of ministers representing developing countries at an Intergovernmental Group of Twenty-four on International Monetary Affairs still argued that 'a system of stable exchange rates based on adjustable par values . . . constitutes an essential element of a satisfactory international monetary order' (Crockett and Nsouli 1977, 125).

While Dornbusch's (1976b) contribution to the literature suggested that currency misalignment might be greater under floating than fixed rates, developing countries who chose to remain on a fixed-rate regime after 1973 faced formidable problems. In a clear theoretical exposition, Edwards (1988) has argued that to understand properly real exchange rate (RER) misalignment, it is essential to understand the way in which the equilibrium real exchange rate (ERER) behaves and evolves. Consider first the real exchange rate, defined as:

$$RER = \frac{EP_T^*}{P_N}$$

where E is the nominal exchange rate defined as units of domestic currency per unit of foreign currency, P_T^* is the world price of tradables and P_N is the domestic price of non-tradables. Misalignment of the real exchange rate occurs in two ways. First, when the actual RER departs from its equilibrium value because of inconsistencies in macroeconomic policies (for example, monetary or fiscal disturbances) and the official nominal exchange rate system. For example, an expansionary monetary policy will place pressures on P_N and the real exchange rate will experience a decline (real appreciation).

The second type of misalignment is known as a structural misalignment. To consider this, we need to identify the ERER, which is that relative price of tradables to non-tradables that, for given long-run equilibrium (or sustainable) values of other relevant variables such as trade taxes, international prices, capital and aid flows, and technology, results in the simultaneous attainment of internal and external equilibrium. The ERER is a function of a number of variables (for example, import tariffs, export taxes, real interest rates) which are known as real exchange rate fundamentals. Structural misalignment occurs when changes in the long-run sustainable values of the fundamentals of the ERER are not translated into the short-run changes of the actual RER. So if a country's terms of trade worsen, there will be a change in the ERER because a higher relative price of tradables will be required to maintain equilibrium in the economy. If the actual RER is not adjusted to reflect this change in the ERER, then as a result of the terms of trade shock, the real exchange rate would become structurally misaligned. The difficulty for policymakers is whether the changes in the fundamentals of the ERER are of a temporary or permanent nature.

For many developing nations, a devaluation to correct a significant real exchange rate misalignment has often been seen to represent an admission of policy failure. Empirical work by Edwards (1985) and others has also shown that a lasting real devaluation can only be expected to work when the nominal devaluation is accompanied by a sound macroeconomic package and devaluation is implemented at a time of disequilibrium. Further evidence collected by Edwards and Montiel (1989) from 16 developing countries supports this earlier work. Prior to devaluation crises, they found that the vast majority of countries had 'loose and inconsistent macroeconomic policies' and that the international terms of trade significantly worsened, suggesting that some collapses may have been caused by exogenous external shocks.

Table 5.5 gives estimates of the size of the 1974 and 1975 terms-of-trade shock in relation to the GDP and exports of the previous year. The three groupings are in descending order of the size of the terms-of-trade shock in relation to GDP. The first group consists of the seriously affected, with a total effect exceeding 3 per cent of GDP. The second group consists of five countries where the terms-of-trade effect was very small in relation to GDP but large in relation to exports (except Colombia). The final group of three countries gained from the terms-of-trade shift. From this table, it is worth examining the experience of Nigeria and Indonesia, which made positive gains from the terms-of-trade shock but who then devalued for different reasons and had divergent GDP performances in the 1980s.

The implications of an exchange rate misalignment can be shown by the experiences of Nigeria. From the mid-1970s, oil revenues produced a large fiscal income but affected the balance of payments, causing problems for the non-oil sector (the 'Dutch disease' effect). By the early 1980s, capital flight was a problem for the Nigerian authorities. Inflation was about 23 per cent in 1983 and rose to 40 per cent in 1984. The exchange rate remained fixed. From the end of 1982 to the end of 1984, the real exchange rate appreciated by 64 per cent and import restrictions were tightened. Following a nominal devaluation in 1985, the earlier real

Table 5.5 Terms-of-trade shocks, 1974 and 1975 (percentages)

Country	Total effect on GDP		Total effect on Exports		Change in debt (PPG)/ GNP	GDP growth rate			
	1974	1975	1974	1975	1973– 1975*	1973	1974	1975	1976
Chile	−12.4	−5.1	−48.2	−27.8	+32.0	−5.5	0.8	−13.2	3.6
Cameroon	−3.8	−3.7	−20.3	−16.7	+0.6	5.5	10.7	−0.8	4.3
Ivory Coast	−0.9	−6.4	−2.6	−16.1	+1.4	4.3	6.2	10.2	5.8
Kenya	−4.1	−3.0	−13.4	−8.0	+2.5	5.8	3.6	1.3	2.2
Costa Rica	−5.1	−1.0	−22.6	−4.0	+7.2	7.8	5.4	2.0	5.4
Pakistan	−3.1	−2.8	−21.4	−22.0	−18.9	7.1	3.4	4.1	5.3
Korea, Rep.	−4.0	+0.9	−16.6	+4.0	+0.8	15.2	8.9	7.7	13.5
Sri Lanka	−3.1	−0.6	−21.9	−3.8	−1.1	9.5	3.8	6.5	3.5
Thailand	−0.8	−3.0	−5.3	−16.6	+0.7	9.8	4.3	4.8	9.4
Brazil	−2.6	−0.5	−33.3	−7.0	+3.0	14.4	9.0	5.2	9.8
Mexico	−0.9	−0.6	−22.5	−15.8	+1.5	8.2	6.1	5.7	4.2
Turkey	−1.1	−0.3	−18.1	−5.2	−5.1	4.2	8.6	8.9	8.8
Argentina	−0.9	−0.3	−19.5	−7.7	+8.1	3.8	5.5	−0.5	−0.2
India	−0.9	+0.0	−25.0	+1.0	0.0	3.4	1.2	9.2	1.7
Colombia	+0.9	−1.1	+7.6	−9.5	−1.6	6.7	5.7	2.1	4.8
Morocco	+3.0	+1.3	+20.8	+5.9	+2.5	3.5	5.4	6.7	11.0
Indonesia	+17.0	−3.0	+90.9	−11.1	−5.6	8.7	7.7	5.0	6.9
Nigeria	+23.1	−2.6	+136.7	−9.8	−3.5	7.6	11.2	−3.2	9.2

Notes:
*Percentage points.

The effect on the terms-of-trade must be regarded as giving an order of magnitude only: there are considerable divergences in several cases between World Bank data and those given in the country studies. Only in the case of Kenya were World Bank data clearly wrong.

Source: Little et al. (1993, 30).

appreciation was more than reversed but was still too high in real terms because of the fall in the price of oil in 1986. This was followed by a protracted public debate about whether Nigeria should accept IMF aid. Most of the opinion was highly critical and attacked the aid as three Trojan horses: devaluation, trade liberalisation and the removal of petroleum subsidies (James 1996, 542). Thus, 'the first two will facilitate the admission of the Greeks into Troy and the last will ensure that Troy does not recover from the pandemonium that will come' (Callaghy 1990, 306).

While the IMF approach was rejected following a referendum, the Nigerian government negotiated a one year SDR 650 million standby arrangement (this money was used to reschedule debts with Paris and London Clubs) and implemented a structural adjustment programme in 1987. Import licensing was abolished and a fiscal restraint and wage freeze was coupled to the floating of the exchange rate. A massive nominal and real devaluation followed. Unfortunately, the trade liberalisation programme was opposed by some foreign countries with plants in Nigeria while the trade unions were against the wage freeze. Inevitably, the government budget deficit increased in the late-1980s and the architects of the plan admitted that they had been wrong to reject formal IMF assistance.

A devaluation which was not seen as an admission of failure was the Indonesia devaluation of November 1978. According to Woo (1988), this is a classic example where exchange rate policy was determined by the 'technocrats', who had anticipated forthcoming events. Although the rupiah was fixed to the dollar between 1970 and 1978, there was a substantial real appreciation over this period as a result of double-digit inflation. The decision to devalue took most commentators by surprise, as oil export earnings had been buoyant and the non-oil export sector showed steady growth, despite the deleterious effects of Dutch disease. In short, there was no balance of payments crisis, although Kincaid (1984) has suggested that the decision to devalue was taken because a balance of payments constraint was imminent.

Thus far, much of the discussion has ignored the unique experiences of the Latin-American countries. Table 5.6 shows the decline in per capita income growth in the years after 1979 and the remarkable rise in inflation in 15 heavily indebted countries (ten of which are Latin American) up to the mid-1980s. As Sachs (1989) has indicated, many of the factors which contributed to the debt crisis in these countries would have impeded economic performance in most circumstances: the large budget deficits; overvalued exchange rates; trade regimes which were biased against exports in general and agriculture in particular. But the debt problem was exacerbated by shocks to world interest rates, exchange rates and commodity prices in the early 1980s coupled to the perverse financing policies of international commercial banks between 1979 and 1982.

Table 5.6   The economic crisis in the heavily indebted countries[1]

	Average 1969–78	1979	1980	1981	1982	1983	1984	1985	1986
Per capital GDP (annual change)	3.6	3.6	2.6	–1.6	–2.7	–5.5	–0.1	0.9	1.4
Inflation (annual rate)[2]	28.5	40.8	47.4	53.2	57.7	90.8	116.4	126.9	76.2
Gross capital formation (percentage of GDP)	n.a	24.9	24.7	24.5	22.3	18.2	17.4	16.5	16.8
Debt–export ratio	n.a	182.3	167.1	201.4	269.8	289.7	272.1	284.2	337.9

Notes:
1. Argentina, Bolivia, Brazil, Chile, Colombia, Ivory Coast, Equador, Mexico, Morocco, Nigeria, Peru, Philippines, Uruguay, Venezuela, Yugoslavia.
2. Inflation refers to the consumer price index.

Source: Sachs (1989, 2).

Table 5.6 does not illustrate fully the traumatic events which afflicted Argentina, Brazil, Chile and Mexico in the early 1980s. Yet the debt crisis, according to James (1996, 347):

> brought home the consequences of the internationalisation of finance: the vulnerability of producers in Latin America (and elsewhere) to interest changes decided by the Federal Reserve System in Washington and to alterations in sentiment in the banking community. But it also showed that bank depositors, bank customers, and, indeed, whole national economies in advanced industrial countries could be affected by policy shifts in Mexico City or Manila or Warsaw. For a time, a major banking crisis appeared imminent in industrial countries.

Undoubtedly the most famous case of inconsistency between macroeconomic policies and exchange rate alignment post-1973 occurred in Argentina. While the authorities tried to eliminate inflation and reduce fiscal deficits from the mid-1970s, their efforts were unsuccessful and prompted a popular backlash. The unwise attempt to reduce inflation through a preannounced rate of devaluation (the *tablita*) between 1978 and 1981 exacerbated an unstable economic situation. The preannounced rate was inconsistent with the inflation tax required to finance the fiscal deficit and generated a real appreciation. Moreover, as Calvo (1986) has shown, it also encouraged the public to bet on when the *tablita* would be abandoned. The overvaluation of the exchange rate combined with capital flight and prompted foreign borrowing on a massive scale. As Table 5.7 shows, the external debt accumulated in the late-1970s was huge but only half was owed by the public sector by 1980. According to some critics (Dornbusch and de Pablo 1989), the cause of Argentina's debt crisis was 'almost exclusively' the result of mismanagement of the exchange rate and unrestricted capital mobility.

Table 5.7 Argentina's external debt ($ billion and percentages)

	1975	1978	1979	1982	1985
Total external debt ($)	7.9	12.5	19.0	43.6	48.3
Public ($)	4.0	8.4	10.0	28.6	40.0
Reserves ($)	0.6	5.8	10.1	3.0	6.0
Net debt/exports (%)	260	110	120	540	520
Debt/GDP (%)	18.6	23.9	30.2	60.3	64.5
Interest payments/GDP (%)	0.7	1.4	1.4	2.4	5.7

Source: Dornbusch and de Pablo (1989, 41).

Argentina's unsuccessful experiment with an active crawling peg in this period was a result of a failure in domestic policy and can be contrasted to the experience of Chile. In the Chilean case, the exchange rate was fixed to the dollar from the end of 1979 to 1981 to bring inflation down (to about 7 per cent by the end of 1981). Although there was a substantial real appreciation and unemployment remained high, domestic monetary and fiscal policies were not out of line. The overvaluation was intensified by the increase in oil prices and the collapse in copper prices. The structural misalignment of the exchange rate that resulted was caused by the exogenous shocks (the fall in the terms-of-trade and the decline in lending) and required a real devaluation. The problems for Chile arose as a consequence of excessive private borrowing in the late 1970s and early 1980s which was followed by the withdrawal of credits in early 1983 in the wake of the Mexican crisis.

While the Mexican economy experienced a phase of high growth and low inflation in the 14 years after the devaluation of the peso in 1954, the 1970s was a decade of more radical economic policy shifts. The first half of the decade witnessed an enormous fiscal expansion and inflation rose above 20 per cent in 1973 and 1974. The real exchange rate fell rapidly and by 1975 the current account deficit was 5.1 per cent of GDP. Following extensive large-scale capital flight ($3.6 billion in 1975 and 1976), the authorities were forced to impose import controls and in August of 1976, devalued the peso by nearly 100 per cent. Yet because the authorities refused to curb their excessive spending and allowed the money supply to grow unchecked, macroeconomic policy was inconsistent with the devaluation. Moreover, after agreeing to an IMF stabilisation plan, the Lopez Portillo administration soon dropped its commitment to monetary and fiscal austerity as Mexico's oil wealth was greater than had initially been thought. The oil boom allowed Mexican costs and prices to rise faster than those in the United States, resulting in a real appreciation and the symptoms of Dutch disease. Despite a depreciation of the peso relative to the dollar in late 1980, higher inflation in Mexico still contributed to an overvalued real exchange rate. The real exchange rate appreciation combined with trade liberalisation and lowered the real price of imported goods by approximately 28 per cent from 1977 to 1981, provoking huge increases in demand (Buffie and Krause 1989, 151). Perversely, every time the peso was devalued, the government granted special pay awards to public sector employees, which made for larger deficits.

When the bubble burst in August 1982, it caught the US by surprise. Just two months before, the Bank of America had organised a $2.5 billion loan on the basis that 'we are confident that Mexico's vast natural resources, its industrial labour force, its dynamic private initiative as well as the efficient public administration, will pull Mexico out of its current troubles' (James 1996, 363). A more balanced analysis of Mexico's situation would have found it difficult to concoct such a description, let alone conclude that Mexico should have been granted such a huge sum of money which was merely plugging the dyke in the forlorn hope of preventing the dam from bursting. The bulk of the debt which Mexico accumulated in the 1978–81 period was contracted by the public sector, most of which took the form of medium- or long-term commercial loans. Yet short-term debt had also grown rapidly to account for 20.3 per cent of the total public sector debt by 1981. Private debt had tripled in the same period to stand at $21.9 billion in 1981, over half of which was short-term borrowing. Thus despite the large windfall from oil discoveries and the high rates of GDP growth between 1978 and 1981, the increase in foreign debt was excessive (Buffie and Krause 1989). Despite the fact that Mexico introduced a successful *tablita* in the late-1980s, the peso became overvalued by the early 1990s and this was followed by a mismanaged devaluation. By the end of 1994, there was a further loss of confidence in the economy as a result of large imbalances.

While the escalation of the debt crisis in Latin America and then into middle-income countries did prompt various initiatives (for example, the Baker Plan of 1986; the Brady Plan of 1989), debt overhang is still a problem for many of the largest debtors in the late-1990s.

International economic policy coordination in the 1980s and 1990s
As we have seen, during the first decade of floating rates there was little stability in foreign exchange markets. Plans to reform the international

monetary system came to nothing and the rhetoric from some members of the OECD became decidedly protectionist in tone. Moreover, the attempt at 'internationally coordinated Keynesianism' (James 1996, 414) following the Bonn summit of 1978 is generally assumed to have soured German enthusiasm for further international cooperation (compare Holtham 1989). Even the outbreak of the debt crisis in the early 1980s did little to inspire the international community towards settling problems collectively.

By the early 1980s, the United States had shifted decisively away from the aegis of cooperation, following the election of Ronald Reagan. It was quickly made apparent to the rest of the world that America intended to form its domestic policy with little regard to the repercussions on the international community. In April 1981, the United States Treasury Secretary, Donald Regan, and his Under-Secretary for Monetary Affairs, Beryl Sprinkel, announced that the Treasury was no longer going to intervene in the foreign exchange market to stabilise the dollar, except on extraordinary occasions. As the US administration was following a mixture of loose fiscal policy and moderate monetary policy this raised real interest rates and attracted capital, placing upward pressure on the dollar which made the US less competitive.

By 1982, the French became among the keenest supporters of greater policy coordination, requesting intervention in the foreign exchange markets to reduce currency instability. In part this reflected France's fear that sudden swings in currencies would put the EMS under strain; in part President François Mitterrand was concerned that sharp currency movements would unsettle his macroeconomic strategy. In contrast, Regan and Sprinkel espoused views which were the binary opposite of the French. The two disparate views were graphically illustrated at Rambouillet in April 1982, which was a preparatory meeting for the Versailles summit in June. According to James (1996, 422) the American negotiators:

> saw the most important task as securing a new disinflationary convergence of monetary policy and an orientation toward price stability. Treasury Secretary Donald Regan had little sympathy for intervention in exchange rates, or for Mitterrand's reflationary ideas. One French official remembers an American claiming that he could detect no difference between the economy policy of France and that of the Soviet Union.

The outcome of the Versailles summit attempted to appease conflicting interests and in so doing, was something of a curate's egg. The final communiqué stressed that to reduce real interest rates, it was necessary for the Group of Five (G5) to pursue prudent monetary and fiscal policies. Yet the US continued to deny that there existed any link between the budget deficit, the strong dollar and the growing trade deficit. However, by agreeing to set up a study group on exchange market intervention, there was hope that there would be a general commitment to stabilise exchange rates. Even here, Regan's entrenched position made this less of a reality and the United States' belief that intervention could not be used to establish greater currency stability appeared to be confirmed by the Jurgensen Report of 1983. The Report did not have any clear conclusions but it did argue that sterilised intervention was ineffective and that unsterilised intervention could be inflationary or deflationary. According to the President of the Bundesbank, Karl Otto Pöhl, interviewed at the time the Report was published:

> I think we should not exclude occasional intervention to avoid erratic fluctuations, but I am no fan of large-scale intervention. It can't change the fundamentals, as recent experience shows, and we ourselves have never urged the United States to intervene. (Pöhl 1983, 46)

Slowly, the inflexible attitude of the US towards the strong dollar did subside. In October 1983, there was an attempt to decrease the yen/dollar exchange rate. Moreover, as the dollar appreciated by another 20 per cent between mid-1984 and February 1985, several studies argued that the foreign exchange market was being carried away by an irrational 'speculative bubble' (Krugman 1985). With the trade deficit and budget deficit continuing to widen, even those in the Reagan administration were forced to admit that freely floating exchange rates did not appear to be the panacea for domestic economic harmony, let alone a salvation for harmonious international economic relations.

Following Reagan's re-inauguration in 1985, Regan and Sprinkel were replaced by James Baker and Richard Darman. Baker in particular proved to be 'less doctrinaire' (Lawson 1992, 475) than Regan and was very concerned about the impact of the high dollar on American business and industry. Baker also realised that cooperation to bring down the dollar might appease the protectionist sentiment in Congress and enable Europe and the Japanese to be seen as allies. On 17 January 1985, the G5 finance ministers committed themselves to coordinated intervention in the foreign exchange markets when it was considered necessary. On 22 September 1985 at the Plaza Hotel in New York – mainly at the instigation of Baker – the G5 finance ministers agreed to cooperate further on currency misalignments. By the time of the Louvre Accord on the 21 and 22 February 1987, fears had been expressed by some countries over the slide in the dollar. These had been made most forcefully by Germany and Japan at the Tokyo summit in May 1986, but a year later, this concern was more widespread. Concomitantly, the communiqué issued by the G7 on the 22 February pledged further international cooperation to 'foster stability of exchange rates around current levels' (Funabashi 1989, 280).

Despite the greater consensus in international cooperation from the mid-1980s, discussions did not proceed altogether smoothly. The US was eager to achieve a correction in its current account and in vain tried to encourage Germany and Japan to give a Keynesian stimulus to the world economy. The 1985–87 period also saw a return to the macroeconomic conflict of the 1970s as James Baker threatened to withhold support for currency stabilisation unless Germany and Japan agreed to stimulate their economies. Meanwhile, the main burden of intervention rested with the Europeans and the Japanese. As Henning (1994) illustrates, from the beginning of November 1985 through to the end of January 1987, the American authorities engaged in not a single instance of intervention. For 1987 as a whole, foreign central banks financed almost two-thirds of the record $163.5 billion US current account deficit while the US financed only about $8.5 billion through sales of foreign exchange (Bank for International Settlements 1988, 188–9).

By the time of the Tokyo summit, James Baker was against focusing solely on exchange rate issues which he regarded as too narrow. Instead, he proposed that the G7 should set out a range of indicators which they could use to guide policy. The seven eventually chosen were growth, inflation, unemployment, budget deficits, trade balances, monetary conditions and exchange rates. According to Lawson (1992, 546), the motive behind this stemmed from a US preoccupation with 'misplaced worries that global economic growth was slowing down'. In short, by launching this initiative, Baker believed that he could alter economic policy in other countries. The Europeans and the Japanese thought otherwise. Lawson (ibid., 547) noted that:

> there was never any agreement – or even proper discussion – of what to do if the various indicators pointed in different directions . . . I found it impossible to take the exercise very seriously – and it certainly played no part, for all Jim Baker's combination of nagging and enthusiasm, in the subsequent course of world economic policy.

The Japanese Vice-Minister of Finance for International Affairs commented that: 'the thrust of the whole argument revolved around this one consideration [expansionary measures]. We're not going to allow indicators to meddle into the domestic politics and sovereignty' (Funabashi 1989, 135), and Karl Otto Pöhl (1987, 20–22) remarked that:

> those who wish to replace persons and ad hoc decisions by regulatory mechanisms and indicators apparently have no perfectly clear idea about the nature of monetary policy decisions and the difficulties of reaching them . . . There are, I think, very few situations in the area of international monetary policy in which a depersonalized, predetermined decision-making process could have covered up, much less resolved, such conflicts of aim.

Despite the fact that the dollar was stabilised, the dollar peaked in February 1985 and had already depreciated by 13 per cent by the time of the Plaza meeting. This led one economist to comment that 'for West Germany and the other G5 countries, the Plaza meeting was essentially a non-event, and even the change in Japanese monetary policy was soon abandoned' (Feldstein 1987, 799). More supportive evidence on the benefits of intervention can be found in the work of Catte et al. (1992) who identified 17 episodes of concerted intervention by at least two of the three major countries (Germany, Japan and the United States) since 1984. Their study found that nine of the 17 episodes were 'definitely successful' in reversing the trend of the dollar, while the other eight enjoyed temporary success.

While many of the supporters of exchange rate management claim that world welfare has been raised as a result of coordination, they tend to overlook the fact that some countries pursued coordination at the expense of their own welfare. The work of Hughes-Hallet et al. (1988) has touched on this issue: they find gains to be asymmetrically distributed among the G5 countries in the late 1980s although it is extremely difficult to find ways of improving the lot of those countries that benefit least from coordination. For some countries the costs of intervention were particularly high, and the experience of the United Kingdom is a good case in point.

Nigel Lawson, British Chancellor of the Exchequer between 1983 and 1989, had remarked in 1985 that he had 'never believed in intervention in the foreign exchange market as a way of life, still less as a substitute for firm fiscal and monetary action' (Congdon 1989, 20). Yet by the time Lawson attended the G5 meeting at the Louvre in 1987, a French delegate noted that 'there was a change in Great Britain in favor of more concerted management of exchange rate fluctuations and it developed up to the Louvre Agreement. In fact, they were anxious for stability between pound sterling and European currencies' (quoted in Funabashi 1989, 175).

In some ways, it could be said that Lawson's 1985 proclamation could be reconciled with his 1987 viewpoint by arguing that in the Louvre Accord, Lawson had promised that the UK would continue to follow firm fiscal and monetary action. However, between March 1987 and March 1988, the conduct of UK economic policy was highly dubious as Chancellor Lawson followed a policy of shadowing the Deutschmark at DM 3 to the pound. By maintaining this rate, Lawson was forced to keep interest rates low to prevent the exchange rate from rising. This was accompanied by massive interventions by the Bank in the foreign-exchange markets, which ultimately grew to such a level that Treasury and Bank officials were becoming worried about sustaining them. For some critics, the (inappropriate) low interest rates during the shadowing period increased the inflationary pressure within the British economy (Walters 1990). Monetary policy was loosened in the UK following the Black Monday crash of 17 October 1987, which in retrospect was not a wise response. While the Federal Reserve tightened monetary policy in 1987, the shadowing exercise being pursued by the British Chancellor effectively ruled out higher interest rates.

By the end of the 1980s, policy cooperation had evaporated again and it is not hard to agree with the view of Currie et al. (1989, 22–3) that by this date there was:

> the spectacle of countries solemnly declaring that current exchange rates are appropriate without offering any supporting evidence, apart from the fact that these rates are what they are. Should the market . . . then drive exchange rates somewhere else, the authorities can be relied upon to announce that the new levels are appropriate too.

Indeed, while the initial desire for international coordination in the early 1980s stemmed from economic objectives, by the late-1980s observers were noting that 'it is politics rather than economics which now dominates official policy towards exchange rates' (Stephens 1988, 1). By the mid-1990s, the Bretton Woods Commission (1994, A5) had also picked up on this point, noting that the G7 process was 'unlikely to ensure future exchange rate stability, or to support economic policies that are sound internationally as well as domestically'. As Currie (1993) has suggested, it is little wonder that in areas such as fiscal policy, national self-interest has taken precedence over international decisionmaking. Indeed, it is rather chimerical to imagine that in the absence of legally binding requirements, it would even be possible to make some countries conform to rigid monetary and fiscal targets. As we shall argue in the next chapter, this could have important implications for regional currency groupings.

Conclusion

Since 1973, the major currencies have been floating with respect to one another, although the floating has frequently been subjected to market intervention by the authorities to influence the movement of exchange rates. Moreover, while the early supporters of floating arrangements had argued that the main mechanism of adjustment would be changes in real exchange rates, brought about by market-induced changes in nominal rates (supported where appropriate by changes in fiscal policy), experience has suggested otherwise.

As we have seen, the adoption of floating rates in the 1970s did not herald an era of international economic harmony, nor did it allow economies to undergo the economic miracles claimed by their supporters.

Since the early 1970s there have been two broad problems which have arisen under floating rates.

First, the international economy has generally been destabilized by numerous endogenous and exogenous shocks which have placed pressure on currencies. Undoubtedly, the turbulence of the international economy in the 1970s and the botched attempts at coordination had parallels with the 1930s. While there were more valiant endeavours to stabilise exchange rates in the 1980s, this momentum had all but vanished at the beginning of the 1990s.

Second, the floating rate has been more volatile and its consequences more dramatic than predicted. As countries experienced different growth trajectories and were inflating and deflating diversely throughout the 1970s, exchange rates were varying in response to the size of the income movement divergences. Many nations did not realise that to obtain exchange rate stability they should be inflating and deflating simultaneously, which was basically impossible under a floating rate.

It is because of this volatility that there has been a movement back towards a fixed exchange rate system in Europe. However, in the final analysis, in spite of the difficulties associated with floating rates and the attraction of the European Monetary System, it is highly unlikely that in the foreseeable future the generalised float could be replaced by a new Bretton Woods.

6 The evolution of the European Monetary System

Following the breakdown of Bretton Woods in the early 1970s, the monetary system of the Western European countries can be broadly characterised as two exchange rate regimes. The first – the managed float – was dealt with at some length in the previous chapter while the second – the fixed, but adjustable, peg in the EMS – is examined in this chapter. By the late-1970s, most of Western Europe had opted for fixed but adjustable exchange rate regimes, motivated by a desire to guarantee the stability of intra-European trade. The progress of the EMS since 1979 has included a set of arrangements which were designed to limit currency fluctuations through the ERM and is the driving force behind European Monetary Union (EMU).

According to Giavazzi and Giovannini (1989, 1):

> The European Monetary System is simply a recent step in the historical quest for exchange rate stability in Europe. Europeans dislike exchange rate fluctuations for three reasons. First, they all live in relatively open countries. Second, many of them hold the floating rates of the 1920s and 1930s responsible for the ensuing collapse of national economies and of the international trading and monetary systems. Third, postwar European institutions – particularly the common agricultural market – depend for their survival on exchange rate stability.

While previous chapters have argued that it is unfair to blame the chaos in the international monetary system during the twentieth century on floating exchange rates, many European countries in their quest for exchange rate stability have wanted to pursue fixed exchange rates. Perhaps the biggest institutional reason for this, as Giavazzi and Giovannini suggest, is the common agricultural market, or more accurately, the Common Agricultural Policy (CAP). As the CAP is closely connected to European exchange rate policy, our account of the evolution of EMS has to begin by a consideration of this development.

The CAP and green exchange rates

The CAP was developed in the early 1960s by national officials, European Community (EC) administrators and representatives of agriculture (Commission of the European Communities 1987). The goal was the creation of a European customs union in agricultural products, with the intention of standardising prices for agricultural products across the EC. There was an array of instruments to support prices, including internal price subsidies, export subsidies and external third country tariffs. These instruments were financed out of the EC budget, to which all the members contributed.

The architects of the EC had recognised agriculture as an area of common concern in the Treaty of Rome (Harris et al. 1983). The CAP was a priority among European governments, spurred by memories of food shortages in the wake of two world wars, a growing European farm lobby and the view that agriculture was the best candidate for progress towards European integration. Because agriculture was one area where there already was widespread national intervention, it seemed both natural and necessary that the national programmes be replaced by EC-level programmes if a unified Common Market was to operate effectively.

However, the basic problem with the working of the CAP was caused by the incompatibility of a collective pricing system in the context of sovereign national economies, each with its own currency. Prices could be set at one point in time so as to be equal across all currencies, but once the value of one currency moved up or down, the price would no longer be in line with the others, defeating the purpose of the collective programme. To achieve a common pricing system among countries with different currencies, all the members needed to have a fixed exchange rate relative to one another, denominated in some common unit, in order to limit exchange rate turbulence. Thus, when drawing up the CAP, commission officials created a new EC instrument, called the agricultural unit of account, to fill this need. The values assigned to each of the national currencies in this account were called 'green monies'. Green money was not real currency but an accounting device, a separate exchange rate used for agricultural purposes.

At the outset, the CAP pricing system operated within the stable confines of the Bretton Woods system, which facilitated the working of the CAP. The accounting value of the agricultural unit of account was also fixed at 0.88867088 grams of fine gold, identical to the value of a US dollar at the time. Since the dollar was the basis for the Bretton Woods system, the green exchange rate would be the same, at least initially, as the regular, non-agricultural rates pegged to the dollar.

Indeed, for the first few years of the CAP, the green money exchange rate system worked smoothly and so did the EC-wide agricultural price-support scheme. The CAP system of fixed green currency values was stabilised, as were the general European exchange rates, by the larger Bretton Woods system, which in turn rested on the economic and political strength of the United States and the administrative capacity of the IMF. As long as the larger monetary system remained stable, the agricultural programmes functioned without any serious difficulties.

The first significant challenge to the CAP pricing system occurred when the French government, without consulting the other EC members, devalued the franc in August 1969. The value of the franc against gold, and thus against all the currencies in the Bretton Woods system, was reduced by 12.5 per cent. The drop in value was too large to be smoothed over by allowing the green rate to remain the same, as had previously been the case for minor fluctuations which caused only a small gap between the green franc and the general franc value. If the EC devalued the 'green franc' by the same amount, the common price of all agricultural commodities covered by the CAP agreement would automatically rise by 12.5 per cent in terms of the French franc. But a large rise in food prices threatened to worsen an already undesirable level of inflation in France, and the French government received permission from the Council of Ministers to phase in the new, higher price level over two seasons, despite the French farm lobby's desire for a shorter transition period to higher prices. In effect, the result was that agricultural products were exempted from the overall economic policy changes that the French government had put into effect with its initial devaluation.

However, the special status of French agricultural prices created unwanted effects throughout the EC system. The gradual upward adjustment of French prices had the unintended result of giving the French an artificial trade advantage over the other CAP members during the time that French prices were below the common CAP price. To adjust for the trade effects of the diverging green money rates, agricultural experts in the Commission devised monetary compensatory amounts (MCAs) as a temporary measure to help smooth the systemic effects caused by the French desire to phase in green money changes and higher food prices. MCAs were an elaborate programme of border levies and subsidies paid out of the EC budget that would bring French exports up to the EC-level prices (the levies) and lower the price of EC food imports into France (the subsidies). They also were used to standardise the prices of agricultural goods from third countries. In effect, MCAs were border controls that insulated the French agricultural market from the rest of the EC, keeping prices lower than they would have been in the wake of the devaluation of the franc.

MCAs solved the immediate problem of speculation and arbitrage across European agricultural markets, but the MCAs reintroduced the very levies and subsidies that the European Common Market had been set up by the Treaty of Rome to do away with. The French MCAs set a precedent, allowing the suspension of free trade among EC members when nominal exchange rates changed – a step that ran contrary to the basic assumptions of European integration. They also set a precedent of allowing two sets of agricultural prices (one at the national level and one at the common price level) instead of forcing an immediate adjustment on the part of farmers and consumers when an overall exchange rate change was made.

Within a few months, the CAP system was again challenged, this time by the upward revaluation of the German mark by 9.29 per cent in October of 1969. The potential domestic price effects were the opposite of the French devaluation: CAP prices in terms of marks would fall, reducing the intervention prices paid to German farmers. Heeding the protests of its farm sector, Germany asked for the gradual lowering of the intervention prices until they reflected the new exchange rate, with the EC-funded MCAs again compensating for the trade effects. The clash of two differing goals – agricultural price stability and the need for overall national currency adjustment – would have increasing repercussions for the EC's budget and its institutions in the coming years.

The problems that currency realignments brought to the working of the CAP were minimised by the relative currency stability of the 1960s, which kept green rates roughly in line with general exchange rates. However, the breakdown of the Bretton Woods system in the 1970s had severe consequences for the working of the common agricultural policy and showed that a European food policy system developed in a time of fixed, stable exchange rates would not necessarily work when the larger system around it was transformed into a floating-rate regime.

From the snake to the EMS
Johnson (1973) has argued that the unstable dollar and the disorderly revaluation of European currencies would endanger the EC, and it was these fears that prompted the Werner Report of 1970. The report detailed how EMU could be achieved in stages by 1980. The report did not recommend a single European currency or a European Central Bank (ECB) but it did call for the centralisation of members' macroeconomic policies, politically responsible to the European Parliament. Ultimately, monetary union would entail 'the total and irreversible fixing of parity rates and the complete liberation of movements of capital' (Werner et al. 1970, Ch. 3, 10).

The Werner Plan was never implemented for several reasons. First, while the exchange rate stability of the first half of the 1960s was achieved when domestic policy targets did not have to be sacrificed, in the 1970s European countries were desperate to hold on to their independence in setting macroeconomic policy in the wake of international disturbances (Gros and Thygesen 1992, 15). Second, the Community was also widened in 1973, when the original six members were joined by Denmark, Ireland and the UK. This enlargement further complicated integration efforts. Finally, but by no means least, the initial implementation stages of the Werner Plan would have coincided with the breakup of Bretton Woods.

The attempts to salvage the Bretton Woods system through the Smithsonian Agreement in December 1971 allowed member currencies to fluctuate by plus or minus 2.25 per cent, creating a band of 4.5 per cent around the dollar. Intra-European exchange rates were able to fluctuate by as much as plus or minus 4.5 per cent, or a 9 per cent variation. There was widespread agreement among EC officials and agricultural representatives that this potential 9 per cent variation was too wide to work alongside the CAP pricing system, as it would require large and continual MCA adjustments. This need for increased exchange rate stability was reinforced by the belief among economists and business leaders that growing intra-European trade flows would be disrupted by the potentially wide variance in European exchange rates.

Consequently, in March 1972, the six members of the EC and the three prospective members agreed to limit exchange rate fluctuations among the European currencies to plus or minus 1.123 per cent relative to one another. This became known as the 'snake in the tunnel' (or more formally, the European Common Margins Agreement). The snake was the European currencies fluctuating within a narrow range of plus or minus 2.25 per cent (the snake), against the wider world of 4.5 per cent (the tunnel). While the European currencies would continue to fluctuate against the US dollar and other non-European currencies within the wider band, their intra-European fluctuations would be decreased.

As can be seen from Table 6.1, the evolution of the snake in the 1970s did not bequeath Europe with solid foundations for EMU. Not only did the snake lose its tunnel when the European currencies accepted a joint float with the dollar in March 1973 but the snake soon mutated into little more than a Deutschmark zone (Tsoukalis 1997, 141–2). Concomitantly, there were frequent and large exchange rate adjustments and several countries showed schizophrenic tendencies by entering and then leaving the system. As a mid-1970s assessment of the prospects for EMU emphasised:

> Europe is no nearer to EMU than in 1969. In fact, if there has been an movement, it has been backward. The Europe of the 1960s represented a relatively harmonious and monetary entity which was undone in the course of recent years; national economic and monetary policies have never in 25 years been more discordant, more divergent, than they are today. (Commission of the European Communities 1975)

Table 6.1   Chronological history of the European Common Margins Agreement (the 'snake')

1972	24 Apr.	Basle Agreement enters into force; participants: Belgium, France, Germany, Italy, Luxembourg, the Netherlands.
	1 May	The UK and Denmark join
	23 May	Norway becomes associated
	23 June	The UK withdraws
	27 June	Denmark withdraws
	10 Oct.	Denmark returns
1973	13 Feb.	Italy withdraws
	19 Mar.	Transition to the joint float. Interventions to maintain fixed margins against the dollar ('tunnel') are discontinued. Sweden becomes associated
	3 Apr.	Establishment of a European Monetary Cooperation Fund is approved
	29 June	The DM is revalued by 5.5 per cent
	17 Sep.	The HFL is revalued by 5 per cent
	16 Nov.	The NKR is revalued by 5 per cent
1974	19 Jan.	France withdraws
1975	10 July	France returns
1976	15 Mar.	France withdraws again.
	17 Oct.	Agreement on exchange rate adjustment ('Frankfurt realignment'): the DKR is devalued by 6 per cent, the HFL and BLF by 2 per cent and the NKR and SKR are devalued by 5 per cent
1977	1 Apr.	The SKR is devalued by 6 per cent and the DKR and NKR are devalued by 3 per cent
	28 Aug.	Sweden withdraws, the DKR and NDR are devalued by 5 per cent
1978	13 Feb.	The NKR is devalued by 8 per cent
	17 Oct.	The DM is revalued by 4 per cent, the HFL and BLF by 2 per cent
	12 Dec.	Norway announces decision to withdraw
1979	13 Mar.	The European Monetary System becomes operational

Source: Gros and Thygesen (1992, 17).

It was perhaps unrealistic for the members of the snake to have expected anything less than disaster. As the previous chapter has shown, loose fiscal and monetary policies in several European countries in the mid-1970s were generating budget deficits and inflation. National governments ignored the prescriptions of the Werner Report for the harmonization of fiscal and monetary policies for domestic reasons and were able to do this because the authorities in Brussels did not have the jurisdiction to press for the necessary adjustments (Gros and Thygesen 1992). However, during the course of the succeeding four years, EMU once again became part of the EC's agenda. How can this revival of interest be explained?

The first stage was the initiative taken by the Dutch on assuming presidency of the EC in July 1976. To counter the violent movements in the lira and sterling which had occurred in the first half of the year, the Dutch government suggested that EC countries should move towards the adoption of so-called 'target zones' for their exchange rates. The idea was that countries would declare a zone within which they were aiming to contain their trade-weighted exchange rate and if the rate moved outside the declared zone, there would be consultation at the EC level. While this proposal was rejected by Germany, the Council of Ministers encouraged the Commission, the Committee of Governors and the Monetary Committee to extend their consultation on exchange rate matters.

Second, the political climate was beginning to change, which slowly added momentum to the process (Ludlow 1982). The centre right coalition in France was re-elected following the national parliamentary election in March 1978. This allowed President Valéry Giscard d'Estaing to continue with the Plan Barre which was designed to stabilise the French economy. Germany was encouraged by this development and, coupled to the growing conflicts with the US, Chancellor Helmut Schmidt sought to establish a firmer and wider alliance within the EC. Chancellor Schmidt also recognised that political developments in Italy, where the Communist Party was brought into the government's parliamentary majority, called for a wider, more stable European political and economic framework. Schmidt later recalled that 'I had always regarded the EMS not only as a mere instrument to harmonise the economic policies of the EC member countries, but also as part of a broader strategy for political self-determination in Europe' (Fratianni and von Hagen 1992, 17–18).

Consequently, Germany became keener to link the Deutschmark to as many of the individually floating major EC currencies as possible, thereby insulating the German economy from the effects of a renewed dollar depreciation. While the UK favoured a more global approach, the dollar's instability and the political inclination of France and Germany concentrated discussions on a regional solution to exchange rate instability. Both France and Germany were more realistic than the British in making the assumption that the prospect of a reformed international monetary system was remote, although the British President of the European Commission, Roy Jenkins, was the catalyst for the relaunching of monetary integration. Thus the relaunching of monetary union in the late-1970s combined political and economic factors. On a political level, Germany felt unease after the Bonn summit in July 1978 that the US had abdicated its role of Western leadership and something had to be done to fill the vacuum. On the macroeconomic level, Germany and France, in particular, wanted exchange rate stability to be backed by an increased convergence between national economies with greater emphasis placed on control of inflation.

The EMS was intended by the Commission and the main participants to lead on to a full exchange rate mechanism from which would emerge a European Monetary Fund (or European Central Bank). The European Monetary Fund would ultimately replace the European Monetary Cooperation Fund and manage the combined foreign exchange rate reserves of the members, to intervene in currency markets and to create ecu (European Currency Unit) reserves to serve as European SDRs. When domestic policies threatened currency pegs, strong-currency countries would expand and weak-currency countries would contract. Those that agreed to be part of the ERM would be required to have their currencies held within 2.25 per cent bands (those countries in a weak financial position were allowed to operate wider 6 per cent bands for a transitional period). Capital controls were permitted to allow governments to negotiate realignments while providing them with a degree of policy autonomy.

While eight of the nine EC countries participated in the EMS from the beginning, only Britain decided not to join the ERM. For the majority of the EC, the time was now ripe to proceed to the next level of EMU.

The EMS, 1979–1989

In 1979, many observers would not have predicted the longevity of the ERM given Europe's chequered history with regional integration. The durability of the system rests on two crucial developments in the 1980s: first, that the mechanism to deal with exchange rate instability strengthened during the first half of the 1980s, largely as a response to the US policy of 'benign neglect' towards the dollar; and second, because there was a promise of further political integration (James 1996). Yet as this section will show, this does not imply that only membership of the ERM offered economic success during the 1980s. For one thing, the ERM allowed countries to follow a gradualist approach rather than shock therapy, which throws into question the claims that the mechanism was a disciplinary device making a less costly disinflation possible than other exchange rate regimes. Moreover, pegged exchange rates can only be sustained if shocks requiring frequent and sizeable relative price adjustments are infrequent; if individual wages and prices adjust smoothly; or if changes in nominal exchange rates are allowed in the event of exceptional shocks. As we shall see, the first two conditions were not met, while by the late-1980s the authorities traded the third condition for the added credibility of a fixed exchange rate system, hoping that infrequent shocks and tranquil domestic adjustments would follow (Eichengreen and Wyplosz 1993). Unfortunately, they did not, as the events of August 1992 made clear.

Before the 1980s, it was argued that higher inflation in some European countries (France, Italy and the UK) had resulted from credibility problems, that is, the governments in these countries lacked a commitment to monetary discipline. As the previous chapter has shown, in the 1970s there was a variety of incentives for governments to inflate such as domestic political pressure, strong trade unions and expansionary government policies. To this extent, Giavazzi and Giovannini (1989, 85) have described the EMS as 'an arrangement for France and Italy to purchase a commitment to low inflation by accepting German monetary policy'. But how does the EMS provide commitment for disinflation?

Frattiani and von Hagen (1992) have summarised the literature in this area into disciplinary and cooperative interpretations of the EMS. The former interpretation stresses the strong 'spillover effects' which stem from the presence of the Bundesbank in the system, while the latter assumes that monetary policies were formed as a joint effort of member governments. The cooperative approach is expected to maximise the role of domestic policies and subsequently, domestic shocks, in determining the success of the domestic disinflation policy in the high-inflation countries of the EMS. In contrast, the disciplinary approach is expected to maximise the role of the German monetary policy, and subsequently German monetary shocks in determining the success of the domestic disinflation policy in the high-inflation countries of the EMS.

There are strong points that argue for the validity of both approaches. The establishment of the EMS was the result of efforts of a number of countries that aimed at establishing joint monetary policy as the outcome of a cooperative decisionmaking process of all member countries. Indeed, some authors (Melitz 1988; Fratianni and von Hagen 1992) are of the opinion that the EMS was characterised by cooperation in terms of monetary policies. However, advocates of the disciplinary view recall that previous fixed exchange rate arrangements were characterised by a hegemonic solution in which one country, usually the largest one, independently determined monetary policy for the system as a whole.

Similar to the position of the Great Britain in the classical gold-standard period, or the United States in the Bretton Woods period, Germany in the EMS is seen as the hegemonic country, the inflationary anchor of the system. Giavazzi and Giovannini (1989, 195) have declared that the EMS 'has worked effectively as a DM-zone' and assert that 'Germany by and large has retained the ability to set monetary policy independently'.

From a practical standpoint, it is possible for the German dominance to arise within the EMS. If there is a fixed exchange rate arrangement among n countries, there are only $n-1$ exchange rates to be fixed. Thus, assuming that $n-1$ countries exhibit monetary policy aimed at maintaining the pegged exchange rate, then the nth country could pursue an independent monetary policy. The arguments for the German hegemonic role centre around the size of the German economy and the high credibility of the Bundesbank. As Barro and Gordon (1983) have shown, the credibility of the monetary authority is crucial in determining the inflationary trend in a country. It is, therefore, plausible to perceive a scenario in which countries with traditionally higher inflation, by joining the EMS, actually delegated part of their monetary autonomy to the Bundesbank and achieved lower inflation in return. As Thygesen suggests (1988, 5–6):

> By pegging to the less inflationary currencies over long intervals, with the prospect that they cannot fully devalue in accordance with their excess inflation on the infrequent occasions of a realignment, the authorities of the weaker currencies gain credibility for their disinflationary stance.

If the EMS is an asymmetric system, and Germany is the nth country in the system able to determine its monetary policy unilaterally, there is still an incentive for Germany to be a member of the ERM and not 'go it alone' outside the mechanism. As Melitz (1988) has argued, Germany gains from membership of the ERM because between realignments Germany's competitiveness improves. These competitiveness gains were not eliminated, as the exchange rate realignments in the other ERM member countries were not large enough to completely offset inflation rate differentials between them and Germany.

However, the view that the EMS is a highly asymmetric system dominated by Germany has attracted a number of criticism in recent years. The leading opponents of the thesis, Fratianni and von Hagen (1992) use a vector autoregressive model to estimate cross-country monetary base growth rates and rely on Granger causality tests. They refute the hypothesis of German dominance, concluding that the EMS 'appears to be more interactive than hierarchical', although 'asymmetries exist in the system' (Fratianni and von Hagen 1992, 89). The main asymmetry is German long-run monetary independence.

De Grauwe's (1991) investigation into whether the EMS had developed into a Deutschmark zone during the 1980s led him to focus on the effect of speculative disturbances on interest rates. If the EMS had developed into an asymmetric system then speculative disturbances would have no impact on German interest rates and only the weak country's interest rate would increase. *Per contra*, if the EMS had operated symmetrically, the speculative disturbances would lead to a decline in Germany's interest rate and a rise in the weak country's rate of interest. If the weak country had effective exchange and capital controls then it could avoid changes in its money supply and interest rates following the emergence of speculative pressures. In this case, such controls would generate a *de facto* symmetry in the system even though Germany pursued independent monetary policies. The system's asymmetry would re-emerge if speculative pressures were to persist and intensify as exchange and capital controls could not insulate the weak country indefinitely.

De Grauwe examined the behaviour of the onshore (domestic) and offshore interest rates for a number of countries during the 1980s. He found that when there were periods of foreign exchange market turmoil, the offshore interest rate was more variable in France, Italy and Belgium while the domestic rates were largely unaffected as exchange and capital controls insulated against speculative disturbances. While Giavazzi and Giovannini (1989) have argued that Germany was the only member country in the EMS whose domestic monetary conditions were relatively unaffected by the events originating from other member countries, De Grauwe found that in the case of the Netherlands, speculative disturbances resulted in both Dutch and German domestic interest rates adjusting. De Grauwe also found that the French and Belgian interest rates were significant in explaining the German interest rate. Neither finding supports a German dominance thesis and De Grauwe concluded against the proposition that Germany dominated monetary policy in the EMS, transforming the system into a Deutschmark zone.

As to the success of the disinflation policy within countries of the EMS, even the leading proponents have been able to isolate only 'very weak evidence of a shift in expectations associated with the institution of the EMS' (ibid., 196). De Grauwe (1990) was equally unsuccessful in detecting an impact on inflation expectations in EMS member countries following the introduction of the system. Table 6.2 reports his finding based on the 'misery index' (the sum of unemployment and inflation rates) in comparing the costs of the reduction of inflation during the 1980s in EMS countries and in countries outside the system.

Table 6.2 Misery index in OECD countries

	1974–1979	1980–1988	Index of centralisation of wage bargaining*
EMS countries			
Belgium	13.7	16.1	8
Germany	8.1	9.9	6
Denmark	16.3	15.9	4
France	15.7	16.8	11
Italy	23.3	21.1	13
Netherlands	12.5	15.2	7
Average	14.9	15.8	
Non-EMS countries			
Australia	17.8	16.2	10
Austria	7.9	7.3	1
Canada	15.9	15.8	17
Switzerland	4.5	4.0	15
Finland	17.5	12.6	5
United Kingdom	19.9	17.2	12
Japan	11.4	4.8	14
Norway	10.4	11.0	2
New Zealand	14.9	16.7	9
Sweden	11.9	10.7	3
United States	14.7	12.8	16
Average	13.7	11.7	

Note: *Countries are ranked from high (1) to low (17).

Source: De Grauwe (1990, 157).

These findings show that the misery index was on average higher in the EMS countries than in the non-EMS countries during both periods. More specifically, the average EMS misery index increased during the 1980s, whereas it declined in the non-EMS countries. De Grauwe's analysis extends the findings of Collins (1988) who agreed that there is no overwhelming evidence that the EMS members performed substantially better than non-EMS members in decreasing inflation rates in the period under consideration.

Moreover, as Dornbusch (1989) and Giovanni (1990) among others have argued, the EMS forces countries who wanted to disinflate to choose a gradual approach. In contrast to the UK and the US who let their exchange rates float, the EMS countries could not use 'shock therapy'. Shock therapy has the advantage of establishing the anti-inflation reputation of the authorities, thereby leading to a quicker reduction of inflationary expectations. In the EMS arrangement, gradualism has the disadvantage that the authorities gain an anti-inflation reputation slowly, with the result that inflationary expectations decline only slowly. Concomitantly, this forces the authorities to apply deflationary policies for a longer period than if they had used shock therapy.

The persistence of inflation differentials across EMS countries during the first half of the 1980s meant that there was a need for exchange rate realignments. As can be seen from Table 6.3, there were eleven EMS realignments from the inception of the EMS to January 1987 and a twelfth on 8 January 1990, when the Italian lira's wide band was replaced with the narrow EMS band. What becomes clear from this table is that over half the realignments for the entire period were clustered around the first five years of the EMS.

With the second oil shock which raised inflation, coupled to the deteriorating current accounts, stagnating output and rising unemployment in European countries, it was perhaps surprising that the ERM did manage to survive the first five years. Although the realignments were frequent, they were not always large enough to offset inflationary differentials with Germany. While the divergences which began after the first oil shock have not been eliminated, Figure 6.1 shows that from the mid-1980s, there was a greater convergence of inflation rates.

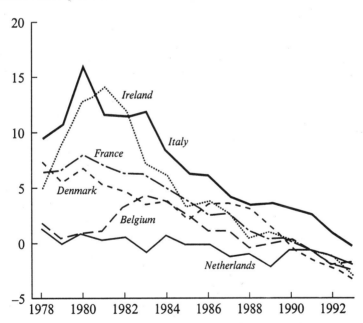

Note: *Difference between national and German CPI inflation rates.

Source: OECD, *Main Economic Indicators*.

*Figure 6.1 Inflation convergence in the EMS, 1978-1993**

Table 6.3 *EMS realignments and selected policy changes, 1979–1990*

Year	Date	Event
1979	13 Mar.	**EMS**: ERM starts to operate; initial currency weights in ecu currency basket: DM 32.0%, FF 19.0%, UKL 15.0%, LIT 10.2%, HFL 10.1%, BF 8.5%, DKR 2.7%, DRA 1.3%, IRL 1.2%
	24 Sep.	**EMS**: realignment (DM +2%, DKR −2.9%)
	30 Nov.	**EMS**: realignment (DKR−4.8%) **Denmark**: short-term price and wage freeze
1981	9 Mar.	**Belgian–Luxembourg Economic Union (BLEU)**: convention for BLEU (fixed parity without bands) renewed for 10 years
	22 Mar.	**EMS**: realignment (LIT−6%) **Italy**: government spending cut plans
	July	**Italy**: Banca d'Italia freed from the obligation to purchase unsold public debt at the Treasury auctions, which gave the government preferential access to monetizing fiscal deficits
	July	**Netherlands**: the Nederlandsche Bank abandons control of domestic liquidity and gears its monetary policy towards the external constraint, in particular the DM exchange rate
	5 Oct.	**EMS**: realignment (DM +5.5%, FF −3%, LIT −3%, HFL +3.5%) **France**: temporary price and profit freeze
1982	22 Feb.	**EMS**: realignment (BF −8.5%, DKR −3%) **Belgium**: general price freeze until end of March, selective freeze thereafter; freeze of wage indexation (until May); also longer-run measures to impede complete wage indexation
	25 Mar.	**Ireland**: tight budget by Fianna Fail government; initiation of an austerity and fiscal consolidation programme
	14 June	**EMS**: realignment (DM +4.25%, FF −5.75%, LIT −2.75%, HFL +4.25%) **France**: temporary freeze of prices, wages, rents and dividends until October; reduction in 1983 budget deficit plans
	23 June	**Italy**: announcement of budgetary austerity measures
	21 Oct.	**Ireland**: proposal for elimation of budget deficits by 1986
	16 Oct.	**Denmark**: comprehensive stabilisation package: automatic wage indexation suspended; wage freeze until March1983; tight fiscal policy; progressive dismantling of capital controls
	30 Dec.	**Belgium**: selective price freeze extended until end of 1983; wage restraint (flat rate indexation) until the end of 1984
1983	21 Mar.	**EMS**: realignment (DM +5.5%, FF −2.5%, LIT −2.5%, HFL +3.5%, BF +1.5%, DKR +2.5%, IRL −2.5%)
	28 Mar.	**France**: stringent austerity programme aiming at bringing down inflation via monetary restraint. restoring external balance via foreign exchange controls and reducing the public budget deficit by cutting expenditures and raising taxes
	12 Apr.	**Denmark**: government announces further liberalisation of capital movements to take place on 1 May
	April	**Denmark**: government guidelines for an upper limit of 2% for the annual wage increase in the new two-year wage agreement
	Dec.	**EC**: target dates for the expiry of capital restrictions set for France (end of 1986) Italy and Ireland (end of 1987) in order to allow for a gradual relaxation of the controls
1984	17 Sep.	**EMS**: revision of currency weights in ecu currency basket (DM 32.0%, FF 19.0%, UKL 15.0%, LIT 10.2%, HFL 10.1%, BF 8.5%, DKR 2.7%, DRA 1.3%, IRL 1.2%)

Year	Date	Event
1985	1 Jan.	**France**: start of a two-year transition of monetary policy operating procedures from quantitative credit controls to a more market-based system of reserve requirements
	12 Mar.	**EMS**: Council of Central Bank Governors decides on a package to strengthen role of the ecu in the EMS
	April	**Denmark**: government enforces a 2% legal upper limit for the annual wage increase in the new two-year wage agreement
	22 July	**EMS**: realignment (DM +2%, FF +2%, LIT −6%, HFL +2%, BL +2%, DKR +2%, IRL +2%)
	July	**Italy**: announcement of revenue-raising measures to contain the increase in the budget deficit
1986		**Italy**: modification of wage indexation mechanism, *scala mobile*
	Feb.	**EC**: European Single Act sets 31 December 1992 as target date for completion of internal market with free movement of goods, persons, services and capital
	17 Apr.	**EMS**: realignment (DM +3%, FF −3%, HFL+3%, BF +1%, DKR +1%)
		France: steps to slow nominal wage growth; plans to reduce government budget deficit; relaxation of exchange controls
	June	**Denmark**: wage indexation law (suspended 1982) is abolished
	4 Aug.	**EMS**: realignment (IRL −8%)
		Ireland: sharp monetary tightening to offset the destabilising effects of British pound sterling weakness
1987	12 Jan.	**EMS**: realignment (DM +3%, HFL +3%, BF +2%, DKR +2%)
	12 Sep.	**EMS**: Basle–Nyborg Agreement of the Committee of Central Bank Governors to strengthen the exchange rate mechanism of the EMS; measures include a wider use of fluctuation bands, an extension of the very short-run financing facilities and the use of ecu for inframarginal intervention.
1989	17 Apr.	**EMS**: Delors Committee Report proposes a three-stage transition to Economic and Monetary Union: stage 1: extension of ERM to all EMS member countries, reduction of fluctuation bands to narrow range, infrequent realignments subject to mutual agreement, full capital mobility; stage 2: creation of new Community institution, increasing coordination of national monetary policies; stage 3a: irrevocably fixed exchange rates without bands, new Community institutions (EuroFed) functioning: stage 3b: single currency monetary union at a later date
	19 June	**EMS**: Spain enters the exchange rate mechanism of the EMS with a wide fluctuation margin of ±6%
	27 June	**EMS**: European Council decision to enter the first stage of EMU from the Delors Committee Report on 1 July 1990
	21 Sep.	**EMS**: revision of currency weights in ecu currency basket (DM 30.1%, FF 19.0%, UKL 13.0%, LIT 10.15%, HFL 9.4%, BF 7.9%, PES 3%, DKR 2.45%, IRL 1.1%, DRA 0.8%, ESC 0.8%)

Notes: At realignments, + (−) indicate a revaluation (devaluation) in % against those currencies whose bilateral parities remained unchanged, except for the two general realignments (March 1983, July 1985), for which the percentages from the official communiqué are shown.

Source: Weber (1991).

157

Further evidence on the interaction between exchange rate changes and inflation can be found in Table 6.4, which reports the annual rates of change in unit labour costs and the annual rates of change in the franc–mark and lira–mark exchange rates. Up to 1986, large exchange rate depreciations in France and Italy accompanied large divergences in the growth rates of unit labour costs relative to Germany. In France, there was a major increase in the minimum wage, a shortening of the working week and a fiscal stimulus after the socialist government took office in 1981. This was accompanied by a big devaluation so that *in toto*, between March 1979 and March 1983, the central rate of the Deutschmark against the French franc rose by 33 per cent. While the Italian authorities announced several austerity measures in 1981–82 (Table 6.3), some authors have pointed out that this did not justify the large devaluations of the lira (Gros and Thygesen 1992, 81). Moreover, as Table 6.5 shows, the stabilisation of exchange rates has been accompanied by a loss in competitiveness relative to Germany which, in the case of Italy, was due to both a rapid rise in relative wages and an appreciating exchange rate.

Table 6.4   *Changes in unit labour costs and in the exchange rate, France and Italy relative to Germany, 1980–1989 (percentages)*

	France and Germany		*Italy and Germany*	
	Relative unit labour costs[a]	*Exchange rate*[b]	*Relative unit labour costs*[a]	*Exchange rate*[b]
1980	6.9	−0.7	12.3	2.3
1981	8.0	10.6	16.9	12.0
1982	8.3	11.0	13.4	8.3
1983	8.3	8.3	14.9	5.7
1984	5.2	−0.6	8.1	0.9
1985	2.8	0.8	6.4	10.9
1986	−0.4	8.3	2.9	2.6
1987	−0.4	1.5	4.3	5.7
1988	0.8	0.8	5.9	−0.8

Notes:
a. The change in relative unit labour costs is the difference between the growth rate of unit labour costs in each country and that in Germany.
b. The change in the exchange rate is the annual rate of change of the franc–mark and lira–mark exchange rates.

Source: Giovannini (1990, 235).

Despite the poor outlook for economic growth in the recessionary conditions of the early 1980s, Western Europe subsequently experienced nearly a decade of unbroken growth, weak at first in 1982–83, but averaging about 2.5 per cent (of GDP) a year over 1984–87 and then rising to 3 per cent or more in the latter years of the 1980s. Unemployment remained stubbornly high, however, and there was a growing belief that unless the flexibility and efficiency of the labour market was improved, 'Eurosclerosis' would inevitably slow down the growth momentum.

Table 6.5   Adjusted relative wages and terms of trade, France and Italy relative to Germany, 1979–1989 (ratio)

	France and Germany		*Italy and Germany*	
	Relative wages[a]	*Terms of trade[b]*	*Relative wages[a]*	*Terms of trade[b]*
1979	98.6	103.0	90.5	97.4
1980	104.8	100.0	97.8	100.0
1981	108.7	101.3	106.1	98.9
1982	105.1	100.3	108.5	101.3
1983	102.8	100.2	117.4	103.4
1984	105.3	100.9	122.2	104.2
1985	109.3	103.0	123.6	104.1
1986	104.1	102.0	121.3	105.6
1987	99.7	98.4	121.4	104.3
1988	99.9	98.8	126.9	104.5

Notes:
a. Adjusted relative wages are the ratio of adjusted wage shares (total economy) in GDP, multiplied by the (exchange rate adjusted) ratio of GDP deflators, for France and Italy relative to Germany.
b. Terms of trade are the ratio of export unit values to import unit values, indexed with 1982=100, for France and Italy relative to Germany.

Source: Giovannini (1990, 237).

This fear, coupled to the reduced number of realignments in the EMS after 1983 and falling inflation rates, edged several European governments to begin a renewed drive for European integration.

This drive culminated in the 1986 Single European Act which sought to create an integrated market, free of obstacles to the unimpeded movement of commodities, capital and labour by the end of 1992. Proponents of the Act argued that eliminating currency conversion costs was the only way of removing hidden barriers to internal economic flows, while abolishing the opportunity for countries to manipulate their exchange rates would prevent protectionist opposition to the liberalisation of trade. Consequently, the Act contained a reference to the October 1972 statement by heads of state and government approving the objective of economic and monetary union; this was followed by the setting up of the Delors Committee to examine how a single currency could be achieved within ten years.

Unlike the Werner Report, the Delors Report (Committee for the Study of Economic and Monetary Union 1989) recommended that capital controls should be abolished at the start of the transition to monetary union and that a centralised institution, the European Central Bank, should be responsible for executing the common monetary policy and for issuing a single European currency. As for fiscal policy, the Report did not propose transferring control of national budgets to the EC, but recommended rules imposing a ceiling on budget deficits and excluding governments' access to direct central bank credit and other forms of money financing.

Concurrent to the moves towards EMU, the ERM had also evolved from the mid-1980s. After the general realignment of parities in July 1985, and the devaluation of the French franc in 1986, 1987 marked the end of the 'old EMS' with a new realignment (Giavazzi and Spaventa 1990). The authorities argued that this realignment was necessary because of the declining dollar and self-fulfilling speculative expectations. What followed was a revision of EMS arrangements to strengthen intervention and to encourage policy coordination, with the resulting Basle–Nyborg Agreement in September 1987 allowing for the support of intermarginal intervention through Very Short-term Financing (VSTF) and lengthening VSTF from one to three-and-a-half months. This agreement provided for small realignments more frequently, but apart from the 1990 realignment of the lira, this option was discarded by policymakers (Eichengreen and Wyplosz 1993). Consequently, by the start of the 1990s, the evolution of the EMS was about to take another turn which few saw at the time.

The breakdown of the ERM, 1990–1993

With hindsight, it is now clear that the apogee of the ERM was reached in the final years of the 1980s. Not only had the major participants achieved a substantial reduction in exchange rate variability over the 1980s, but the credibility of the mechanism steadily increased throughout its first ten years (Giavazzi and Giovannini 1989). By 1 July 1990, most members of the EMS had removed exchange and capital controls (Table 6.6). Ironically, it was the removal of capital controls as part of the requirement of fulfilling the Single European Act which fatally undermined the viability of the 'old' EMS.

Table 6.6 EMS realignments and selected policy changes, 1990–1997

Year	Month	Event
1990	Jan.	EMS: realignment (LIT –3.7%), narrowing of band to ±2.25%
	June	Belgium: central bank declares German mark exchange rate as its main official policy target
	1 July	EMS: complete removal of all capital controls except for Ireland, Spain, Portugal and Greece (deadline 1992)
	1 July	Germany: monetary union between West and East Germany
	3 Oct.	Germany: six East German federal states join the Federal Republic of Germany
	8 Oct.	UK: Sterling enters the exchange rate mechanism of the EMS with a wide fluctuation margin of ±6%
1991	Dec.	EC: Heads of states and government of the EC decided, in Maastricht, to create the Economic and Monetary Union no later than 1999
1992	Apr.	Portugal: ESC enters the exchange rate mechanism of the EMS with a wide fluctuation margin of ±6%
	16 Sep.	EMS: £ and LIT withdraw from the exchange rate mechanism, realignment of PES (–5%)
	22 Nov.	EMS: Portugal realigns (–6%); Spain shifts its ERM band (by 6%)
	10 Dec.	EMS: Norway abandons its ecu peg
1993	30 Jan.	EMS: Irish punt devalued by 10%
	May	EMS: Realignment of PES and ESC; Danes vote for Maastricht in second referendum
	1 Aug.	EMS: Extension of the system to ±15% with the exception of DM and HFL which continue with a narrow fluctuation margin of ±2.25%
	Nov.	Maastricht Treaty enters into force; composition of ecu basket frozen
1994	1 Jan.	EMS: Stage 2 of EMU begins; the European Monetary Institute (EMI) is set up as a forerunner of the European Central Bank; member states strive to fulfil convergence criteria; final deadline of 1 January 1999 agreed for beginning Stage 3 of EMU, regardless of the number of member states qualifying and of general economic climate
1995	Jan.	EMS: Austria enters the exchange rate mechanism of the EMS
		EC: Austria, Sweden and Finland join EU
	Mar.	EMS: Realignment of PES and ESC
	Dec.	EC: The name 'Euro' agreed for the single currency
1996	14 Oct.	EMS: Finland enters the exchange rate mechanism of the EMS
	25 Nov.	EMS: LIT re-enters the ERM
	Dec.	EC: Agreement reach on stability and growth pact, setting the framework for the coordination of the single currency
1997	May	EC: New uncertainty over EMU focusing on stability and growth pact
	Sep.	EC: Finance ministers agree to fix bilateral conversion rates between participating countries in advance, when qualifying countries chosen in May 1998; EMU effectively to start six months in advance
	Oct.	UK is unlikely to enter EMU before 2002/3

Source: Weber (1991) and updated from various issues of OECD *Economic Survey.*

As is well known, the old EMS was a mixture of pegged and adjustable exchange rate regimes. Periods of exchange rate stability provided many of the benefits of fixed exchange rates and the realignments readdressed serious competitiveness problems. The periods of exchange rate stability with the occasional realignment were only possible, however, because capital controls protected central banks' reserves against speculative attacks driven by anticipations of realignment (Eichengreen 1993a). In the first ten years of the existence of the EMS, the authorities did at least retain limited policy autonomy. Yet the 'new' ERM was described by some economists as 'half-baked' (Walters 1988) and Tommaso Padoa-Schioppa (1988) pointed out that there was now an 'inconsistent quartet' of policy objectives: free trade, capital mobility, fixed (managed) exchange rates and independent monetary policies. Thus Spain, the UK and Portugal all joined the ERM just when the system became more volatile but appeared more stable. While the strategy of no realignments and no controls did seem to work for a while, the Jeremiah's predictions eventually unfolded during the early 1990s.

On 3 June 1992, sterling, the Italian lira, the French franc and the Danish krone all came under pressure in foreign exchange markets. Italy raised its interest rate on 5 June, and in the succeeding weeks the lira was allowed to depreciate against the DM within the narrow band, while the Italian authorities intervened heavily in the foreign-exchange market. Despite these measures, speculation continued and intensified on the Italian currency. While the initial EMS agreement did commit central banks to unlimited intervention when currencies reached their fluctuation margins (which was further strengthened by the Basle–Nyborg Agreement), there had not been a case when this commitment was tested. An emergency meeting of the Bundesbank Council on 11 September proposed a package of measures with the Italian government in which the lira would be devalued by 3 per cent and the Deutschmark revalued by 3 per cent against the other EMS currencies. As this was a *de facto* devaluation of all currencies relative to the Deutschmark, these measures were rejected by France (which had a crucial referendum pending on the Maastricht Treaty) and the UK (Prime Minister John Major argued that sterling's parity was correctly valued). Italy was forced to go it alone and devalued by 7 per cent on 13 September and was forced out of the ERM on 17 September.

Following the devaluation of the lira, the speculative pressures on sterling grew in intensity. Given the UK's long opposition to ERM entry (mainly because of ideological reasons espoused by Margaret Thatcher) there had been a question mark over the seriousness of the Conservative government's commitment to the system. This credibility was further undermined by

Margaret Thatcher (1993, 723), who made it clear that membership would not be 'at the expense of domestic monetary conditions' and upon entry, demanded that interest rates were cut by one percentage point.

Whether the pound was overvalued when it entered the ERM is a moot point which has already led to several academic studies into the question. In the year leading up to entry, work carried out at the National Institute of Economic and Social Research used the concept of fundamental equilibrium exchange rates to suggest that a lower entry rate might have been appropriate (Wren-Lewis 1990; Wren-Lewis et al. 1990). This analytical framework was developed by John Williamson (1983), who used it to support the arguments of the National Institute team that sterling was between 10 and 15 per cent overvalued upon entry into the ERM (Williamson 1991; Wren-Lewis, et al. 1991).

Those who opposed this view argued that analysis based on purchasing power parity (PPP) indicated either that sterling had entered at the 'right rate' (Davies 1990), or that sterling was undervalued when it joined the ERM (Brittan 1995). When challenged about the rate of entry by a member of the Treasury and Civil Service Committee on 5 December 1990, Chancellor Norman Lamont defended the rate of entry and argued that 'the 2.95 rate is, of course, very close to the average real exchange rate against the Deutschmark over the last 10 years' (Lamont 1990, 30).

Unfortunately, the timing of the British entry also coincided with the start of a major recession. On 2 January 1991, Alan Walters (1991) argued that membership of the ERM was exacerbating a recession and that 'the only feasible, let alone humane, policy is to engineer a substantial devaluation of sterling'. However, while interest rates were gradually reduced, it was only a matter of time before Britain's commitment to the ERM would be severely challenged. During the summer of 1992, when the Bundesbank raised interest rates to curb post-unification inflation in Germany, the UK authorities simply tried to wait until the tensions in the mechanism had eased. The authorities repeatedly ruled out devaluation and refused to raise interest rates, which gave confusing signals to the financial markets.

By the end of August 1992, it was estimated that the Bank of England had used at least $1.3 billion of reserves to prevent sterling falling through the floor of its wide band, while during the first week in September, it borrowed $14.5 billion to finance further intervention. On 16 September, the Bank of England extended its support for sterling, by reportedly using half its total foreign exchange reserves. The discount rate was raised from 10 to 15 per cent, but these measures were not sufficient to stem the orgy of speculation which was only quelled when sterling withdrew from the ERM on the same day.

After the exit of the UK, Chancellor Lamont (1992, 6) told the Treasury Select Committee that 'the Italians had devalued on the Monday and had been under intense pressure ever since and, frankly, the game was up by Wednesday and we had no option but to withdraw'. With hindsight, it is difficult to envisage what other policy the British government could have implemented other than withdrawal from the ERM in the autumn of 1992. During the summer of 1992, the pound was not that far off the central rate within the ERM (DM2.90–2.91/£) and there was widespread agreement that interest rates were too high. Although Cobham (1997) has suggested that a rise in UK interest rates in mid-July would have indicated unequivocally the UK's commitment to the mechanism, such a decision would have been over-zealous. Given that the economy was in recession, higher interest rates would have been polit-ically insensitive and economically absurd. After all, over the period since October 1990 inflation had fallen from nearly 11 per cent to less than 4 per cent; interest rates had been cut from 15 per cent to 10 per cent and Britain's trade performance had improved.

However, as Table 6.7 shows, it is not clear from data on unit labour costs and producer prices that sterling was overvalued. Among the other members of the ERM, Italy post-1987 shows an obvious deterioration in competitiveness; Germany's labour costs rose but she did not suffer a speculative attack and there is little in the table which justifies the attacks on the French franc, Belgian franc, Danish krone and Irish punt in the wake of Britain's exit from the ERM. As Eichengreen (1996, 177) notes, the evidence for Spain and Portugal is less clear-cut as both countries experienced more inflation than their ERM partners, but this was to be expected of rapidly growing countries moving into the production of higher-value goods.

Some authors have suggested that the foreign exchange market turbu-lence which led to the September 1992 episode reflected the failure of the ERM member countries to agree after Germany's unification in 1990 on a policy course which would have been consistent with maintaining the cred-ibility of the EMS (Branson 1994). The ERM member countries did not accept that the mark should appreciate, despite the opinion of economists. With the appreciation of the mark ruled out, adjustment to the asymmet-ric shock of Germany's unification had then to involve the revaluation of the mark through an increase in Germany's rate of inflation relative to the rate of inflation in the other ERM member countries. This was effectively achieved through a small rise in Germany's rate of inflation and a fall in the inflation rates of other ERM member countries. In other words, Germany forced the other ERM countries to deflate. Eichengreen and Wyplosz (1993) have presented evidence suggesting that apart from Italy,

Table 6.7 Indicators of cumulative competitiveness changes, 1987–August 1992 (percentages)

	Relative to other EC countries[a]		Relative to industrial countries	
	Producer prices	Unit labour costs[b]	Producer prices	Unit labour costs[b]
Belgium	4.0	5.6	1.3	2.7
Denmark	3.6	6.4	–0.5	3.8
Germany (Western)	1.7	0.5	–3.8	–5.5
Greece	n.a	n.a	–10.2	–15.6
France	7.9	13.3	3.3	7.2
Ireland	6.4	35.7	1.3	27.9
Italy	–0.3	–7.0	–6.4	–9.8
Netherlands	1.5	5.2	–1.4	1.9

From ERM entry-August 1992[c]

Spain	–2.1	–7.5	–8.1	–13.8
Portugal	n.a	–4.6	n.a	–6.9
United Kingdom	–1.7	–0.4	–4.0	8.3

Notes:
a. Excluding Greece.
b. Manufacturing sector.
c. Spain = June 1989; Portugal = April 1992; UK = October 1990.

Source: Eichengreen (1996, 176).

the other ERM members had already moved a long way towards adjusting to the unification shock by September 1992; moreover, a time span of two years had elapsed between Germany's unification and the events of September 1992, and this cannot be considered an adequate explanation of the upheaval in 1992 of the intra-European exchange rates.

Perhaps a more satisfactory explanation which can explain the turmoil on the foreign exchanges between June 1992 and early August 1993 is the theory of self-fulfilling speculative attacks. The work of Flood and Garber (1984) and Obstfeld (1986) has shown that there exist multiple equilibria in foreign-exchange markets. Although the prevailing exchange rate may be perfectly consistent with economic fundamentals, a self-fulfilling speculative attack may shift the exchange rate to a different equilibrium value. The speculative attack then induces the country whose currency has been devalued to adopt more expansionary fiscal and monetary policies.

As numerous authors have argued (Eichengreen and Wyplosz 1993; Rose and Svennsson 1994; Obstfeld 1996), the Maastricht Treaty provided such an environment conducive to self-fulfilling speculative attacks. One of the criteria that the Treaty outlines is if countries are to qualify for membership of the monetary union then their currencies have to be within the ERM's narrow band without severe tension for at least two years. The Treaty suggested that the third and final stage should begin any time after 1 January 1994. Even if a country is following sound financial policies, an exchange rate crisis that forces it to devalue its currency could prevent it from qualifying for monetary union. The country will then have no incentive to continue with austere policies, and thus it will be likely to adopt more expansionary fiscal and monetary policies as the prospects of qualifying for membership of the monetary union become remote. Even in the absence of a speculative attack and assuming that the economic fundamentals are sound, once an attack occurs the government has an incentive to move towards expansionary macroeconomic policies, fulfilling speculators' expectations.

The Danish referendum on 2 June was the turning point in this instance, because the 'no' vote raised serious questions about whether the Maastricht Treaty would come into effect. If the Treaty was abandoned, the incentive for countries to hold their currencies within their ERM bands in order to qualify for monetary union would then be weakened, and high-debt countries like Italy would have less reason to cut their deficits. After the devaluation of the lira on 13 September 1992, the markets realised that changes in EMS exchange rates were still possible. Pressure mounted on Britain, Spain, Portugal and Italy until either a currency left the ERM (Italy and Britain) or until capital controls were tightened (Ireland, Spain and Portugal).

The following six months witnessed periods of instability on the foreign exchanges and the French franc came under renewed pressure at the end of 1992. Stability was returned in the foreign exchanges following a statement by the French and German authorities supporting their commitment to the prevailing exchange rate, and calm returned more generally following the endorsement of the Maastricht Treaty by the Danish electorate in May 1993. The French franc and other weak ERM currencies strengthened following the Bundesbank's decision to lower its discount and Lombard rates. As inflation in France was running below that of Germany, French officials suggested that the franc had assumed the role of anchor currency in the ERM and persuaded the Bank of France to reduce interest rates to alleviate high unemployment. The Bundesbank did not follow suit and when it finally cut its rate the reduction was very small. A scheduled Franco-German meeting to coordinate interest rate reductions was cancelled by German officials and the foreign-exchange markets became jittery. Speculative pressures on the ERM, particularly against the franc, developed during July 1993. On Friday 23 July, the Bank of France was forced to raise its interest rates sharply to prevent the franc falling through its ERM lower band. A coordinated statement by the German and French authorities could not contain the speculative pressure on the franc this time and the pressures peaked at the end of July 1993 with massive sales of French francs and also the Belgian franc, the Danish krone, the peseta and the escudo. This forced EC monetary officials to decide on 2 August against an exchange rate realignment but in favour of widening the permitted band of fluctuation from 2.25 per cent to 15 per cent.

As Eichengreen (1996, 175) notes, the irony was that European currencies were now set to float more freely than they had ever before under Bretton Woods, the snake and the central rates of the ERM.

The approach to EMU
With the advantage of five years of hindsight, the perverse outcome of the collapse of the ERM in 1993 was that it made monetary unification inevitable. In the 'old EMS', capital controls guarded central banks' reserves from speculators but once these had been abolished in the 'new EMS', the system collapsed. To resolve this problem, there were two solutions. One was to return to floating exchange rates. Arguably, with floating rates, countries can still integrate their economies while retaining monetary autonomy (for example, Canada, Mexico and the US in the North American Free Trade Area). However, in Europe the calls for greater exchange rate stability arose because of the problems associated with floating rates and the CAP, coupled to the *sentiment* that fixed rates are preferable to floating. The second solution was to fix irrevocably exchange rates between existing national currencies. Yet in this instance there will always be the possibility that exchange rates may change in the future under dire circumstances (the 'escape clause') and because such circumstances are often unobservable, nominal exchange rates may end up being destabilised (Obstfeld 1992). In short, an irrevocably fixed exchange rate system has less credibility than a system in which the countries share a common currency.

Stage Three of the Maastricht Treaty inaugurates monetary union. While the Treaty proposed that Stage Three should begin not earlier than 1 January 1997, the Madrid summit in 1995 recognised that 1999 was a more realistic date. To qualify for entry, the Maastricht Treaty cited four basic criteria as a guideline. Those countries which can satisfy the four entry criteria (which would be available by early 1998) would be allowed to proceed to monetary union (Table 6.8). The four necessary criteria do allow a degree of flexibility.

Table 6.8 EMU timetable post-1998

Year	Date	Event
1998	1 Jan.	UK presidency begins
	May	Probable Dutch General Election
	1 July	Deadline for the Council, in the composition of heads of state or government, to decide on initial members of the Euro-zone
		Austrian presidency begins
	Sep.	French election of the Senate
		Latest date for Danish Election
		Swedish General Election
	Oct.	German election of the Bundestag
	Year end	Appointment of Executive Board of the ECB
		Set the day for the introduction of Euro banknotes and coins
		Start production of Euro banknotes and coins
		Final preparation of the ECB/ESCB (adoption of a secondary legislation and rendering it operational)
1999	1 Jan.	Irrevocable fixing of the conversion rates and entry into force of legislation related to the introduction of the Euro (legal status, continuity of contracts, rounding, etc.)
		From this date: definition and execution of the single monetary policy into Euro
		Conduct of foreign exchange operations in Euro
		Operation of TARGET payment system
1998	1 Jan.	Issue new public debt in Euro
	May	Belgium General Election
	June	European Parliment Elections
		Luxembourg General Elections
		Portuguese General Election
	1 July	Finnish presidency begins
	Dec.	Austrian General Election
2000	1 Jan.	Start circulation of the Euro banknotes and coins and withdrawal of national banknotes and coins
		Portuguese presidency begins
	Mar.	Spanish elections
	1 July	Greek presidency begins
	Sept.	Greek General Election
2001	1 Jan.	Swedish presidency begins
	April	Latest date for Italian General Election
	1 July	Belgian presidency begins
2002	1 Jan.	Latest date for issue of Euro notes and coins
		Greek presidency begins
	30 June	Latest date for abolition of national notes and coins
	1 July	Danish presidency begins

Source: European Commission, various.

First, it is expected that the price performance is sustainable, with an average rate of inflation observed over a period of one year before the examination which does not exceed by more than 1.5 per cent that of, at most, the three best-performing member states in terms of price stability.

Second, it is expected that a government should not have an 'excessive' budget deficit. This will be assessed by reference to whether the ratio of the planned or actual government deficit to GDP exceeds 3 per cent, unless either the ratio has declined substantially and continuously and reached a level that comes close to this value; or alternatively, the excess over 3 per cent is only exceptional and temporary and the ratio remains close to this value. Second, whether the ratio of the government debt to GDP exceeds 60 per cent, unless the ratio is sufficiently diminishing and approaching this value at a satisfactory pace.

The third criterion is concerned with exchange rate stability and requires the observance of the normal fluctuation margins provided for by the ERM (for at least two years), without devaluing against the currency of any other member state, on its own initiative and without severe tensions.

Finally, it is expected that for one year before the examination, a member state must have an average nominal long-term interest rate that does not exceed by more than 2 percentage points that of, at most, the three best performing member states in terms of price stability. Interest rates shall be measured on the basis of long-term government bonds or comparable securities.

At this stage, there is some uncertainty about the initial composition of EMU. As Table 6.9 shows, some countries do not yet meet all the criteria. Table 6.10 makes three assumptions based on this table: first, that Germany, France, the Benelux countries, Austria and Ireland join (EU7); second a larger group joins that excludes the United Kingdom, Denmark, Greece and Sweden (EU11); third, all 15 join (EU15).

From an aggregate perspective, the single currency area will be larger than Japan in terms of population and GDP even if only a small group of countries join initially. In terms of GDP, the EU15 would encompass an economy which based on 1991 PPP rates was roughly the same size as the United States and based on 1996 PPP rates, 12 per cent larger. Little wonder that some American economists are concerned about the impact of EMU, leading Feldstein (1997, 73) to remark that 'the Europeans, guided by a combination of economic self-interest, historical traditions, and national pride, may seek alliances and pursue policies that are contrary to the interests of the United States'.

Table 6.9   Convergence criteria for the EU15 (1997 forecasts)

	Inflation %	Government debt %	Fiscal deficit %	Bond yields %	ERM stability[*]	1999 joiner
EMU Target	2.8	60	3.0	7.9		
Ireland	1.5	66	0.0	6.3	Y	Y
Austria	1.9	66	2.9	5.7	Y	Y
Belgium	1.8	125	2.7	5.8	Y	Y
Denmark	2.1	67	+1.2	6.3	Y	N
Finland	1.1	59	1.5	6.0	Y	Y
France	1.3	57	3.1	5.6	Y	Y
Germany	1.8	62.5	3.0	5.7	Y	Y
Greece	5.7	109	4.2	n.a.	N	N
Italy	2.2	123	3.0	6.8	Y	Y
Luxembourg	1.6	6.7	+1.6	5.8	Y	Y
Netherlands	2.1	73.4	2.1	5.7	Y	Y
Portugal	2.3	62	2.8	6.4	Y	Y
Spain	2.2	68	2.9	6.4	Y	Y
Sweden	1.8	77	1.9	6.7	N	N
United Kingdom	2.8	54.7	1.5	7.0	N	N

Notes:
[*] Determined by observance of 15% fluctuation bands within the ERM in the two years prior to membership.
Shading indicates meeting of convergence criteria

Source: European Commission.

On a final note, because of the size of the EMU area, its fiscal and monetary policies are likely to have a significant impact on the macro-economic environment of the rest of the world. Assuming that the three major areas in Table 6.9 pursue more stable macroeconomic policies than they have since the late-1960s, the bilateral exchange rates among the three major economies could be more stable than they have been since generalised floating began in the early 1970s. However, it is clear that the ability of the EMU economy to adjust smoothly and relatively quickly to shocks will make it even more imperative for it to adopt structural changes in labour and product markets, as the US has successfully done.

Table 6.10 Economic indicators: United States, Japan, European Union

	Population (thousands)	GDP[a] 1991 PPP rates ($US billion)	GDP[a] December 1996 exchange rates ($US billion)	Average real GDP growth 1990–96 (%)	Average unemployment rate 1990–96 (%)	Public sector debt, % of GDP 1990–96[b]	Trade balance, % of GDP 1990–94	Average gross national saving, % of GDP 1990–94
United States	263,057[c]	7575	7575	2.0	2.7	61.9	–1.6	15.4
Japan	124,960[d]	2571	4377	1.7	0.8	71.4	2.5	33.4
EU7[e]	176,806[d]	3647	4732	2.5	2.6	60.4	–0.7[h]	21.3
EU11[f]	287,254[g]	5818	6743	1.9	3.5	71.4	–0.8[h]	20.7
EU15	369,834[g]	7430	8504	1.8	3.6	68.9	–0.9[h]	19.3

Notes:
a. 1996 projected. Total Germany from 1991 onwards.
b. General government gross financial liabilities as a percentage of nominal GDP.
c. 1995.
d. 1994.
e. Germany, France, Austria, Belgium, Luxembourg, Ireland and the Netherlands.
f. Current EU15 members except Denmark, Greece, Sweden and the United Kingdom.
g. 1993.
h. Excluding intra-EU trade.

Source: OECD Secretariat.

7 Do monetary systems matter?

The twentieth century has seen virtually every conceivable form of monetary regime possible. Starting with the final phase of the classical gold standard in the years before 1914, it was followed by a period of free floating after the war and then came the restoration of the gold standard, or rather the gold exchange standard. This collapsed in the financial crisis of the early 1930s when managed floats (with currency blocs or zones) became the order of the day. After the second world war, a system of fixed but adjustable rates under the Bretton Woods arrangements came into force which lasted until the early 1970s. This was followed by a period of free floating, but eventually a wide variety of different systems came into being so much so that it has been labelled a non-system. Although the most recent period is often referred to as the post-1973 float, it includes independent floats, pegging to key currencies, conditional flexibility and, of course, the EMS. In fact, most of the world's currencies since the later 1970s have been pegged in one form or another and only a small number of countries (about 20 in the 1980s rising to 27 in 1991 and 56 in 1995) have operated independent floats (Kenen 1994, 148, 151–4; Baxter and Stockman 1989, 386–7). The next major change will be the European single currency, the forerunner of which occurred under the Roman Empire.

In view of the approach of European Monetary Union and the single currency, the historical experience of different exchange rate regimes may seem to be of somewhat academic interest. This, however, is an erroneous conception. Even when in place, the European single currency will still have to work alongside many other exchange systems outside the area. Second, the benefits of European monetary integration could well be outweighed by the costs. Transaction cost benefits are likely to be modest and unequally distributed and these could easily be offset by resource misallocation arising out of fiscal bargaining for regional aid to counteract the impact of a unified monetary policy (Foreman-Peck 1991, 17; A.P. Thirlwall in *The Times* 29 October 1997). Moreover, there is no certainty that European monetary integration will produce net benefits for the whole world. Third, the commitment to a common currency could give rise to the same sort of policy constraints as arose under the gold standard in the event of severe exogenous shocks, which might precipitate the world into depression. Fourth, the burdens of a single currency may eventually be too great to be accommodated within a federalist structure dominated by sovereign rights, especially when the number of participants increases. Nor, as Foreman-Peck (1991, 18) notes, can we be certain that the greater economic and political centralisation in Europe which monetary union presages will lead to better policies and institutional structures. Indeed, there are already signs that the opposite is happening.

While economists continue to disagree about the respective merits of different exchange rate regimes, especially between floating and fixed, it would probably be true to say that politicians and the general public – in so far as the latter ever consider the matter at all except when going on holiday – would tend to favour fixed regimes, especially in times of violent disturbances which, of course, is when they are least likely to prevail. There are still those, moreover, who have a nostalgic attachment to anything based on gold with the classical gold standard set as the model. In the words of Scammell (1965, 45):

> There can be no doubt that the international gold standard as it evolved in the nineteenth century, provided the growing industrial world with the most efficient system of adjustment for balances of payments which it was ever to have, either by accident or conscious planning. No wonder that in 1918 the monetary wishes of the world were 'to get back to normal', normalcy implying above all the use of gold-based currencies.

Kemp (1962, 149–50) waxed lyrical over the virtues of a full gold coin standard, while Yeager (1962, 7) felt that it provided a good test of financial management: 'By standing ready to demand redemption, the citizens can control their government more directly and effectively than they could at the ballot box alone'. European citizens may in time realise the powers they have lost in the course of a century.

How, therefore, have different exchange rate regimes fared in practice? Do they have much influence on nominal and real variables? Do some systems perform better than others? Very general impressions would suggest that fixed exchange rate regimes have proved more successful than floating or intermediate systems. From this conclusion it would follow that the classical gold standard, the exchange standard of the later 1920s and the Bretton Woods system produced better outturns in terms of nominal and real variables than the floating or intermediate regimes of the early 1920s, the 1930s or since the early 1970s.

If we examine the respective systems in terms of exchange rate behaviour, prices and real variables, these conclusions are broadly confirmed, although with some notable exceptions.

It is convenient to start with the interwar years since this period had three major regimes – general floating in the years 1919–25, the gold exchange standard, 1926–31 and managed floating in the 1930s. As might be expected, exchange rates were most volatile in the first of these periods. Measured by the standard deviation, nominal rates in European countries (10) and the United States were four times as variable in the early 1920s than under the managed float of the 1930s, while in turn the latter were equally volatile in comparison with those under the gold exchange standard. Nominal rate behaviour was reflected in real exchange rates, although the volatility was less severe (Eichengreen 1988a, 366–8). The first half of the 1920s was also more turbulent than the 1970s (De Grauwe, Janssens and Leliaert 1985, 29). In fact, this period was the most turbulent of the twentieth century when exchange rates experienced the largest departure from purchasing power parities, especially in the hyperinflationary bursts.

Aside from the interwar years, exchange rates (both nominal and real) were the most stable during the gold-standard period followed by Bretton Woods, and these periods also recorded the lowest rate of divergence in rates of change. However, the pre-convertible Bretton Woods years, which no doubt were heavily influenced by the major realignment of European currencies in 1949, experienced almost as much volatility as occurred in the post-1973 period. The nominal rate pattern also tended to be reflected in real exchange rate behaviour for most periods, although under the gold standard the mean rates and the degree of volatility are much higher than those of the nominal magnitudes (Bordo and Jonung 1996, 181–2, 201).

As far as prices are concerned, fixed exchange rate regimes perform quite well. The classical gold standard had the lowest rate of inflation of any system, even though there were quite sharp short- to medium-term variations in prices. During the Bretton Woods era, inflation was persistent but fairly trendless until late on in the period and, on average, inflation was a good deal lower than in the semi-floating period after 1973. Inflation rates also had a more marked tendency to converge during the classical period and the Bretton Woods era than in the floating and mixed regimes of the interwar period and in comparison with the post-1973 period. Similarly, prices were more stable under the gold exchange standard than either before or after, although overall the interwar period was characterised by mild deflation (ibid., 176; Alogoskoufis 1990, 461–2; Bordo and Schwartz 1996, 45). The greater degree of price stability under fixed regimes is consistent with the view that monetary accommodation is less responsive to exogenous shocks. It might also be due to the presence of milder shocks, although Bayoumi and Eichengreen (1996, 175) question whether disturbances were less intense under the pre-1914 gold standard than under later regimes.

While exchange rate and price behaviour are better under fixed regimes than under floating ones, the position is less clear-cut when it comes to real variables. More specifically, real per capita growth was lower under the classical gold standard than in any other period barring the interwar years, while its volatility was also rather high. The pure gold standard may have been fine for exchange rate and price stability – although more in the long term than the short since there were some quite significant movements in prices – but this was probably at the expense of growth and employment. This was one reason, no doubt, why many countries along the periphery were not prepared to commit themselves to such a rigid system (Nugent 1973, 1130). By contrast the Bretton Woods era, especially the convertible period, saw the highest rates of income and employment growth of any regime (Bordo and Jonung 1996, 177–8, 188). However, although post-1973 growth slowed down appreciably in many parts of the world, there is little evidence to suggest that movements in real economic variables, except real exchange rates, were systematically related to the type of exchange rate regime. Taking a sample of 49 countries, Baxter and Stockman (1989) found that the choice of exchange rate regime (pegged, floating, cooperative) had little significance in explaining differences in the pre- and post-1973 behaviour of economic variables.

Do convertibility regimes constrain countries in their fiscal and monetary policies to the extent that they produce a superior performance in nominal variables? The fiscal outturn under the classical gold standard and Bretton Woods is certainly good; measured as a proportion of GNP, fiscal deficits in the major countries are very small on average, especially in the Bretton Woods convertible years, and compare very favourably with the high deficits recorded between 1974 and 1990, and to a lesser extent in the interwar years. On the other hand, the rate of growth of real government spending does not appear to have been unduly constrained since it was very similar under Bretton Woods and before 1914 as after 1973 (Eichengreen 1993b, 630–32). Money growth did not, however, follow the fiscal pattern exactly. It was much more rapid under Bretton Woods (with little difference between convertible and pre-convertible phases) than during the interwar years and after 1973 (Bordo and Jonung 1996, 178–83, 191, 208).

Overall, the interwar years as a whole records the worst performance in both nominal and real variables. Given the violent upheavals in this period and the short life of each currency regime it is difficult to make strict relative comparisons, although on balance the early 1920s were probably the least attractive. In nominal terms, Bretton Woods and classical gold score highly, but the latter performed poorly in terms of real variables. In fact, real growth post-1973 was slightly better on average in the major countries than under the gold standard. In other words, commitment to convertibility may produce commendable results in terms of prices and financial variables but there is no guarantee that it does the same for real magnitudes. Bretton Woods was very successful in the latter respect, but the gold standard was not. It might be suggested, therefore, that real economic performance is not systematically related to the type of exchange regime in force in the long run.

No system is perfect; nor could it ever be without constant adaptation and change unless economies and their structures remained completely static. The failure to adapt is presumably one reason why fixed exchange rate regimes have a tendency to terminal decline, however successful they may be initially. Thus the collapse of the Bretton Woods system has been attributed to its increasing inability to adjust to shocks over time (Bayoumi and Eichengreen 1994, 292). The speed of adjustment was certainly slower than under the classical gold standard, whose flexibility is often extolled as one of its main virtues, but even the classical system showed signs of creaking in its later years and its anchor currency, sterling, was said to be overvalued. Thus, even had the war not intervened, it is quite possible that it would have disintegrated in time as it became less responsive to external shocks. If the hegemon's role is regarded as crucial to the maintenance of broad-based fixed regimes this would provide an additional factor in their disintegration. Similarly, the narrow bands of the ERM collapsed under speculative pressure and the weakening of the regional leadership and the wide bands which replaced them meant that currencies had more room to float than was the case under either Bretton Woods or the snake.

Do fixed exchange rate regimes involve costs to the participants or to non-members? In the long run the classical gold standard has been seen as a deflationary force in which the growth potential of its members was not fully realised. Exchange rate and price stability were achieved at the expense of growth and employment. Moreover, in so far as it was very much a Euro- or Western-centred system, some of the costs were thrown on to the periphery. This is one reason, no doubt, why many peripheral countries opted out and remained on silver, so that they could secure the benefits of depreciated currencies (Nugent 1973). On the surface, the Bretton Woods system seems to have avoided the growth problem. One suspects that its adjustable peg could have helped here, especially in 1949 when there was a wholesale devaluation of West European currencies against the dollar, but probably more important in the longer term was the inherent underlying strength of the postwar boom, which no doubt would have transpired whatever type of regime had been in force. There is also some evidence to suggest that Third World countries were not specially well served by what were still basically Western international monetary institutions, particularly in terms of their access to international capital markets (Williamson 1994, 62).

Floating rate regimes, which in theory should be the most flexible, are not generally regarded with great favour. Unfortunately, there is relatively little experience of pure floats on which to draw. The chief one is that of the early 1920s, but since conditions were dominated by postwar reconstruction and the violent inflationary outbursts in much of Europe it has done more to discredit than to recommend the virtues of floating. Exchange rates and prices were extremely volatile in this period and exchange rates had a tendency to overtrack, thus accentuating the inherent instability of these years. Nurkse's report on interwar currency experience, written under the auspices of the League of Nations (1944), was anything but sympathetic to the cause of floating exchange rates.

The remaining systems of the twentieth century have been a sort of half-way house between fixed and floating regimes. During the 1930s, after a brief spell of floating, the exchanges were extensively managed and the majority of currencies were linked to or associated with currency blocs or zones – sterling, gold, Reichsmark blocs and the dollar and yen zones. These also included the colonial appendages of the key powers. For the most part, exchange rates remained remarkably stable within the blocs and changes that did occur were mainly between the rates of the blocs or zones. The system was neat and reasonably stable but one has to bear in mind that external transactions between countries and regions were extensively controlled and regulated by tariffs, quotas, exchange controls and the like. Whether the system of regional groupings under leader countries – Britain, France, Germany, the United States and Japan – would have survived had the war not intervened is a moot point.

In some ways the more recent system, that is from the 1970s, has similarities with that of the 1930s. Most currencies are managed in one way or another and many are pegged to key currencies or to a composite basket of currencies, while the EMS revolves round the Deutschmark. The regional orientation is less clearly defined than in the 1930s, while the degree of intervention in market transactions (that is, trade controls, exchange restrictions and so on) is far less widespread. However, whether the system is more stable than that of the 1930s is something that will repay further research.

Assuming that the single currency comes into operation, this will leave most of the world's currencies within three main systems or currency zones – the European, the dollar and the yen. Whether this produces a more stable world exchange rate system remains to be seen. The presence of three large zones whose exchange rates float freely against one another could lead to more volatile and damaging exchange rate movements than in the past. This is because the sheer size of the zones may exert an inordinate impact on each other. For Europe itself there is an additional problem. Since a single currency will entail a single monetary policy, the establishment of which will be no mean feat, there is the thorny issue of what happens when the ecu currency weakens significantly against the outside world. The European Central Bank would no doubt respond to a significant depreciation by raising interest rates and this would hit all countries irrespective of the state of their domestic economies. Those countries with structural problems and already high levels of unemployment would be especially disadvantaged, and they would have no means to rectify the situation other than fiscal redress through European institutions, which may prove slow and cumbersome.

Finally, in the quest for greater financial and monetary integration among the European nations, the Third World seems to have been almost forgotten. It is doubtful whether they can draw much comfort from the latest developments in international monetary relations and as we have argued, those low-income countries which have adapted more successfully in the last quarter of a century have done so usually because they have undergone large-scale industrial and political adjustment. Until widespread structural adjustments are undertaken in these economies, it is arguable that even if a new global exchange rate regime were to be assembled, it would be largely irrelevant to the needs of the poorer nations.

References

Abelshauser, W. (1995), 'Between myth and reality: the concept of Mitteleuropa', in M. Petricioli (ed.), *Une occasion manquée? 1922: la reconstruction de l'Europe*, Bern: Peter Lang.

Aldcroft, D.H. (1970), 'The impact of British monetary policy, 1919–1939', *Revue Internationale d'Histoire de la Banque*, **3**.

Aldcroft, D.H. (1977), *From Versailles to Wall Street, 1919–1929*, London: Allen Lane.

Aldcroft, D.H. and Morewood, S. (1995), *Economic Change in Eastern Europe Since 1918*, Aldershot: Edward Elgar.

Alesina, A. and Drazen, A. (1991), 'Why are stabilisations delayed?', *American Economic Review*, **81**.

Alford, B.W.E. (1996), *Britain in the World Economy Since 1880*, London: Longman.

Aliber, R.Z. (1962), 'Speculation in the foreign exchanges: the European experience, 1919–1926', *Yale Economic Essays*, **2**.

Alogoskoufis, G.S. (1990), 'Monetary accommodation, exchange rate regimes and inflation persistence', *Economic Journal*, **102**.

Angell, J.W. (1929), *The Recovery of Germany*, New Haven, CT: Yale University Press.

Arndt, H.W. (1944), *The Economic Lessons of the Nineteen-thirties*, London: Oxford University Press.

Arrighi, G. (1994), *The Long Twentieth Century*, London: Verso.

Asselain, J.-C. and Plessis, A. (1995), 'Exchange-rate policy and macroeconomic performance: a comparison of French and Italian experience between the wars', in C.H. Feinstein (ed.), *Banking, Currency, and Finance in Europe Between the Wars*, Oxford: Oxford University Press.

Bairoch, P. (1976), 'Europe's gross national product: 1800–1975', *Journal of European Economic History*, **5**.

Balderston, T. (1994), 'The banks and the gold standard in the German financial crisis of 1931', *Financial History*, **1**.

Balderston, T. (1995), 'German and British monetary policy, 1919–1932', in C.H. Feinstein (ed.), *Banking, Currency, and Finance in Europe Between the Wars*, Oxford: Oxford University Press.

Bandera, V.N. (1964), *Foreign Capital as an Instrument of National Economic Policy: A Study Based on the Experience of East European Countries Between the Two World Wars*, The Hague: Nijhoff.

Bank for International Settlements (1934), *Fourth Annual Report, 1 April 1933–31 March 1934*, Basle: Bank for International Settlements.

Bank for International Settlements (1935), *Fifth Annual Report, 1 April 1934–31 March 1935*, Basle: Bank for International Settlements.

Bank for International Settlements (1988), *Fifty-eighth Annual Report*, Basle: Bank for International Settlements.

Bank for International Settlements (BIS), various issues.

Bareau, P. (1938), 'The Belgium, Dutch and Swiss exchange funds', *The Banker*, **45**.

Bareau, P. (1945), 'The sterling area – its use and abuse', *The Banker*, **73**.

Barro, R.J. and Gordon, D.B. (1983), 'Rules, discretion and reputation in a model of monetary policy', *Journal of Monetary Economics*, **12**.

Basch, A. (1944), *The Danube Basin and the German Economic Sphere*, London: Kegan Paul, Trench, Trubner.

Baudhuin, F. (1946), *Histoire économique de la Belgique, 1914–1939*, two vols, Brussels: Emily Bruylant.

Baxter, M. and Stockman, A.C. (1989), 'Business-cycles and the exchange-rate regime', *Journal of Monetary Economics*, **23**.

Bayoumi, T. and Eichengreen, B. (1994), 'Economic performance under alternative exchange rate regimes: some historical evidence', in P.B. Kenen, F. Papadia and F. Saccomanni (eds), *The International Monetary System*, Cambridge: Cambridge University Press.

Bayoumi, T. and Eichengreen, B. (1996), 'The gold standard and the international monetary system', in T. Bayoumi, B. Eichengreen and M.P. Taylor (eds), *Modern Perspectives on the Gold Standard*, Cambridge: Cambridge University Press.

Bean, C. and Crafts, N. (1996), 'British economic growth since 1945: relative economic decline . . . and renaissance?', in N. Crafts, and G. Toniolo (eds), *Economic Growth in Europe Since 1945*, Cambridge: Cambridge University Press.

Berend, I.T. and Ranki, G. (1974a), *Hungary: A Century of Economic Development*, Newton Abbot: David & Charles.

Berend, I.T. and Ranki, G. (1974b), *Economic Development in East Central Europe in the 19th and 20th Centuries*, New York: Columbia University Press.

Bernanke, B. and James, H. (1991), 'The gold standard, deflation, and financial crises in the great depression: an international comparison', in R. Glen Hubbard (ed.), *Financial Markets and Financial Crises*, Chicago, IL: Chicago University Press.

Berridge, W.A. (1934), 'The world's gold supply again considered', *Review of Economic Statistics*, **16**.

Bird, G. (1990), 'The international financial regime and the developing world', in Graham Bird (ed.), *The International Financial Regime*, London: Surrey University Press/Academic University Press.

Black, S.W. (1978), 'Policy responses to major disturbances of the 1970s and their transmission through international goods and capital markets', *Weltwirtschaftliches Archiv*, **114**.

Blainey, G. (1958), *Gold and Paper: A History of the National Bank of Australasia Ltd*, Melbourne: Georgian House.

Block, F.L. (1977), *The Origins of International Economic Disorder: A Study of United States International Monetary Policy from World War II to the Present*, Berkeley, CA: University of California Press.

Bloomfield, A.I. (1944), 'Operations of the American exchange stabilisation fund', *Review of Economic Statistics*, **26**.

Bloomfield, A.I. (1959), *Monetary Policy Under the International Gold Standard, 1880–1914*, New York: Federal Reserve Bank.

Bloomfield, A.I. (1968), 'Rules of the game of international adjustment', in C.R. Whittlesey and J.S.G. Wilson (eds), *Essays in Money and Banking in Honour of R.S. Sayers*, Oxford: Clarendon.

Boltho, A. (1996), 'Convergence, competitiveness and the exchange rate', in N. Crafts and G. Toniolo (eds), *Economic Growth in Europe Since 1945*, Cambridge: Cambridge University Press.

Bond, M.E. (1980), 'Exchange rates, inflation and vicious circles', *IMF Staff Papers*, **27**.

Bonnell, A.T. (1940), *German Control Over International Economic Relations 1930–1940*, Urbana, IL: University of Illinois Press.

Bordo, M.D. (1981), 'The classical gold standard: some lessons for today', *Federal Reserve Bank of St Louis Review*, **63**.

Bordo, M.D. (1984), 'The gold standard: the traditional approach', in M.D. Bordo and A.J. Schwartz (eds), *A Retrospective on the Classical Gold Standard, 1821–1931*, Chicago, IL: University of Chicago Press.

Bordo, M.D. (1993), 'The Bretton Woods International Monetary System: a historical overview', in M.D. Bordo and B. Eichengreen (eds), *A Retrospective on the Bretton Woods System: Lessons for International Monetary Reform*, Chicago, IL: University of Chicago Press.

Bordo, M.D. and Ellison, R.W. (1985), 'A model of the classical gold standard and deflation', *Journal of Monetary Economics*, **16**.

Bordo, M.D. and Jonung, L. (1996), *Monetary Regimes, Inflation and Monetary Reform*, Stockholm: Stockholm School of Economics Reprint Series, No. 156.

Bordo, M.D. and Kydland, F.E. (1995), 'The gold standard as a rule: an essay in exploration', *Explorations in Economic History*, **32**.

Bordo, M.D. and Kydland, F.E. (1996), 'The gold standard as a commitment mechanism', in T. Bayoumi, B. Eichengreen and M.P. Taylor (eds), *Modern Perspectives on the Gold Standard*, Cambridge: Cambridge University Press.

Bordo, M.D. and Redish, A. (1990), 'Credible commitment and exchange rate stability: Canada's interwar experience', *Canadian Journal of Economics*, **23**.

Bordo, M.D. and Rockoff, H. (1996), 'The gold standard as a "good housekeeping seal of approval"', *Journal of Economic History*, **56**.

Bordo, M.D. and Schwartz, A.J. (1996), 'The operation of the specie standard: evidence for core and peripheral countries, 1880–1990', in J. Braga de Macedo, B. Eichengreen and J. Reis (eds), *Currency Convertibility: The Gold Standard and Beyond*, London: Routledge.

Boross, E.A. (1994), *Inflation and Industry in Hungary 1918–1929*, Berlin: Haude & Spener.

Boyle, A. (1967), *Montagu Norman: A Biography*, London: Cassell.

Brandon, H. (1966), *In the Red: The Struggle for Sterling 1964–66*, London: André Deutsch.

Branson, G. (1994), 'German reunification, the breakdown of the EMS, and the path to Stage Three', in D. Cobham (ed.), *European Monetary Upheavals*, Manchester: Manchester University Press.

Braun, A.R. (1976), 'Indexation of wages and salaries in developed economies', *IMF Staff Papers*, **23**.

Bresciani-Turroni, C. (1937), *The Economics of Inflation: A Study of Currency Depreciation in Post-war Germany*, London: Allen & Unwin.

Bretton Woods Commission (1994), 'Commission Report', in *Bretton Woods: Looking to the Future*, Washington, DC: Bretton Woods Committee.

Brittan, S. (1995), *Capitalism With a Human Face*, Cheltenham: Edward Elgar.

Broadberry, S.N. (1984), 'The North European depression of the 1920s', *Scandinavian Economic History Review*, **32**.

Broadberry, S.N. (1987), 'Purchasing power parity and the pound–dollar rate in the 1930s', *Economica*, **54**.

Broadberry, S.N. (1989), 'Monetary interdependence and deflation in Britain and the United States between the wars', in M. Miller, B. Eichengreen and R. Portes (eds), *Blueprints for Exchange Rate Management*, London: Academic Press.

Brown, B. (1988), *Monetary Chaos in Europe: The End of an Era*, London: Croom Helm.

Brown, W.A. (1940), *The International Gold Standard Reinterpreted, 1914–1934*, two vols, New York: National Bureau of Economic Research.

Bruton, H.J. (1961), 'Inflation in a growing economy', *Series in Monetary and International Economics*, No. 2, Bombay: Bombay University Press.

Budd, A. and Dicks, G. (1982), 'Inflation – a monetarist interpretation', in A. Boltho (ed.), *The European Economy: Growth and Crisis*, Oxford: Oxford University Press.

Buffie, E.D. and Krause, A.S. (1989), 'Mexico 1958–86: from stabilizing development to the debt crisis', in J.D. Sachs (ed.), *Developing Country Debt and the World Economy*, Chicago, IL: The University of Chicago Press.

Cagan, P. (1956), 'The monetary dynamics of hyperinflation', in M. Friedman (ed.), *Studies in the Quantity Theory of Money*, Chicago, IL: University of Chicago Press.

Cain, P.J. (1996), 'Gentlemanly imperialism at work: the Bank of England, Canada and the sterling area, 1932–1936', *Economic History Review*, **49**.

Cain, P.J. and Hopkins, A.G. (1993), *British Imperialism: Crisis and Deconstruction 1914–1990*, London: Longman.

Cairncross, A. (1995), *Managing the British Economy in the 1960s: A Treasury Perspective*, London: Macmillan.

Cairncross, A. (1997), *The Wilson Years: A Treasury Diary, 1964–1969*, London: The Historians' Press.

Cairncross A. and Eichengreen, B. (1983), *Sterling in Decline: the Devaluations of 1931, 1949 and 1967*, Oxford: Blackwell.

Cairncross, A. and Watts, N. (1989), *The Economic Section 1939–1961: A Study in Economic Advising*, London: Routledge.

Callaghy, T.M. (1990), 'Lost between state and market: the politics of economic adjustment in Ghana, Zambia, and Nigeria', in J. Nelson (ed.), *Economic Crisis and Policy Choice: The Politics of Adjustment in the Third World*, Princeton, NJ: Princeton University Press.

Calvo, G. (1986), 'Fractured liberalism: Argentina under Martinz de Hoz', *Economic Development and Cultural Change*, **34**.

Campa, J.M. (1990), 'Exchange rates and economic recovery in the 1930s: an extension to Latin America', *Journal of Economic History*, **50**.

Cassel, G. (1936), *The Downfall of the Gold Standard*, Oxford: Oxford University Press.

Cassiers, I. (1995), 'Managing the franc in Belgium and France: the economic consequences of exchange rate policies, 1925–1936', in C.H. Feinstein (ed.), *Banking, Currency and Finance in Europe Between the Wars*, Oxford: Oxford University Press.

Catte, P., Galli, G. and Rebecchini, S. (1992), 'Concerted interventions and the dollar: an analysis of daily data', Paper presented to the Rinaldo Ossola Memorial Conference, Perugia, July.

Caves, R.E. and Jones, R.W. (1972), *World Trade and Payments*, Boston, MA: Little, Brown & Company.

Chandler, L.V. (1970), *America's Greatest Depression 1929–1941*, New York: Harper & Row.

Choudhri, E.V. and Kochin, L.A. (1980), 'The exchange rate and the international transmission of business cycle disturbances: some evidence from the great depression, *Journal of Money, Credit and Banking*, **12**.

Clarke, S.V.O. (1967), *Central Bank Cooperation, 1924–31*, New York: Federal Reserve Bank.

Clarke, S.V.O. (1973), *The Reconstruction of the International Monetary System: The Attempts of 1922 and 1933*, Princeton, NJ: Princeton University Press.

Clarke, S.V.O. (1977), *Exchange Rate Stabilization in the Mid-1930s: Negotiating the Tripartite Agreement*, Princeton, NJ: Princeton University Press.

Clavin, P. (1991), 'The World Economic Conference 1933: the failure of British internationalism', *Journal of European Economic History*, **20**.

Clavin, P. (1992), 'The fetishes of so-called international bankers: central bank cooperation for the World Economic Conference, 1932–3', *Contemporary European History*, **1**.

Clavin, P. (1996), *The Failure of Economic Diplomacy: Britain, Germany, France and the United States, 1931–36*, Basingstoke: Macmillan.

Clay, H. (1957), *Lord Norman*, London: Macmillan.

Clements, K.W. and Frenkel, J.A. (1980), 'Exchange rates, money and relative prices: the dollar–pound in the 1920s', *Journal of International Economics*, **10**.

Cleveland, H. van (1976), 'The international monetary system in the interwar period', in B.M. Rowland (ed.), *Balance of Power or Hegemony: the Interwar Monetary System*, New York: New York University Press.

Cobham, D. (1997), 'Inevitable disappointment? The ERM as the framework for UK monetary policy, 1990–92', *International Review of Applied Economics*, **11**.

Cohen, B.J. (1977), *Organising the World's Money: The Political Economy of International Monetary Relations*, London: Macmillan.

Cohen, J.H. (1972), 'The 1927 revaluation of the lira: a study in political economy', *Economic History Review*, **25**.

Collins, S.M. (1988), 'Inflation and the European Monetary System', in F. Giavazzi, S. Micossi and M. Miller (eds), *The European Monetary System*, Cambridge: Cambridge University Press.

Commission of the European Communities (1975), *Report of the Study Group 'Economic and Monetary Union 1980'*, Brussels: Commission of the European Communities.

Commission of the European Communities (1987), *The Agricultural Situation in the Community*, 1986 Report, Luxembourg: CEC Publication Office.

Committee for the Study of Economic and Monetary Union (1989), *Report on Economic and Monetary Union in the European Community* ('Delors Report'), Luxembourg: Office of Publication of the European Communities.

Condliffe, J.B. (1941), *The Reconstruction of World Trade: A Survey of International Economic Relations*, London: Allen & Unwin.

Congdon, T. (1989), *Monetarism Lost and Why It Must Be Regained*, London: Centre For Policy Studies.

Cooper, R.N. (1982), 'The gold standard: historical facts and future prospects', *Brookings Papers on Economic Activity*, **1**.

Cooper, R.N. (1987), 'Gold: does it provide a viable basis for the monetary system?', in R.Z. Aliber, (ed.), *The Reconstruction of the International Monetary Arrangements*, Basingstoke: Macmillan.

Cooper, R.N. (1992), 'Fettered to gold? Economic policy in the interwar period', *Journal of Economic Literature*, **30**.

Corden, M. (1985), *Inflation, Exchange Rates and the World Economy: Lectures on International Monetary Economics*, Oxford: Clarendon Press, 3rd edn.

Costigliola, F.C. (1977), 'Anglo-American financial rivalry in the 1920s', *Journal of Economic History*, **37**.

Costigliola, F.C. (1984), *Awkward Dominion: American Political, Economic and Cultural Relations with Europe, 1919–1933*, Ithaca, NY: Cornell University Press.

Crockett, A.D. and Nsouli, S.M. (1977), 'Exchange rate policies for developing countries', *Journal of Development Studies*, **13**.

Currie, D. (1993), 'International cooperation in monetary policy: has it a future?', *Economic Journal*, **103**.

Currie, D.A., Holtham, G. and Hughes-Hallett, A.J. (1989), 'The theory and practice of international policy coordination: does coordination pay?', in R. Bryant, D.A. Currie, J.A. Frenkel, P. Masson and R. Portes (eds), *Macroeconomic Policies in an Interdependent World*, Washington, DC: International Monetary Fund.

Dahmén, E. (1970), *Entrepreneurial Activity and the Development of Swedish Industry, 1919–1939*, Homewood, IL: Irwin.

Dale, E.L. (1971), 'Nixon hails pact', *New York Times*, 19 December.

Dam, K.W. (1982), *The Rules of the Game: Reform and Evolution in the International Monetary System*, Chicago, IL: University of Chicago Press.

David, T. (1995), 'Un indice de la production industrielle de la Suisse durant l'entre-deux guerres', *Schweizerische Zeitschrift für Geschichte*, **45**.

David, T. (1996), 'Indices de la production industrielle Suisse', in H. Ritzmann (ed.), *Statistique historique de la Suisse*, Zurich: Charonos.

Davidson, D. (1933), *The Rationalization of the Gold Standard*, Stockholm: Almquist & Wicksells.

Davies, G. (1990), 'Memorandum: The Autumn Statement', in Treasury and Civil Service Committee, *The 1990 Autumn Statement*, First Report, HC 41, London: HMSO.

de Cecco, M. (1984), *The International Gold Standard: Money and Empire*, London: Frances Pinter.

de Cecco, M. (1995), 'Central bank cooperation in the interwar period: a view from the periphery', in J. Reis, (ed.), *International Monetary Systems in Historical Perspective*, Basingstoke: Macmillan.

De Grauwe, P. (1990), 'The cost of disinflation and the European Monetary System', *Open Economies Review*, **1**.

De Grauwe, P. (1991), 'Is the EMS a DM-zone?', in A. Steinherr and D. Weiserbs (eds), *Evolution of the International and Regional Monetary Systems*, London: Macmillan.

De Grauwe, P. (1996), *International Money: Postwar Trends and Theories*, Oxford: Oxford University Press.

De Grauwe, P., Janssens, M. and Leliaert, H. (1985), *Real Exchange-rate Variability from 1920 to 1926 and 1973 to 1982*, Princeton, NJ: Princeton University Press.

de Vegh, I. (1939), *The Pound Sterling*, New York: Scudder, Stevens & Clark.

de Vries, M.G. (1996), 'Bretton Woods fifty years later: a view from the International Monetary Fund', in O. Kirshner (ed.), *The Bretton Woods–GATT System: Retrospect and Prospect After Fifty Years*, New York: M.E. Sharpe.

Dick, T.J.O., Floyd, J.E. and Pope, D. (1996), 'Balance of payments adjustment under the gold standard policies: Canada and Australia compared', in T. Bayoumi, B. Eichengreen and M.P. Taylor (eds), *Modern Perspectives on the Gold Standard*, Cambridge: Cambridge University Press.

Dimsdale, N.H. (1981), 'British monetary policy and the exchange rate', *Oxford Economic Papers, Supplement*, **33**.

Dornbusch, R. (1976a), 'The theory of flexible exchange rate regimes and macroeconomic policy', *Scandinavian Journal of Economics*, **78**.

Dornbusch, R. (1976b), 'Expectations and Exchange Rate Dynamics', *Journal of Political Economy*, **84**.

Dornbusch, R. (1983), 'Flexible exchange rates and interdependence', *IMF Staff Papers*, **30**.

Dornbusch, R. (1987), 'Lessons from the German inflation experience of the 1920s', in R. Dornbusch, S. Fischer and J. Bossons (eds), *Macroeconomics and Finance: Essays in Honor of Frank Modigliani*, Cambridge, MA: MIT Press.

Dornbusch, R. (1989), 'Credibility, debt and unemployment: Ireland's failed stabilization', *Economic Policy*, **8**.

Dornbusch, R. (1992), 'Monetary problems of post-communism: lessons from the end of the Austro-Hungarian Empire', *Weltwirtschaftliches Archiv*, **128**.

Dornbusch, R. and de Pablo, J.C. (1989), 'Debt and macroeconomic instability in Argentina', in J.D. Sachs (ed.), *Developing Country Debt and the World Economy*, Chicago, IL: The University of Chicago Press.

Dornbusch, R. and Fischer, S. (1986), 'Stopping hyperinflations past and present', *Weltwirtschaftliches Archiv*, **122**.

Drummond, I.M. (1979), *London, Washington and the Management of the Franc, 1936–39*, Princeton, NJ: Princeton University Press.

Drummond, I.M. (1981), *The Floating Pound and the Sterling Area*, Cambridge: Cambridge University Press.

Drummond, I.M. (1987), *The Gold Standard and the International Monetary System*, Basingstoke: Macmillan.

Dulles, E.L. (1929), *The French Franc 1914–1928: The Facts and Their Interpretation*, New York: Macmillan.

Dutton, J. (1984), 'The Bank of England and the rules of the game under the international gold standard: new evidence', in M.D. Bordo and A.J. Schwartz (eds), *A Retrospective on the Classical Gold Standard, 1821–1931*, Chicago: University of Chicago Press.

Eastman, H.C. (1955), 'French and Canadian exchange rate policy', *Journal of Economic History*, **15**.

Edwards, S. (1985), 'Exchange rate misalignment in developing countries: analytical issues and empirical evidence', *CPD Working Paper*, Washington, DC: World Bank, Country Policy Department.

Edwards, S. (1988), *Exchange Rate Misalignment in Developing Countries*, Baltimore, MD: Johns Hopkins University Press.

Edwards, S. and Montiel, P. (1989), 'Devaluation crises and the macroeconomic consequences of postponed adjustment in developing countries', *IMF Staff Papers*, **36**.

Edwards, S. and Santaella, J.A. (1993), 'Devaluation controversies in the developing countries: lessons from the Bretton Woods era', in M.D. Bordo and B. Eichengreen (eds), *A Retrospective on the Bretton Woods System: Lessons for International Monetary Reform*, Chicago, IL: The University of Chicago Press.

Eichengreen, B. (1982), 'Did speculation destabilise the French franc in the 1920s?', *Explorations in Economic History*, **19**.

Eichengreen, B. (1984), 'Central bank cooperation under the interwar gold standard', *Explorations in Economic History*, **21**.

Eichengreen, B. (ed.) (1985a), *The Gold Standard in Theory and History*, New York: Methuen.

Eichengreen, B. (1985b), 'International policy coordination in historical perspective: a view from the interwar years', in W.H. Buiter and R.C. Marston (eds), *International Economic Policy Coordination*, Cambridge: Cambridge University Press.

Eichengreen, B. (1986a), 'Understanding 1921–1927: inflation and economic recovery in the 1920s', *Rivista di Storia Economica*, **3**.

Eichengreen, B. (1986b), 'The Bank of France and the sterilization of gold, 1926–1932', *Explorations in Economic History*, **23**.

Eichengreen, B. (1987), 'Conducting the international orchestra: Bank of England leadership under the classical gold standard', *Journal of International Money and Finance*, **6**.

Eichengreen, B. (1988a), 'Real exchange rate behaviour under alternative monetary regimes: interwar evidence', *European Economic Review*, **32**.

Eichengreen, B. (1988b), 'The Australian recovery of the 1930s in international comparative perspective', in R.E. Gregory and N.G. Butlin (eds), *Recovery from the Depression: Australia in the World Economy in the 1930s*, Cambridge: Cambridge University Press.

Eichengreen, B. (1989), 'Hegemonic stability theories of the international monetary system', in R.N. Cooper, B. Eichengreen, C.R. Henning, G. Holtham and R. Putnum (eds), *Can Nations Agree? Issues in International Economic Cooperation*, Washington, DC: The Brookings Institution.

Eichengreen, B. (1990a) *Elusive Stability: Essays in the History of International Finance 1919–1939*, Cambridge: Cambridge University Press.

Eichengreen, B. (1990b), 'International monetary instability between the wars: structural flaws or misguided policies', in Yoshio Suzuki, Junichi Miyake and Mitsuaki Okabe (eds), *The Evolution of the International Monetary System*, Tokyo: University of Tokyo Press.

Eichengreen, B. (1991), 'Relaxing the external constraint: Europe in the 1930s', in G. Alogoskoufis, L. Papademos and R. Portes (eds), *External Constraints on Macroeconomic Policy: The European Experience*, Cambridge: Cambridge University Press.

Eichengreen, B. (1992a) 'The gold standard since Alec Ford', in S.N. Broadberry and N.F.R. Crafts (eds), *Britain in the International Economy*, Cambridge: Cambridge University Press.

Eichengreen, B. (1992b), *Golden Fetters: The Gold Standard and the Great Depression, 1919–1939*, Oxford: Oxford University Press.

Eichengreen, B. (1992c), 'The origins and nature of the Great Slump revisited', *Economic History Review*, **45**.

Eichengreen, B. (1993a), 'European monetary unification', *Journal of Economic Literature*, **31**.

Eichengreen, B. (1993b), 'Epilogue: three perspectives on the Bretton Woods system', in M.D. Bordo and B. Eichengreen (eds), *A Retrospective on the Bretton Woods System: Lessons for International Monetary Reform*, Chicago, IL: University of Chicago Press.

Eichengreen, B. (1995), 'The endogeneity of exchange-rate regimes', in P. Kenen (ed.), *Understanding Interdependence: The Macroeconomics of the Open Economy*, Princeton, NJ: Princeton University Press.

Eichengreen, B. (1996), *Globalizing Capital: A History of the International Monetary System*, Princeton, NJ: Princeton University Press.

Eichengreen, B. and Flandreau, M. (1996), 'Blocs, zones and bands: international monetary history in the light of recent theoretical developments', *Scottish Journal of Political Economy*, **43**.

Eichengreen, B. and Irwin, D.A. (1995), 'Trade blocs, currency blocs and the reorientation of world trade in the 1930s', *Journal of International Economics*, **38**.

Eichengreen, B. and Kenen, P. (1994), 'Managing the world economy under the Bretton Woods system: an overview', in P.B. Kenen (ed.), *Managing the World Economy: Fifty Years After Bretton Woods*, Washington, DC: Institute for International Economics.

Eichengreen, B. and Portes, R. (1987), 'The anatomy of financial crises', in R. Portes and A.K. Swoboda (eds), *Threats to International Financial Stability*, Cambridge: Cambridge University Press.

Eichengreen, B. and Sachs, J. (1985), 'Exchange rates and economic recovery in the 1930s', *Journal of Economic History*, **45**.

Eichengreen, B. and Wyplosz, C. (1993), 'The unstable EMS', *Brookings Papers on Economic Activity*, **1**.

Einzig, P. (1932), *Montagu Norman: A Study in Financial Statesmanship*, London: Kegan Paul, Trench, Trubner & Co.

Einzig, P. (1933), *The Sterling–Dollar–Franc triangle*, New York: Macmillan.

Einzig, P. (1935), *World Finance Since 1914*, London: Kegan Paul, Trench, Trubner & Co.

Einzig, P. (1937), *World Finance 1935–1937*, London: Kegan Paul, Trench, Trubner.

Einzig, P. (1938), *Bloodless Invasion: German Economic Penetration into the Danubian States and the Balkans*, London: Duckworth.

Einzig, P. (1970), *The History of Foreign Exchange*, London: Macmillan, 2nd edn.

Ellis, H.S. (1939), 'Exchange control in Austria and Hungary', *Journal of Economics*, **54**.

Ellis, H.S. (1941), *Exchange Control in Central Europe*, Cambridge, MA: Harvard University Press.

Fearon, P. (1987), *War, Prosperity and Depression: The US Economy 1917–45*, Oxford: Philip Allan.

Feavearyear, A.E. (1963), *The Pound Sterling*, Oxford: Clarendon Press, rev. edn.

Feinstein, C.H., Temin, P. and Toniolo, G. (1995), 'International economic organisation: banking, finance and trade in Europe between the wars', in C.H. Feinstein, (ed.), *Banking, Currency, and Finance in Europe Between the Wars*, Oxford: Oxford University Press.

Feldman, G.D. (1975), 'Economic and social problems of German demobilisation, 1918–19', *Journal of Modern History*, **47**.

Feldman, G.D. (1993), *The Great Disorder: Politics, Economics, and Society in the German Inflation 1914–1924*, Oxford: Oxford University Press.

Feldstein, M. (1987), 'Correcting the trade deficit', *Foreign Affairs*, **65**.

Feldstein, M. (1997), 'EMU and international conflict', *Foreign Affairs*, November/December.

Ferguson, N. (1995), *Paper and Iron: Hamburg Business and German Politics in the Era of Inflation, 1897–1927*, Cambridge: Cambridge University Press.

Fink, C. (1984), *The Genoa Conference: European Diplomacy 1921–1922*, Chapel Hill: University of North Carolina Press.

Fishlow, A. (1985), 'Lessons from the past: capital markets during the 19th century and the interwar period', *International Organization*, **39**.

Flandreau, M. (1997), 'Central bank cooperation in historical perspective: a sceptical view', *Economic History Review*, **50**.

Fleisig, H.W. (1975), *Long-term Capital Flows and the Great Depression: The Role of the United States, 1927–1933*, New York: Arno Press.

Flood, R. and Garber, P. (1984), 'Gold monetization and gold discipline', *Journal of Political Economy*, **92**.

Floyd, J. E. (1985), *World Monetary Equilibrium: International Monetary Theory in an Historical-Institutional Context*, Oxford: Philip Allan.

Ford, A.G. (1989), 'International financial policy and the gold standard, 1870–1914', in P. Mathias and S. Pollard (eds), *The Cambridge Economic History of Europe*, Vol. VIII, Cambridge: Cambridge University Press.

Foreman-Peck, J. (1983), *A History of the World Economy: International Economic Relations Since 1850*, Brighton: Wheatsheaf Books.

Foreman-Peck, J. (1991), 'The gold standard as a European monetary lesson', in J. Driffil and M. Beber (eds), *A Currency for Europe*, London: Lothian Foundation Press.

Foreman-Peck, J., Hallett, A.G. and Ma, Y. (1992), 'The transmission of the great depression in the United States, Britain, France and Germany', *European Economic Review*, **36**.

Foreman-Peck, J., Hallett, A.G. and Ma, Y. (1996), 'Optimum international policies for the world depression 1919–1933', *Economies et Sociétés*, **22**.

Foreman-Peck, J., Hallett, A.G. and Ma, Y. (1997), 'The end of free trade: protection and the exchange rate regime between the wars', in A. Marrison (ed.), *Free Trade and its Reception, 1815–1960*, London: Routledge.

Forsyth, D.J. (1993), *The crisis of Liberal Italy: Monetary and Financial Policy 1914–1922*, Cambridge: Cambridge University Press.

Fratianni, M. and von Hagen, J. (1992), *The European Monetary System and European Monetary Union*, Boulder, CO: Westview Press.

Fremling, G.M. (1986), 'A specie-flow model of the gold standard', *Journal of International Money and Finance*, **5**.

Frenkel, J.A. (1977), 'The forward exchange rate, expectations and the demand for money: the German hyperinflation', *American Economic Review*, **67**.

Frenkel, J.A. (1978), 'Purchasing power parity: doctrinal perspective and evidence from the 1920s', *Journal of International Economics*, **8**.

Frenkel, J.A. (1980), 'Exchange rates, prices and money: lessons from the 1920s', *American Economic Review, Papers and Proceedings*, **70**.

Frenkel, J.A. and Mussa, M.L. (1980), 'The efficiency of foreign exchange markets and measures of turbulence', *American Economic Review*, **70**.

Freris, A.F. (1986), *The Greek Economy in the Twentieth Century*, London: Croom Helm.

Friedman, M. (1988), 'A proposal for resolving the US balance of payments problem: confidential memorandum to President-elect Richard Nixon', in L. Melamed (ed.), *The Merits of Flexible Exchange Rates: An Anthology*, Fairfax, VA: George Mason University Press.

Friedman, M. and Schwartz, A.J. (1963), *A Monetary History of the United States, 1867–1960*, Princeton, NJ: Princeton University Press.

Friedman, P. (1974), *Impact of Trade Destruction on National Incomes: A Study of Europe 1924–1938*, Gainesville: University Presses of Florida.

Friedman, P. (1976), 'The welfare costs of bilateralism: German–Hungarian trade 1933–38', *Explorations in Economic History*, **13**.

Fuentes Quintana, E. (1984), 'El Plan de Estabilización económica de 1959, veinticinco años después', *Información Comercial Española*, **612–13**.

Funabashi, Y. (1989), *Managing the Dollar: From the Plaza to the Louvre*, Washington, DC: Institute for International Economics.

Furtado, C. (1970), *Economic Development of Latin America*, Cambridge: Cambridge University Press.

Garber, P.M. (1993), 'The collapse of the Bretton Woods fixed exchange rate system', in M.D. Bordo and B. Eichengreen (eds), *A Retrospective on the Bretton Woods System: Lessons for International Monetary Reform*, Chicago, IL: University of Chicago Press.

Gayer, A.D. (1934), 'The nature and functioning of the postwar gold standard', in R.M. McIver (ed.), *Economic Reconstruction: Report of the Columbia University Commission*, New York: Columbia University Press.

Gayer, A.D. (ed.) (1937), *The Lessons of Monetary Experience: Essays in Honour of Irving Fisher*, New York: Farrer & Rinehart.

Giavazzi, F. and Giovannini, A. (1989), *Limiting Exchange Rate Flexibility: The European Monetary System*, Cambridge, MA: MIT Press.

Giavazzi, F. and Spaventa, L. (1990), 'The "new" EMS', in P. De Grauwe and L. Papademos (eds), *The European Monetary System in the 1990s*, London: Longman.

Gilbert, M. (1939), *Currency Depreciation and Monetary Policy*, Philadelphia, PA: University of Pennsylvania Press.

Giovannini, A. (1986), 'Rules of the game during the international gold standard: England and Germany', *Journal of International Money and Finance*, **5**.

Giovannini, A. (1989), 'How do fixed-exchange-rate regimes work? Evidence from the gold standard, Bretton Woods and the EMS', in M. Miller, B. Eichengreen and R. Portes (eds), *Blueprints for Exchange Rate Management*, London: Academic Press.

Giovannini, A. (1990), 'European monetary reform: progress and prospects', *Brookings Papers on Economic Activity*, **2**.

Giovannini, A. (1993), 'Bretton Woods and its precursors: rules versus discretion in the history of international monetary regimes', in M.D. Bordo and B. Eichengreen (eds), *A Retrospective on the Bretton Woods System: Lessons for International Monetary Reform*, Chicago, IL: University of Chicago Press.

Glynn, S. and Lougheed, A.L. (1973), 'A comment on United States economic policy and the "dollar gap" of the 1920s', *Economic History Review*, **26**.

Goldstein, M. (1984), *The Exchange Rate System: Lessons of the Past and Options for the Future – A Study by the Research Department of the International Monetary Fund*, IMF Occasional Paper, No. 30.

Goodman, J.B. (1992), *Monetary Sovereignty: The Politics of Central Banking in Western Europe*, Ithaca, NY: Cornell University Press.

Gordon, R.J. (1982), 'Why stopping inflation may be costly: evidence from fourteen historical episodes', in R.E. Hall (ed.), *Inflation: Causes and Effects*, Chicago, IL: University of Chicago Press.

Graham, F.D. (1930), *Exchange, Prices and Production in Hyperinflation Germany, 1920–23*, Princeton, NJ: Princeton University Press.

Gregory, T.E. (1936), 'Memorandum on the experiences of the sterling area', in Carnegie Endowment/International Chamber of Commerce (eds), *The Improvement of Commercial Relations Between Nations and the Problems of Monetary Stabilization*, Paris: International Chamber of Commerce.

Griffiths, R.T. (1987), 'The policy makers', in R.T. Griffiths (ed.), *The Netherlands and the Gold Standard 1931–1936*, Amsterdam: NEHA.

Griffiths, R.T. (1989), 'The economic disintegration of Europe: trade and protection in the 1930s', *European University Institute Colloquium Papers*, 138/89.

Gros, D. and Thygesen, N. (1992), *European Monetary Integration*, London: Longman Group.

Gruber, J. (1924), *Czechoslovakia: A Survey of Economic and Social Conditions*, New York: Macmillan.

Haavisto, T. and Jonung, L. (1995), 'Off gold and back again: Finnish and Swedish monetary policies 1914–1925', in C.H. Feinstein (ed.), *Banking, Currency and Finance in Europe Between the Wars*, Oxford: Oxford University Press.

Hallwood, C.P. MacDonald, R. and Marsh, I.W. (1996), 'Credibility and fundamentals: were the classical and interwar gold standards well-behaved target zones?', in T. Bayoumi, B. Eichengreen and M.P. Taylor (eds), *Modern Perspectives on the Gold Standard*, Cambridge: Cambridge University Press.

Hallwood, C.P. MacDonald, R. and Marsh, I.W. (1997), 'Crash! Expectational aspects of the departure of the United Kingdom and the United States from the interwar gold standard', *Explorations in Economic History*, **34**.

Hamilton, J.D. (1988), 'The role of the international gold standard in propagating the great depression', *Contemporary Policy Issues*, **6**.

Hardach, G. (1995), 'Endogenous versus exogenous causes of stabilisation and crisis in Germany, 1922–1932' , in M. Petriciali (ed.), *Une occasion manquée? 1922: la reconstruction de l'Europe*, Bern: Peter Lang.

Hardy, C.O. (1936), *Is There Enough Gold?*, Washington, DC: The Brookings Institution.

Harris, S.E. (1931), *Monetary Problems of the British Empire*, New York: Macmillan.

Harris, S.E. (1936), *Exchange Depreciation: Its Theory and Its History 1931–35, With Some Consideration of Related Domestic Policies*, Cambridge, MA: Harvard University Press.

Harris, S., Swinbank, A. and Wilkinson, G. (1983), *The Food and Farm Policies of the European Community*, London: John Wiley.

Harrison, J. (1985), *The Spanish Economy in the Twentieth Century*, London: Croom Helm.

Hart, A.G., Kaldor, N. and Tinbergen, J. (1964), 'The case for an international commodity reserve currency', in *Proceedings of the UN Conference on Trade and Development*, Vol. III, New York: United Nations.

Hauser, J.D. (1973), 'Britain, France, and the United States at the World Economic Conference of 1933: a study in futility', PhD thesis, Washington State University Department of History.

Hawke, G. (1971), 'New Zealand and the return to gold in 1925', *Australian Economic History Review*, **11**.

Hawtrey, R.G. (1939), *The Gold Standard in Theory and Practice*, London: Longmans, Green, 4th edn.

Heckscher, E.F. (1930), *Sweden, Norway, Denmark and Iceland in the World War*, New York: Oxford University Press.

Heilperin, M.A. (1931), *Le problème monétaire d'après-guerre at sa solution en Pologne, en Autriche et en Tchécoslovaquie*, Paris: Recueil Sirey.

Henning, C.R. (1994), *Currencies and Politics in the United States, Germany and Japan*, Washington, DC: Institute for International Economics.

Heuser, H. (1939), *Control of International Trade*, London: Routledge.

Hicks, J. (1950), *A Contribution to the Theory of the Trade Cycle*, Oxford: Clarendon.

Hiden, J. (1977), *Germany and Europe 1919–1939*, London: Longman.

Hill, R.L. (1956), 'The role of rigidities in the failure of the gold standard', *Weltwirtschaftliches Archiv*, **77**.

Hilton Young, E. (1924), *Report on Financial Conditions in Poland*, London: Waterloo and Sous.

Hjerppe, R. (1996), *Finland's Historical National Accounts 1860–1914: Calculation Methods and Statistical Tables*, Jräskylä: Kari-Pekka Kivirauma.

Hodgson, J.S. (1972), 'An analysis of floating exchange rates: the dollar–sterling rate, 1919–1925', *Southern Economic Journal*, **39**.

Hogan, M.J. (1977), *Informal Entente: The Private Structure of Cooperation in Anglo-American Economic Diplomacy 1918–1928*, Columbia, MO: University of Missouri Press.

Hogg, R.L. (1987), 'Belgium, France and Switzerland and the end of the gold standard', in R.T. Griffiths, *The Netherlands and the Gold Standard 1931–1936*, Amsterdam: NEHA.

Holtfrerich, C.-L. (1986), *The German Inflation 1914–1923*, Berlin: Walter de Gruyter.

Holtham, G. (1989), 'German macroeconomic policy and the 1978 Bonn Summit', in R. Cooper et al., *Can Nations Agree? Issues in International Economic Cooperation*, Washington, DC: Brookings Institute.

Hoptner, J.B. (1962), *Yugoslavia in Crisis, 1934–1941*, New York: Columbia University Press.

Horiuchi, A. (1993), 'Monetary policies: Japan', in H. Fukui, P.H. Merkl, H. Müller-Groeling and A. Watanabe (eds), *The Politics of Economic Change in Postwar Japan and West Germany*, New York: St. Martin's Press.

Horsefield, J.K. (1969), *The International Monetary Fund, 1945–65: Twenty Years of International Monetary Cooperation, Vol. I: Chronicle*, Washington, DC: IMF.

Horsman, G. (1988), *Inflation in the Twentieth Century: Evidence from Europe and North America*, Hemel Hempstead: Harvester-Wheatsheaf.

Howson, S. (1975), *Domestic Monetary Management in Britain 1919–38*, Cambridge: Cambridge University Press.

Howson, S. (1976), 'The managed floating pound, 1932–39', *The Banker*, **126**.

Howson, S. (1980a), 'The management of sterling, 1932–1939', *Journal of Economic History*, **40**.

Howson, S. (1980b), *Sterling's Managed Float: The Operations of the Exchange Accounts 1932–39*, Princeton, NJ: Princeton University Press.

Howson, S. and Winch, D. (1977), *The Economic Advisory Council: A Study in Economic Advice During Depression and Recovery*, Cambridge: Cambridge University Press.

Huffman, W.E. and Lothian, J.R. (1984), 'The gold standard and the transmission of business cycles', in M.D. Bordo and A.J. Schwartz (eds), *A Retrospective on the Classical Gold Standard, 1821–1931*, Chicago, IL: University of Chicago Press.

Hughes, M.L. (1988), *Paying for the German Inflation*, Chapel Hill: University of North Carolina Press.

Hughes-Hallet, A.J., Holtham, G. and Hutson, G. (1988), 'Exchange rate targeting as a surrogate for international policy coordination', in B. Eichengreen, M. Miller and R. Portes (eds), *Blueprints for Exchange Rate Management*, London: Academic Press.

Hurst, W. (1932), 'Holland, Switzerland and Belgium and the English gold crisis of 1931', *Journal of Political Economy*, **40**.

International Monetary Fund (IMF) (1948), *Annual Report*, Washington, DC: IMF.

International Monetary Fund (1951), *Annual Report*, Washington, DC: IMF.

International Monetary Fund (1976), *Summary Proceedings of the Thirty-First Annual Meeting of the Board of Governors*, Washington, DC: IMF.

International Monetary Fund (1979), *International Financial Statistics Yearbook*, Washington, DC: IMF.

International Monetary Fund (1980), *International Financial Statistics*, Washington, DC: IMF.

International Monetary Fund (1982), *International Financial Statistics Yearbook*, Washington, DC: IMF.

International Monetary Fund (1984), *Exchange Rate Volatility and World Trade*, Occasional Paper No. 28: Washington, DC: IMF.

International Monetary Fund (1997), *World Economic Outlook*, October, Washington, DC: IMF.

Jack, D.T. (1927), *The Economics of the Gold Standard*, London: P.S. King.

Jackson, J. (1985), *The Politics of Depression in France 1932–1936*, Cambridge: Cambridge University Press.

Jacobs, R.L. (1977), 'Hyperinflation and the supply of money', *Journal of Money, Credit and Banking*, **9**.

Jacobsson, P. (1958), *Some Monetary Problems: International and National*, London: Oxford University Press.

James, H. (1984), 'The causes of the German banking crisis of 1931', *Economic History Review*, **37**.

James, H. (1986), *The German Slump: Politics and Economics 1924–1936*, Oxford: Clarendon Press.

James, H. (1992), 'Financial flows across frontiers during the interwar depression', *Economic History Review*, **45**.

James, H. (1993), 'Innovation and conservatism in economic recovery: the alleged Nazi recovery of the 1930s', in W.R. Garside (ed.), *Capitalism in Crisis: International Responses to the Great Depression*, London: Pinter.

James, H. (1996), *International Monetary Cooperation Since Bretton Woods*, Oxford: Oxford University Press.

Jèze, G. (1921), 'The economic and financial position of France in 1920', *Quarterly Journal of Economics*, **35**.

Johnson, H.G. (1968), 'The sterling crisis of 1967 and the gold rush of 1968', *Nebraska Journal of Economic and Business*, **7**.

Johnson, H.G. (1972), 'The monetary approach to balance of payments theory', in H.H. Johnson (ed.), *Further Essays in Monetary Economics*, London: Allen & Unwin.

Johnson, H.G. (1973), 'The exchange-rate question for a united Europe', in M. Krauss (ed.), *The Economics of Integration*, London: George Allen & Unwin.

Jones, F.E. (1937), *Hitler's Drive to the East*, London: Gollancz.

Jonung, L. (1981), 'The depression in Sweden and the United States: a comparison of causes and policies', in K. Brunner (ed.), *The Great Depression Revisited*, The Hague: Martinus Nijhoff.

Jonung, L. (1984), 'Swedish experience under the classical gold standard', in M.D. Bordo and A.J. Schwartz (eds), *A Retrospective on the Classical Gold Standard, 1821–1931*, Chicago, IL: University of Chicago Press.

Joslin, D. (1963), *A Century of Banking in Latin America*, London: Oxford University Press.

Kaiser, D.E. (1980), *Economic Diplomacy and the Origins of the Second World War: Germany, Britain, France and Eastern Europe, 1930–1939*, Princeton, NJ: Princeton University Press.

Kaplan, J. and Schleiminger, G. (1989), *The European Payments Union: Financial Diplomacy in the 1950s*, Oxford: Clarendon Press.

Kavka, F. (1960), *An Outline of Czechoslovak History*, Prague: Orbis.

Kemmerer, E.W. (1944), *Gold and the Gold Standard*, New York: McGraw-Hill Book Company.

Kemp, A. (1962), 'The gold standard: a reappraisal', in L.B. Yeager (ed.), *In Search of a Monetary Constitution*, Cambridge, MA: Harvard University Press.

Kemp, T. (1971), 'The French economy under the franc Poincaré', *Economic History Review*, **24**.

Kenen, P.B. (1994), 'Floating exchange rates reconsidered: the influence of new ideas, priorities and problems', in P.B. Kenen, F. Papadia and F. Saccomanni, *The International Monetary System*, Cambridge: Cambridge University Press.

Kenen, P.B., Papadia, F. and Saccomanni, F. (eds) (1994), *The International Monetary System*, Cambridge: Cambridge University Press.

Keyder, C. (1981), *The Definition of a Peripheral Economy: Turkey 1923–29*, Cambridge: Cambridge University Press.

Keynes, J.M. (1930), *A Treatise on Money*, Vol. II: *The Applied Theory of Money*, London: Macmillan.

Killick, J. (1997), *The United States and European Reconstruction, 1945–1960*, Edinburgh: Keele University Press.

Kincaid, R. (1984), 'A test of the efficacy of exchange rate adjustments in Indonesia', *IMF Staff Papers*, **31**.

Kindleberger, C.P. (1973), *The World in Depression 1929–1939*, London: Allen Lane, Penguin Press.

Kindleberger, C.P. (1984), *A Financial History of Western Europe*, London: Allen & Unwin.

Kitchen, J. (1932), 'Gold production', in Royal Institute of International Affairs, *The International Gold Problem: Collected Papers*, London: Oxford University Press.

Kitson, M. and Michie, J. (1994) 'Depression and recovery: lessons from the interwar period', in J. Michie and J. Grieve Smith (eds), *Unemployment in Europe*, London: Academic Press.

Kitson, M. and Solomou, S. (1990), *Protectionism and Economic Revival: The British Interwar Economy*, Cambridge: Cambridge University Press.

Knauerhase, R. (1972), *An Introduction to National Socialism 1920–1939*, Columbus, OH: C.E. Merrill.

Krugman, P.R. (1978), 'Purchasing power parity and exchange rates', *Journal of International Economics*, **8**.

Krugman, P.R. (1985), 'Is the strong dollar sustainable?, in *The US Dollar – Recent Developments, Outlook, and Policy Options*, Kansas City: Federal Reserve Bank of Kansas City.

Kunz, D. (1987), *The Battle for Britain's Gold Standard in 1931*, London: Croom Helm.

Lains, P. and Reis, J. (1991), 'Portuguese economic growth, 1833–1985: some doubts', *Journal of European Economic History*, **20**.

Lamfalussy, A. (1963), *The United Kingdom and the Six*, Homewood, IL: Irwin.

Lamont, N. (1990), 'Minutes of Evidence', in Treasury and Civil Service Committee, *The 1990 Autumn Statement*, First Report, HC 41, London: HMSO.

Lamont, N. (1992), 'Minutes of Evidence', in Treasury and Civil Service Committee, *The Future Conduct of Economic Policy*, HC 201–i, London: HMSO.

Lampe, J.R. and Jackson, M.R. (1982), *Balkan Economic History 1550–1950*, Bloomington, IN: Indiana University Press.

Landau, Z. (1983), 'Inflation in Poland after World War I', in N. Schmukler and E. Marcus (eds), *Inflation Through the Ages*, New York: Brooklyn College Press.

Laursen, K. and Pedersen, J. (1964), *The German Inflation, 1918–1923*, Amsterdam: North-Holland.

Lavka, F. (1960), *An Outline of Czechoslovak History*, Prague: Orbis.

Lawson, N. (1992), *The View From No 11*, London: Bantam Press.

Layton, W. and Rist, C. (1925), *The Economic Situation of Austria*, Geneva: League of Nations.

Lazaretou, S. (1996), 'Macroeconomic policies and nominal exchange rate regimes: Greece in the interwar period', *Journal of European Economic History*, **25**.

League of Nations (1920), *Currencies After the War: A Survey of Conditions in Various Countries*, Geneva: League of Nations.

League of Nations (1926a), *The Financial Reconstruction of Austria*, Geneva: League of Nations.

League of Nations (1926b), *The Financial Reconstruction of Hungary*, Geneva: League of Nations.

League of Nations (1930a), *Principles and Methods of Financial Reconstruction Work Undertaken Under the Auspices of the League of Nations*, Geneva: League of Nations.

League of Nations (1930b), *First Interim Report of the Gold Delegation of the Financial Committee*, Geneva: League of Nations.

League of Nations (1930c), *Ten Years of World Cooperation*, Geneva: League of Nations.

League of Nations (1930–32), *Reports of the Gold Delegation Committee of the Financial Committee*, Geneva: League of Nations.

League of Nations (1931), *The Course and Phases of the World Economic Depression*, Geneva: League of Nations.

League of Nations (1932), *World Economic Survey 1931–32*, Geneva: League of Nations.

League of Nations (1933), *World Economic Survey 1932–33*, Geneva: League of Nations.

League of Nations (1936), *Money and Banking 1935/36*, Geneva: League of Nations.

League of Nations (1937a), *Money and Banking 1936/37*, Geneva: League of Nations.

League of Nations (1937b), *World Economic Survey 1936/37*, Geneva: League of Nations.

League of Nations (1938a), *Report on Exchange Control*, Geneva: League of Nations.

League of Nations (1938b), *World Economic Survey 1937/38*, Geneva: League of Nations.

League of Nations (1939), *World Economic Survey 1938/39*, Geneva: League of Nations.
League of Nations (1942), *Commercial Policy in the Interwar Period*, Geneva: League of Nations.
League of Nations (1943a) *Europe's Overseas Needs 1919–1920 and How They Were Met*, Geneva: League of Nations.
League of Nations (1943b), *Trade Relations Between Free Market and Controlled Economies*, Geneva: League of Nations.
League of Nations (1944), *International Currency Experience: Lessons of the Inter-war Period*, Geneva: League of Nations.
League of Nations (1945), *League of Nations' Reconstruction Schemes in the Inter-war Period*, Geneva: League of Nations.
League of Nations (1946), *The Course and Control of Inflation: A Review of Monetary Experience in Europe After the First World War*, Geneva: League of Nations.
Leith-Ross, F.W. (1968), *Money Talks: Fifty Years of International Finance*, London: Hutchinson.
Lester, R.A. (1937), 'The gold parity depression in Norway and Denmark', *Journal of Political Economy*, **45**.
Lester, R.A. (1939), *Monetary Experiments: Early American and Recent Scandinavian*, Princeton, NJ: Princeton University Press.
Lieberman, S. (1995), *Growth and Crisis in the Spanish Economy: 1940–93*, London: Routledge.
Lindert, P.H. (1969), *Key Currencies and Gold 1900–1913*, Princeton, NJ: Princeton University Press.
Little, I.M.D., Cooper, R.N., Corden, W.M. and Rajapatirana, S. (1993), *Boom, Crisis, and Adjustment: The Macroeconomic Experience of Developing Countries*, Oxford: Oxford University Press.
Llewellyn, D.T. and Presley, J.R. (1995), 'The role of hegemonic arrangements in the evolution of the international monetary system', in J. Reis (ed.), *International Monetary Systems in Historical Perspective*, Basingstoke: Macmillan.
Loveday, A. (1931), *Britain and World Trade*, London: Longmans, Green.
Ludlow, P. (1982), *The Making of the EMS*, London: Butterworth.
Machlup, F. (1964), 'Plans for the reform of the International Monetary System', *Princeton Essays in International Economics*, No. 3, Princeton, NJ: Princeton University Press, rev. edn.
Macmillan Committee (1931), *Report of the Committee on Finance and Industry*, Cmd. 3897, London: HMSO.
Maddison, A. (1962), 'Growth and fluctuation in the world economy, 1870–1960', *Banca Nazionale del Lavoro Quarterly Review*, **15**.
Maddison, A. (1991), *Dynamic Forces in Capitalist Development: A Long-run Comparative View*, Oxford: Oxford University Press.
Maddison, A. (1995), *Monitoring the World Economy 1820–1992*, Paris: OECD.
Maier, C.S. (1975), *Recasting Bourgeois Europe: Stabilisation in France, Germany and Italy in the Decade after the First World War*, Princeton, NJ: Princeton University Press.
Maier, C.S. (1987), 'The politics of inflation in the twentieth century', in C.S. Maier (ed.), *In Search of Stability: Explorations in Historical Political Economy*, Cambridge: Cambridge University Press.
Marjolin, R. (1938), 'The French exchange fund', *The Banker*, **48**.
Matthews, K.G.P. (1986a), 'Was sterling overvalued in 1925?', *Economic History Review*, **34**.
Matthews, K.G.P. (1986b), *The Inter-war Economy: An Equilibrium Analysis*, Aldershot: Gower.
Mazower, M. (1991a), 'Banking and economic development in interwar Greece', in H. James, H. Lindgren and A. Teichova (eds), *The Role of Banks in the Interwar Economy*, Cambridge: Cambridge University Press.
Mazower, M. (1991b), *Greece and the Interwar Economic Crisis*, Oxford: Oxford University Press.
McCloskey, D.N. and Zelcher, J.R. (1976), 'How the gold standard worked, 1880–1913', in J.A. Frenkel and H.G. Johnson (eds), *The Monetary Approach to the Balance of Payments*, London: Allen & Unwin.
McGouldrick, P. (1984), 'Operations of the German central bank and the rules of the game 1879-1913', in M.D. Bordo and A.J. Schwartz (eds), *A Retrospective on the Classical Gold Standard, 1821-1931*, Chicago, IL: University of Chicago Press.

McGuire, C.E. (1927), *Italy's International Economic Position*, London: Allen & Unwin.

McKinnon, R.I. (1993), 'The rules of the game: international money in historical perspective', *Journal of Economic Literature*, **31**.

Melitz, J. (1988), 'Monetary discipline and cooperation in the European Monetary System: a synthesis', in F. Giavazzi, S. Micossi and M. Miller (eds), *The European Monetary System*, Cambridge: Cambridge University Press.

Meltzer, A.H. (1976), 'Monetary and other explanations of the great depression', *Journal of Monetary Economics*, **2**.

Meltzer, A.H. (1991), 'US policy in the Bretton Woods era', *Federal Reserve Bank of St. Louis Review*, **73**.

Meyer, F.V. and Lewis, W.A. (1949), 'The effects of an overseas slump on the British economy', *The Manchester School*, **17**.

Meyer, R.H. (1970), *Bankers' Diplomacy: Monetary Stabilisation in the Twenties*, New York: Columbia University Press.

Mikesell, R.F. (1947), 'The role of international monetary agreements in a world of planned economies', *Journal of Political Economy*, **55**.

Miller, H.E. (1930), 'The franc in war and reconstruction', *Quarterly Journal of Economics*, **44**.

Mintz, I. (1959), *Trade Balances During Business Cycles: US and Britain Since 1880*, New York: National Bureau of Economic Research.

Mitchell, B. (1947), *Prosperity Decade: From the New Era Through to the New Deal 1929–1941*, New York: Holt, Rinehart & Winston.

Mitchell, B.R. (1975), *European Historical Statistics 1750–1970*, London: Macmillan.

Mlynarski, F. (1926), *The International Significance of the Depreciation of the Zloty in 1925*, Warsaw: Polish Economist.

Mlynarski, F. (1931), *The Functioning of the Gold Standard*, Geneva: League of Nations.

Moggridge, D.E. (1969), *The Return to Gold: The Formulation of Economic Policy and its Critics*, Cambridge: Cambridge University Press.

Moggridge, D.E. (1970), 'The 1931 financial crisis: a new view', *The Banker*, **120**.

Moggridge, D.E. (1972), *British Monetary Policy 1924–1931: The Norman Conquest of $4.86*, Cambridge: Cambridge University Press.

Moggridge, D.E. (1981), 'Financial crises and lenders of last resort: policy in the crises of 1920 and 1929', *Journal of European Economic History*, **10**.

Moggridge, D.E. (1989), 'The gold standard and national financial policies 1913–1939', in P. Mathias, and S. Pollard (eds), *The Cambridge Economic History of Europe*, Vol. VIII, Cambridge: Cambridge University Press.

Momtchiloff, N. (1944), *Ten Years of Controlled Trade in South-eastern Europe*, Cambridge: Cambridge University Press.

Morgenstern, O. (1959), *International Financial Transactions and Business Cycles*, Princeton, NJ: Princeton University Press.

Morton, W.A. (1943), *British Finance 1930–1940*, Wisconsin: University of Wisconsin Press.

Mouré, K. (1991), *Managing the Franc Poincaré: Economic Understanding and Political Constraint in French Monetary Policy, 1928–1936*, Cambridge: Cambridge University Press.

Mouré, K. (1992), 'The limits to central bank cooperation 1916–36', *Contemporary European History*, **2**.

Mouré, K. (1996), 'Undervaluing the franc Poincaré', *Economic History Review*, **49**.

Munk, F. (1940), *The Economics of Force*, New York: George W. Stewart.

National Bank of Belgium (1977), *Report on the Activities of the Year 1976*, Brussels.

Neal, L. (1979), 'The economics and finance of bilateral clearing agreements: Germany, 1934–8', *Economic History Review*, **32**.

Néré, J. (1968), *La crise de 1929*, Paris: Colin.

Nevin, E. (1955), *The Mechanism of Cheap Money: A Study of British Monetary Policy, 1931–1939*, Cardiff: University of Wales Press.

Nötel, R. (1986), 'International credit and finance', in M.C. Kaser and E.A. Radice (eds), *The Economic History of Eastern Europe 1919–1975*, Vol. II: *Interwar Policy, The War and Reconstruction*, Oxford: Oxford University Press.

Nove, A. (1969), *An Economic History of the USSR*, London: Allen Lane.

Nugent, J.B. (1973), 'Exchange-rate movements and economic development in the late nineteenth century', *Journal of Political Economy*, **81**.

Nunes, A.B., Mata, E. and Valério, N. (1989), 'Portuguese economic growth 1833–1985', *Journal of European Economic History*, **18**.

Obstfeld, M. (1986), 'Rational and self-fulfilling balance-of-payments crises', *American Economic Review*, **76**.

Obstfeld, M. (1992), 'Destabilising effects of exchange rate escape clauses', *NBER Working Paper*, No. 3606, Cambridge, MA: National Bureau of Economic Research.

Obstfeld, M. (1996), 'Models of currency crises with self-fulfilling features', *European Economic Review*, **40**.

Odell, J.S. (1982), *US International Monetary Policy: Markets, Power, and Ideas as Sources of Change*, Princeton, NJ: Princeton University Press.

OEEC (1960), *Industrial Statistics 1900–1959*, Paris: OEEC.

Officer, L.H. (1996a), *Between the Dollar–Sterling Gold Points: Exchange Rates, Parity, and Market Behaviour*, Cambridge: Cambridge University Press.

Officer, L.H. (1996b), 'Market efficiency and regime efficiency under the 1925–1931 dollar/sterling standard', in T. Bayoumi, B. Eichengreen and M.P. Taylor (eds), *Modern Perspectives on the Gold Standard*, Cambridge: Cambridge University Press.

Ogburn, W.F. and Jaffé, W. (1929), *The Economic Development of Postwar France: A Survey of Production*, New York: Columbia University Press.

Oliver, M.J. (1997), *Whatever Happened to Monetarism? Economic Policy-making and Social Learning in the United Kingdom Since 1979*, Aldershot: Ashgate.

Orde, A. (1990), *British Policy and European Reconstruction After the First World War*, Cambridge: Cambridge University Press.

Organisation for Economic Cooperation and Development (OECD), *Economic Survey*, various issues.

Organisation for Economic Cooperation and Development (OECD), *Main Economic Indictors*, various issues.

Oye, K.A. (1986), 'The sterling–dollar–franc triangle: monetary diplomacy 1929–1937', in K.A. Oye (ed.), *Cooperation Under Anarchy*, Princeton, NJ: Princeton University Press.

Padoa-Schioppa, T. (1988), 'The European Monetary System: a long-term view', in F. Giavazzi, S. Micossi and M. Miller (eds), *The European Monetary System*, Cambridge: Cambridge University Press.

Palyi, M. (1972), *The Twilight of Gold 1914–1936: Myths and Realities*, Chicago, IL: Henry Regnery.

Parker, R.A.C. (1983), 'The pound sterling, the American Treasury and British preparation for war, 1938–1939', *English Historical Review*, **98**.

Patat, J.-P. and Lutfalla, M. (1990), *A Monetary History of France in the Twentieth Century*, Basingstoke: Macmillan.

Patrick, H.T. (1971), 'The economic muddle of the 1920s', in J.W. Morley (ed.), *Dilemmas of Growth in Prewar Japan*, Princeton, NJ: Princeton University Press.

Payne, S.G. (1968), *Franco's Spain*, London: Routledge & Kegan Paul.

Peel, A.G.V. (1925), *The Financial Crisis of France*, London: Macmillan.

Pigou, A.C. (1920), *Memorandum on Credit, Currency and Exchange Fluctuations* (Paper prepared in connection with the Brussels International Conference at the request of the Secretariat of the League of Nations), Geneva: League of Nations.

Pippinger, J. (1984), 'Bank of England operations, 1893–1913', in M.D. Bordo and A.J. Schwartz (eds), *A Retrospective on the Classical Gold Standard, 1821–1931*, Chicago, IL: University of Chicago Press.

Pöhl, K.O. (1983), 'Interview', *Fortune*, 5 September.

Pöhl, K.O. (1987), 'You can't robotize policymaking', *The International Economy*, October/November.

Polak, J.J. (1943), 'European exchange depreciation in the early twenties', *Econometrica*, **11**.

Polak, J.J. (1994), 'The international monetary issues of the Bretton Woods era', in P.B. Kenen, F. Papadia and F. Saccomanni, *The International Monetary System*, Cambridge: Cambridge University Press.

Pollard, S. (1981), *Peaceful Conquest: The Industrialisation of Europe 1760–1970*, Oxford: Oxford University Press.

Poniachek, H.A. (1979), *Monetary Independence Under Flexible Exchange Rates*, Lexington, MA: D. C. Heath.

Prados de la Escosura, L. (1993), *Spain's Gross Domestic Product, 1850–1990*, Madrid: Ministerio de Economía y Hacienda.

Prati, A. (1991), 'Poincaré's stabilisation: stopping a run on government debt', *Journal of Monetary Economics*, **27**.

Pressnell, L.S. (1978), '1925: the burden of sterling', *Economic History Review*, **31**.

Pringle, W.H. (1928), *Economic Problems in Europe To-day*, London: A & C Black.

Pryor, Z.P. (1973), 'Czechoslovak economic development in the interwar period', in V.S. Mamatey and R. Luza (eds), *A History of the Czechoslovak Republic 1918–1948*, Princeton, NJ: Princeton University Press.

Pumphrey, L.M. (1942), 'The exchange equalization account of Great Britain, 1932–1939: exchange operations', *American Economic Review*, **32**.

Ranki, G. (1983a), 'Inflation in post-World War I East Central Europe', in N. Schmukler and E. Marcus (eds), *Inflation Through the Ages*, New York: Brooklyn College Press.

Ranki, G. (1983b), 'Inflation in Hungary', in N. Schmukler and E. Marcus (eds), *Inflation Through the Ages*, New York: Brooklyn College Press.

Ranki, G. (1983c), *Economic and Foreign Policy: The Struggle of the Great Powers for the Hegemony of the Danube Valley, 1919–1939*, New York: Columbia University Press.

Ranki, G. (1985), 'Problems of southern European economic development (1918–38)', in G. Arrighi (ed.), *Semiperipheral Development: The Politics of Southern Europe in the Twentieth Century*, Beverly Hills, CA: Sage.

Rasin, A. (1923), *Financial Policy of Czechoslovakia During the First Year of its History*, London: Clarendon.

Redmond, J. (1980), 'An indicator of the effective exchange rate of the pound in the nineteen-thirties', *Economic History Review*, **33**.

Redmond, J. (1984), 'The sterling overvaluation of 1925: a multilateral approach', *Economic History Review*, **37**.

Redmond, J. (1988), 'Effective exchange rates in the nineteen-thirties: the European gold bloc and North America', *Journal of European Economic History*, **17**.

Redmond, J. (1992), 'The gold standard between the wars', in S.N. Broadberry and N.F.R. Crafts (eds), *Britain in the International Economy*, Cambridge: Cambridge University Press.

Rist, C. (1936), 'Memorandum on the depression experience of gold bloc countries', in Carnegie Endowment/International Chamber of Commerce (eds), *The Improvement of Commercial Relations Between Nations and the Problems of Monetary Stabilization*, Paris: International Chamber of Commerce.

Rist, C. (1953), *Défense de l'or*, Paris: Recueil Sirey.

Rogers, J.H. (1929), *The Process of Inflation in France 1914–1927*, New York: Columbia University Press.

Rose, A.K. and Svensson, L.E.O. (1994), 'European exchange rate credibility before the fall', *European Economic Review*, **38**.

Rothschild, J. (1974), *East Central Europe Between the Two World Wars*, Seattle, WA: University of Washington Press.

Routh, T. (1993), *British Protection and the International Economy: Overseas Commercial Policy in the 1930s*, Cambridge: Cambridge University Press.

Royal Institute of International Affairs (1932), *The International Gold Problem: Collected Papers*, London: Oxford University Press.

Royal Institute of International Affairs (1933), *Monetary Policy and the Depression*, London: Oxford University Press.

Royal Institute of International Affairs (1935), *The Future of Monetary Policy*, London: Oxford University Press.

Royal Institute of International Affairs (1936), *The Balkan States: A Review of the Economic and Financial Development of Albania, Bulgaria, Greece, Romania and Yugoslavia Since 1919*, London: Oxford University Press.

Royal Institute of International Affairs (1938), *The Baltic States: A Survey of the Political and Economic Structure and the Foreign Relations of Estonia, Latvia, and Lithuania*, Oxford: Oxford University Press.

Royal Institute of International Affairs (1939), *South Eastern Europe: A Political and Economic Survey*, London: Oxford University Press.

Ruggie, J. (1991), 'Embedded liberalism revisited: institutions and progress in international economic relations', in E. Adler and B. Crawford (eds), *Progress in International Relations*, New York: Columbia University Press.

Sachs, J.D. (1979), 'Wages, profits and macroeconomic adjustment: a comparative study', *Brookings Papers on Economic Acitvity*, **2**.

Sachs, J.D. (1989), 'Introduction', in J.D. Sachs (ed.), *Developing Country Debt and the World Economy*, Chicago, IL: University of Chicago Press.

Saint-Etienne, C. (1984), *The Great Depression, 1929–1938: Lessons for the 1980s*, Stanford, CA: Hoover Institution Press.

Samuelson, P. (1948), 'Disparity in postwar exchange rates', in S. Harris (ed.), *Foreign Economic Policy for the United States*, Cambridge, MA: Harvard University Press.

Sargent, T.J. (1984), 'Stopping moderate inflations: the methods of Poincaré and Thatcher', in R. Dornbusch and M.H. Simonsen (eds), *Inflation, Debt and Indexation*, Cambridge MA: MIT Press.

Sarti, R. (1970), 'The battle of the lira 1925–27', *Past and Present*, **47**.

Sauvy, A. (1963), 'L'inflation en France jusqu'à la dévaluation de 1928', in A.-M. Piuz and J.F. Bergier (eds), *Mélanges d'histoire économique et sociale en hommage au professeur Antony Babel*, Vol. 2, Geneva.

Sayers, R.S. (1957), *Central Banking after Bagehot*, London: Oxford University Press.

Sayers, R.S. (1960), 'The return to gold, 1925', in L.S. Pressnell (ed.), *Studies in the Industrial Revolution*, London: Athlone Press.

Sayers, R.S. (1976a), *The Bank of England 1891–1944*, Vol. 1, Cambridge: Cambridge University Press.

Sayers, R.S. (1976b), *The Bank of England 1891–1944*, Vol. 2, Cambridge: Cambridge University Press.

Scammell, W.M. (1961), *International Monetary Policy*, London: Macmillan, 2nd edn.

Scammell, W.M. (1965), 'The working of the gold standard', *Yorkshire Bulletin of Economic and Social Research*, **17**.

Scammell, W.M. (1975), *International Monetary Policy: Bretton Woods and After*, London: Macmillan.

Scammell, W.M. (1987), *The Stability of the International Monetary System*, Basingstoke: Macmillan.

Schloss, H.H. (1958), *The Bank for International Settlements: An Experiment in Central Bank Cooperation*, Amsterdam: North-Holland Publishing Company.

Schmid, G.C. (1974), 'The politics of currency stabilisation: the French franc, 1926', *Journal of European Economic History*, **3**.

Schmitz, J. (1930), *Inflation und stabilisierung in Frankreich, 1914–1928*, Bonn: K. Schroeder.

Schubert, A. (1991), *The Credit-Anstalt crisis of 1931*, Oxford: Oxford University Press.

Schuker, S. (1988), *American 'Reparations' to Germany: Implications for the Third World Debt Crisis*, Princeton, NJ: Princeton University Press.

Schwartz, A.J. (1983), 'The postwar institutional evolution of the international monetary system', in M.R. Darby and J.R. Lothian (eds), *The International Transmission of Inflation*, Chicago, IL: University of Chicago Press.

Schwartz, A.J. (1984), 'Introduction', in M.D. Bordo and A.J. Schwartz (eds), *A Retrospective on the Classical Gold Standard, 1821–1931*, Chicago, IL: University of Chicago Press.

Schwarz, L.D. (1993), 'Searching for recovery: unbalanced budgets, deflation and rearmament in France during the 1930s', in W.R. Garside (ed.), *Capitalism in Crisis: International Responses to the Great Depression*, London: Pinter.

Seton-Watson, R.W. (1928), 'Czecho-Slovakia', in W. H. Pringle (ed.), *Economic Problems in Europe To-day*, London: A & C Black.

Shepherd, H.L. (1936), *The Monetary Experience of Belgium 1914–1936*, Princeton, NJ: Princeton University Press.

Shultz, G.P and Dam, K.W. (1977), *Economic Policy Beyond the Headlines*, Stanford, CA: Stanford University Press.

Sicsic, P. (1992), 'Was the franc Poincaré deliberately overvalued?', *Explorations in Economic History*, **29**.

Siegenthaler, H. (1976), 'Switzerland 1920–1970', in C. Cipolla (ed.), *The Fontana Economic History of Europe: Contemporary Economies*, Part Two, London: Collins.

Simmons, B.A. (1993), 'Why innovate? Founding the Bank for International Settlements', *World Politics*, **45**.

Simmons, B.A. (1994), *Who Adjusts? Domestic Sources of Foreign Economic Policy During the Interwar Years*, Princeton, NJ: Princeton University Press.

Simutis, A. (1942), *The Economic Reconstruction of Lithuania After 1918*, New York: Columbia University Press.

Smith, L. (1934), 'The suspension of the gold standard in raw material exporting countries', *American Economic Review*, **24**.

Smith, L. (1936), 'The zloty, 1924–35', *Journal of Political Economy*, **44**.

Solomon, R. (1982), *The International Monetary System, 1945–1981*, New York: Harper & Row.

Solomou, S. (1996), *Themes in Macroeconomic History: The UK Economy, 1919–1939*, Cambridge: Cambridge University Press.

Spulber, N. (1966), *The State and Economic Development in Eastern Europe*, New York: Random House.

Stephens, P. (1988), 'Waiting for November', *Financial Times*, 15 July.

Stolper, W.F. (1948), 'Purchasing power parity and the pound sterling, 1919–1925', *Kyklos*, **2**.

Strakosch, H. (1937), 'The money tangle of the postwar period', in A.D. Gayer (ed.), *The Lessons of Monetary Experience: Essays in Honour of Irving Fisher*, New York: Farrer & Rinehart.

Strange, S. (1971), *Sterling and British Policy: A Political Study of an International Currency in Decline*, London: Oxford University Press.

Svennilson, I. (1954), *Growth and Stagnation in the European Economy*, Geneva: United Nations.

Swoboda, A.K. (1968), 'The Euro-dollar market: an interpretation', *Essays in International Finance*, No. 64, Princeton, NJ: Princeton University Press.

Swoboda, A.K. and Genberg, H. (1982), 'Gold and the dollar: asymmetries in world money stock determination, 1959–1971', in R.N. Cooper (ed.), *The International Monetary System under Flexible Exchange Rates: Global, Regional and National*, Cambridge, MA: Ballinger.

Swoboda, A.K. and Genberg, H. (1993), 'The provision of liquidity in the Bretton Woods system', in M.D. Bordo and B. Eichengreen (eds), *A Retrospective on the Bretton Woods System: Lessons for International Monetary Reform*, Chicago, IL: The University of Chicago Press.

Teichova, A. (1983), 'A comparative view of inflation of the 1920s in Austria and Czechoslovakia', in N. Schmukler and E. Marcus (eds), *Inflation Through the Ages*, New York: Brooklyn College Press.

Temin, P. (1993), 'Transmission of the great depression', *Journal of Economic Perspectives*, **7**.

Temin, P. and Wigmore, B. (1990), 'The end of One Big Deflation', *Explorations in Economic History*, **27**.

Tew, B. (1970), *International Monetary Cooperation, 1945–1970*, New York: Wiley.

Tew, B. (1988), *The Evolution of the International Monetary System, 1944–1988*, London: Hutchinson, 4th edn.

Tew, B. (1997), 'Memorandum', in Treasury and Civil Service Committee, *International Monetary Fund*, Fourth Report, HC 68, London: HMSO.

Thatcher, M.H. (1993), *The Downing Street Years*, London: HarperCollins.

The Economist (1934), 'Back to gold?', 31 March, **118**.

Thomas, B. (1936), *Monetary Policy and Crises: A Study of Swedish Experience*, London: Routledge.

Thomas, L.B. (1972), 'Some international evidence on international currency experience, 1919–1925', *Nebraska Journal of Economics and Business*, **11**.

Thomas, L.B. (1973a), 'Behaviour of flexible exchange rates: additional tests from the post-world war I episode', *Southern Economic Journal*, **40**.
Thomas, L.B. (1973b), 'Speculation in the flexible exchange revisited – another view', *Kyklos*, **26**.
Thygesen, N. (1988), 'Introduction', in F. Giavazzi, S. Micossi and M. Miller (eds), *The European Monetary System*, Cambridge: Cambridge University Press.
Timoshenko, V.P. (1933), *World Agriculture and the Depression*, Ann Arbor, MI: University of Michigan Press.
Traynor, D.E. (1949), *International Monetary and Financial Conferences in the Interwar Period*, Washington, DC: Catholic University of America Press.
Triffin, R. (1946–47), 'National central banking and the international economy', *Review of Economic Studies*, **14**.
Triffin, R. (1960), *Gold and the Dollar Crisis*, New Haven, CT: Yale University Press.
Triffin, R. (1968), *Our International Monetary System: Yesterday, Today and Tomorrow*, New York: Random House.
Triffin, R. (1984), 'How to end the world "infession": crisis management or fundamental reforms?', in R.S. Masera and R. Triffin (eds), *Europe's Money: Problems of European Monetary Co-ordination and Integration*, Oxford: Clarendon Press.
Tsiang, S.C. (1959–60), 'Fluctuating exchange rates in countries with relatively stable economies: some European experiences after world war I', *IMF Staff Papers*, **7**.
Tsokhas, K. (1994), 'The Australian Role in Britain's Return to the Gold Standard', *Economic History Review*, **47**.
Tsoukalis, L. (1997), *The New European Economy Revisited*, Oxford: Oxford University Press, rev. edn.
Tullio, G. and Wolters, J. (1996), 'Was London the conductor of the international orchestra or just a triangle player? An empirical analysis of asymmetries in interest rate behaviour during the classical gold standard 1876–1913', *Scottish Journal of Political Economy*, **43**.
United Nations (1949), *Statistical Yearbook 1948*, New York: United Nations.
van der Wee, H. and Tavernier, K. (1975), *La Banque Nationale de Belgique: l'histoire monétaire entre les deux guerres mondiales*, Brussels: Banque Nationale de Belgique.
Van Walré de Bordes, J. (1924), *The Austrian Crown*, London: P.S. King.
van Zanden, J.L. (1997), 'Old rules, new conditions, 1914–1940', in M. Hart, J. Jonker and J. L. van Zanden (eds), *A Financial History of the Netherlands*, Cambridge: Cambridge University Press.
van Zanden, J.L. and Griffiths, R.T. (1989), *Economische geschiedenis van Nederland in de 20e eeuw*, Utrecht: Aula-paperbacks.
Viner, J. (1932), 'International aspects of the gold standard', in Q. Wright (ed.), *Gold and Monetary Stabilization*, Chicago, IL: University of Chicago Press.
Viner, J. (1945), 'Clapham and the Bank of England', *Economica*, **12**.
Volcker, P. and Gyohten, T. (1992), *Changing Fortunes: The World's Money and the Threat to American Leadership*, New York: Times Books.
Walter, A. (1991), *World Power and World Money: The Role of Hegemony and International Monetary Order*, Hemel Hempstead: Harvester Wheatsheaf.
Walter, J.T. (1951), *Foreign Exchange Equilibrium*, Pittsburgh, PA: University of Pittsburgh Press.
Walters, A.A. (1988), 'Money on a roller-coaster', *The Independent*, July 14.
Walters, A.A. (1990), *Sterling In Danger*, London: Fontana.
Walters, A.A. (1991), 'Dare Major devalue?', *The Times*, 2 January.
Warren, G.F. and Pearson, F.A. (1933), *Prices*, London: Chapman & Hall.
Weber, A.A. (1991), 'Reputation and credibility in the European Monetary System', *Economic Policy*, **12**.
Welk, W.G. (1938), *Fascist Economic Policy*, Cambridge, MA: Harvard University Press.
Werner, P., Ansiaux, H., Brouwers, G., Clappier, B., Mosca, U., Schöllhorn, J.B. and Stammati, G. (1970), *Report to the Council and the Commission on the Realisation by Stages of Economic and Monetary Union in the Community*, Supplement to Bulletin II–1970 of the European Communities, Brussels: European Community.
Whitaker, J.K. and Hudgins, W. (1977), 'The floating pound sterling of the nineteen-thirties: an econometric study', *Southern Economic Journal*, **43**.

Wicker, E. (1986), 'Terminating hyperinflation in the dismembered Habsburg Monarchy', *American Economic Review*, **76**.

Williams, B.A. (1994), *Who Adjusts? Domestic Sources of Foreign Economic Policy During the Interwar Years*, Princeton, NJ: Princeton University Press.

Williams, D. (1959), 'Montagu Norman and banking policy in the 1920s', *Yorkshire Bulletin of Economic and Social Research*, **11**.

Williams, D. (1962–63), 'London and the 1931 financial crisis', *Economic History Review*, **15**.

Williams, D. (1963), 'The 1931 financial crisis', *Yorkshire Bulletin of Economic and Social Research*, **15**.

Williams, J.H. (1953), 'The crisis of the gold standard', in F.C. Lane and J.C. Riemersma (eds), *Enterprise and Secular Change: Readings in Economic History*, Homewood, IL: Richard D. Irwin.

Williamson, J. (1977), *The Failure of World Monetary Reform, 1971–1974*, New York: New York University Press.

Williamson, J. (1983), *The Exchange Rate System*, Washington, DC: Institute for International Economics.

Williamson, J. (1991), 'FEERs and the ERM', *National Institute Economic Review*, **137**.

Williamson, J. (1994), 'The rise and fall of the concept of international liquidity', in P. B. Kenen, F. Papadia and F. Saccomanni (eds), *The International Monetary System*, Cambridge: Cambridge University Press.

Williamson, P. (1992), *National Crisis and National Government: British Politics, the Economy and Empire 1926–1932*, Cambridge: Cambridge University Press.

Wiskemann, E. (1938), *Czechs and Germans: A Study of the Struggle in the Historic Provinces of Bohemia and Moravia*, London: Oxford University Press.

Wolfe, M. (1957), *The French Franc Between the Wars 1919–1939*, New York: Columbia University Press.

Wonnacott, P. (1972), *The Floating Canadian Dollar: Exchange Flexibility and Monetary Independence*, Washington, DC: American Enterprise Institute.

Woo, W.T. (1988), 'Devaluation and domestic politics in developing countries: Indonesia in 1978', *Journal of Public Policy*, **8**.

Woytinsky, W.S. and Woytinsky, E.S. (1955), *World Commerce and Governments*, New York: Twentieth Century Fund.

Wren-Lewis, S. (1990), 'The danger of a high level entry level', *Financial Times*, 17 October.

Wren-Lewis, S., Westaway, P., Soteri, S. and Barrell, R. (1990), 'Choosing the rate: an analysis of the optimum level of entry for sterling into the ERM', *National Institute Discussion Paper*, No. 171.

Wren-Lewis, S., Westaway, P., Soteri, S. and Barrell, R. (1991), 'Evaluating the UK's choice of entry rate into the ERM', *Manchester School of Economic and Social Studies*, **59**.

Wynne, W.H. (1937), 'The French franc, June 1928–February 1937', *Journal of Political Economy*, **45**.

Yamamura, LK. (1972), 'Then came the great depression: Japan's interwar years', in van der Wee, H. (ed.), *The Great Depression Revisited: Essays in the Economics of the Thirties*, The Hague: Nijhoff.

Yeager, L.B. (ed.) (1962), *In Search of a Monetary Constitution*, Cambridge, MA.: Harvard University Press.

Yeager, L.B. (1976), *International Monetary Relations: Theory, History, and Policy*, New York: Harper & Row, 2nd edn.

Yeager, L.B. (1981), *Experience with Stopping Inflation*, Washington, DC: American Enterprise Institute.

Young, J.W. (1997), *Britain and the World in the Twentieth Century*, London: Arnold.

Zamagni, V. (1993), *The Economic History of Italy 1860–1990*, Oxford: Oxford University Press.

Zweig, F. (1944), *Poland Between the Wars: A Critical Study of Social and Economic Changes*, London: Secker & Warburg,

Index